Cast-Iron Cooking

FOR

DUMMIES®

Cast-Iron Cooking

FOR

DUMMIES®

by Tracy Barr

WILEY

Wiley Publishing, Inc.

Cast-Iron Cooking For Dummies®

Published by
Wiley Publishing, Inc.
111 River St.
Hoboken, NJ 07030
www.wiley.com

Copyright © 2004 by Wiley Publishing, Inc., Indianapolis, Indiana

Published by Wiley Publishing, Inc., Indianapolis, Indiana

Published simultaneously in Canada

For general information on our other products and services or to obtain technical support, please contact our Customer Care Department within the U.S. at 877-762-2974, outside the U.S. at 317-572-3993, or fax 317-572-4002.

Wiley also publishes its books in a variety of electronic formats. Some content that appears in print may not be available in electronic books.

Library of Congress Control Number: 2003112837

ISBN: 0-7645-3714-8

Manufactured in the United States of America

16 15 14

WILEY is a trademark of Wiley Publishing, Inc.

About the Author

Tracy Barr has been a part of the *For Dummies* phenomenon for almost a decade. In that time, she has served as editor, editorial manager, writer, and consultant to folks who write and edit *For Dummies* books. Most recently, she helped write *World War II For Dummies,* with Keith D. Dickson, and *Religion For Dummies,* with Rabbi Mark Gellman and Monsignor Thomas Hartman. She also is the coauthor of *Latin For Dummies* and *Adoption For Dummies.* An avid cook, she was introduced to cast iron as a young girl when her mother inherited a few pieces, and she has since made cast iron the workhorse of her own kitchen.

Dedication

To my husband, Larry, who likes everything I cook, and to my children — Adam, Sarah, Mary, and Alex — who are more honest.

Author's Acknowledgments

I would like to thank the following people: From Lodge Manufacturing in South Pittsburg, Tennessee, Jeanne Scholze and Bob Kellerman, who were very generous with their time and expertise; Gayle Allen-Grier, for the Tennessee milkshake recipe, and her husband, Robert, for the tip on how to get through Nashville without getting stuck in traffic. From Wiley: Editors Mike Baker and Esmeralda St. Clair, for the time and effort they gave to this project.

Publisher's Acknowledgments

We're proud of this book; please send us your comments through our Dummies online registration form located at `www.dummies.com/register/`.

Some of the people who helped bring this book to market include the following:

Acquisitions, Editorial, and Media Development

Project Editor: Mike Baker

Acquisitions Editor: Norman Crampton

Copy Editor: Esmeralda St. Clair

Editorial Program Assistant: Holly Gastineau-Grimes

Technical Reviewer and Nutrition Analyst: Patty Santelli

Recipe Testers: Emily Nolan, Kate Brown, and Keith Brown

Editorial Manager: Jennifer Ehrlich

Editorial Assistant: Elizabeth Rea

Illustrator: Liz Kurtzman

Cover Photos: Lodge Manufacturing

Cartoons: Rich Tennant, `www.the5thwave.com`

Composition Services

Project Coordinator: Courtney MacIntyre

Layout and Graphics: Joyce Haughey, Stephanie D. Jumper, Jacque Schneider, Julie Trippetti, Shae Lynn Wilson

Proofreaders: John Greenough, Nancy L. Reinhardt, Aptara

Indexer: Aptara

Publishing and Editorial for Consumer Dummies

    Diane Graves Steele, Vice President and Publisher, Consumer Dummies

    Joyce Pepple, Acquisitions Director, Consumer Dummies

    Kristin A. Cocks, Product Development Director, Consumer Dummies

    Michael Spring, Vice President and Publisher, Travel

    Brice Gosnell, Associate Publisher, Travel

    Kelly Regan, Editorial Director, Travel

Publishing for Technology Dummies

    Andy Cummings, Vice President and Publisher, Dummies Technology/General User

Composition Services

    Gerry Fahey, Vice President of Production Services

    Debbie Stailey, Director of Composition Services

Contents at a Glance

Recips at a Glance

Desserts

Cornbreads

Table of Contents

Part IV: Cast-Iron Cooking for the Great Outdoors — and Beyond 229

Introduction

*I*n some circles, cast iron has a bad reputation. It's old-fashioned, heavy, and hard to take care of. And really, how often do folks nowadays need to hitch up the mule and wagon and leave civilization and Teflon-coated sauté pans behind?

True, cast iron is old. It's been around since the Middle Ages. And it *is* heavy. No one can dispute the fact that even a small pot made of cast iron has a heft to it that no other cookware has. It's also true that most people who set out for parts unknown today are more interested in packing swimsuits, scuba gear, or snow skis than the pots and pans from their kitchens.

Nevertheless, cast-iron cookware has a place in today's kitchens, and I'm not talking about hanging from a wall as a decoration. Cast iron has much to offer modern-day cooks. It's easy to use, easy to care for, economical, versatile, and durable, and let's face it, it has a nostalgic appeal that no other cookware possesses. But more compelling than all those reasons is that it's a great cookware that makes great food.

About This Book

For as simple as cast-iron cooking is, it remains an enigma to many modern cooks. To clear up the mystery, this book tells you just what you need to know. Each chapter contains information about cooking in general and cast-iron cooking in particular, like

- ✔ When and how to season a cast-iron pan
- ✔ How to clean your cast iron (you can't use a dishwasher or soap)
- ✔ What cast-iron pans are available and where you can find them
- ✔ How to get a biscuit to rise
- ✔ How to get that great cornbread crust
- ✔ What to look for when go shopping for ingredients
- ✔ How to recognize quality cast iron — old or new — at a garage sale or the mall

In addition, this book contains many cast-iron recipes, from the traditional fare, such as pineapple upside-down cake, corn bread, and fried chicken, to dishes with a modern flair, such as Apricot-Ginger Glazed Pork Rib Roast with Fruit Stuffing.

Conventions Used in This Book

Simple and straightforward, this book has few conventions that you need to be aware of before you head to the kitchen. In fact, you only need to know a few things about the recipes:

Each recipe indicates a size and type of cast-iron pan to use. But because cast iron is so versatile, you can use just about any cast-iron pan that you have on hand. Just keep the following in mind:

- ✔ Make sure the pan that you use is suitable for the task at hand. If the recipe calls for deep-frying, for example, a skillet won't do because it isn't deep enough, but a Dutch oven will work fine.

- ✔ If the pan that you use is larger or smaller than the one specified in the recipe, especially for baking recipes, such as cakes, you may have to adjust the cooking time. Baking a cake in a 9-inch skillet, for example, takes longer than baking a cake in a 12-inch pan.

So feel free to use whatever cast iron you can. Some good candidates for swapping are as follows:

To Do This		Use Any of These Pans
Roast	Meats	Deep fryer, Dutch oven, fry pan, deep-sided skillet
	Vegetables	Dutch oven, any skillet, casserole dish
Deep-fry		Deep fryer, Dutch oven, fry pan
Pan-fry		Dutch oven, fry pan, skillet
Bake	Cakes, pies	Skillet, Dutch oven, specialty bake pans
	Muffins, cornsticks	Muffin pan, cornstick pans, divided cornbread skillet
	Loaf breads	Loaf pan, Dutch oven, skillet
	Rolls	Dutch oven, skillet, griddle
	Biscuits, cornbread	Skillet, drop-biscuit pan, Dutch oven, cornbread skillet

To Do This	*Use Any of These Pans*
Simmer soups or stews	Dutch oven, deep fryer, deep sauce pan
Sear meats	Skillet, griddle
Stir-fry	Skillet, wok

One of the fun things about cast-iron cooking is that it's as much an art as a science. Many older cast-iron recipes have been handed down from one generation to the next and passed from cook to cook. Many recipes have made it to this book in just that way. So, you're getting authentic cast-iron recipes that have stood the test of time.

Another typical characteristic of these types of recipes is that they often don't use precise measurements or give specific time guidelines. Instead, they tell you to "Add just a smidgeon of salt," or "Simmer the sauce until it's nice and thick." So that anyone from the culinary novice to the seasoned cast-iron cook can have success with the recipes in this book, the impreciseness is kept to a minimum:

- ✔ **Measurements:** The recipes largely give precise measurements (a half teaspoon of this or 1½ tablespoons of that, for example) or indicate a range (½ to 1 teaspoon, for example).

- ✔ **Times:** The recipes also indicate approximate prep and cooking times and times for the tasks within individual recipe steps.

But, at the end of the day, to be true to cast-iron's heritage, some ingredient amounts are occasionally left to your cooking judgment. (Don't worry, I'm talking about things like salt and pepper here.) Continuing a long-standing kitchen tradition, as soon as you make a recipe, that recipe becomes yours to do with as you please. Take advantage of this flexibility and feel free to adjust any of these recipes to suit your own tastes and cooking style.

And now just a few more quick words about the ingredients. Unless otherwise noted,

- ✔ **Butter** is unsalted.
- ✔ **Milk** is whole.
- ✔ **Eggs** are large.
- ✔ **Salt** is common table salt and **pepper** is freshly ground black pepper.
- ✔ **Fruits and vegetables** are washed under cold running water before using.

And all temperatures are Fahrenheit.

What You're Not to Read

This book is full of need-to-know information about cast iron — info that you don't want to skip or miss, because it contains details that are vital to using cast iron successfully. But sprinkled among all this need-to-know stuff is information that's interesting but not vital. Because I assume that you're a fairly busy person (see my assumptions about you in the next section), I've made skipable information easy to recognize. You can safely skip the following text:

- **Text in sidebars.** The sidebars are the shaded boxes that appear here and there throughout the book. They contain historical side notes, more detailed explanations, and other cast-iron related information, but sidebars aren't necessary reading.

- **Anything with a Technical Stuff icon attached.** This information is interesting but not critical to your understanding of cast-iron cooking.

Foolish Assumptions

In the writing of this book, I made some assumptions about you:

- You found yourself the proud owner of cast iron, but you aren't quite sure what to do with it.

- You've had cast iron for a while and are looking to expand your repertoire of cast-iron recipes.

- You've had bad experiences with cast iron but are willing to give it another go.

- You don't own a lick of cast iron, but you've been hearing so much about it (or you've tasted something cooked in it), and you want to give it a try.

- You don't have time for long treatises on the joy of cast-iron cooking and just want practical cooking tips and cut-to-the-chase directions.

If any of the preceding assumptions describe you, you have the right cast-iron cookbook in your hands.

How This Book Is Organized

I wrote this book so that you can find information easily, regardless of whether you're looking for recipes or cast-iron cooking tips.

Part I: Coming Around to Cast-Iron Cooking

Cast iron isn't a hard cookware to figure out, but you do need to know how to season it and how to care for it before you can use it successfully. This part gives you that information. But just knowing the basics isn't enough, not if you really want to enjoy cooking in cast iron. So this part also shares with you the tricks that cast-iron cooks have had up their sleeves for centuries.

Part II: Main-Dish Cast-Iron Recipes

In this part, you can find all sorts of main-dish cast-iron recipes: Roasted dishes, stir-fried dishes, blackened dishes, fried dishes, dishes using poultry, beef, veal, seafood, shellfish, and more. The selection runs the gamut from down-home favorites, such as Southern Fried Chicken, to uptown tastes, such as Chicken Marsala. And yes, I've even included a corn-dog recipe. You can also find tips and suggestions for finding ideal cuts of meat or softening up a tough cut, taking care of prep and presentation tasks, such as carving meat and poultry, and protecting yourself from food-borne illnesses.

Part III: Cast-Iron Sides and Sweet Endings

Some of the best cast-iron dishes are the side dishes, such as roasted vegetables or fried potatoes, breads (corn bread, biscuits, and more), and desserts (pineapple upside-down cake says it all). So, in this part, I gather a bunch of recipes and throw in information that can help you get the results you want.

Part IV: Cast-Iron Cooking for the Great Outdoors — and Beyond

Cast iron is a part of Americana. The first colonists to hit the shores of the New World brought cast iron with them, which may partially explain why their trip across the ocean was so perilous. Then their descendents carried it westward.

With its history as the cookware of adventurers, pilgrims, and pioneers, cast iron is great outdoor cookware even for the modern cook. A quiet twilight, a cast-iron skillet, and a recipe from this part is all that you need to see why cooking outdoors with cast iron is still so popular. Of course, if you're talking about the great outdoors, what better recipes to talk about than fresh game? Those recipes are here — along with tips on how to get fresh game, even if you're not a hunter.

And don't forget that cast iron isn't just an American cookware. It's used in other parts of the world, too. So in this part, you get a mix of recipes from other cultures, as well.

Part V: The Part of Tens

Want to know how to make your cast iron last a lifetime? How about a list of recipes that, ingredient for ingredient, just taste better when they're made in cast iron? Think you need help getting your cast-iron recipes to come out right? This part offers lists of ideas, suggestions, and a few opinions that you may find helpful.

Icons Used in This Book

The icons in this book help you find particular kinds of information that may be of use to you:

You'll see this icon anywhere that I offer a suggestion or a bit of practical advice — such as how to save time or what special tool to use — that can help you with the task at hand.

This icon points out important information about cast-iron cooking or care that (surprise, surprise) I don't want you to forget.

If something can ruin your cast iron, mess up your meal, or prove hazardous to your health, you'll find it highlighted with this icon.

This icon appears beside information that explains the finer points — the technical details (such as how cast iron is made or why yeast works) — that you may find interesting but that you don't need to know to get a handle on cast iron. Feel free to skip this information at will.

Throughout its history, Pilgrims, explorers (think Lewis and Clark), pioneers, and cowboys have cooked under the stars with cast-iron cookware. Today, outdoor enthusiasts, cook-off competitors, and a host of other folks continue that tradition by heading to the hills (or their backyards) with their cast iron. If you're interested in doing the same, this icon flags information that will make your open-air excursions run smoothly.

Where to Go from Here

This book is organized so that you easily find whatever you want to find. Have some potatoes that you need to use and want some recipe ideas? Head to Chapter 10. If you're interested in outdoor recipes, because a camp out is coming up, go to Chapter 14 for that. You can use the table of contents to find broad categories of information, the index to look up more specific items, or the Recipes at a Glance section at the front of this book to find the right recipe.

What's great about this book is that *you* decide where to start and what to read. It's a reference that you can jump into and out of at will.

If you don't currently have any cast iron or you're not sure how to cook with cast iron, you may want to head to Part I. It gives you all the basic info that you need to get started. After you've digested the tidbits in Part I, you can go anywhere your heart — or your taste buds — takes you.

Part I
Coming Around to Cast-Iron Cooking

The 5th Wave   By Rich Tennant

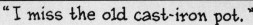

"I miss the old cast-iron pot."

In this part . . .

*E*ven though cast-iron cooking has been around for hundreds of years, cooking in cast iron may be a skill that's new to you. If so, this part is for you. You can find an explanation of all that you need to know about cooking in cast iron: how to season and care for your pans, how to control the temperature and make cast iron's natural heating properties work for you, and how to restore old cast-iron pans. You can also find information on what to look for when you go shopping for cast iron.

Chapter 1

Welcome to Cast-Iron Cooking

Cast iron has a nostalgic appeal. Watch reruns of old TV Westerns or pick up any book chronicling America's past, from colonial times to the settling of the West to more modern portrayals of cowboy round-ups, and you're bound to find at least one domestic scene that features a cook, a fire, and a cast-iron pot. If you're into history, the idea of cooking the same way that your ancestors did may persuade you that cast iron is for you.

Most cooks today, however, want a few more incentives than the rough-around-the-edges charm that cast iron brings. They want cookware that's conducive to healthy eating; that's easy to use and care for; that can be used for a wide range of cooking methods; and that can withstand the abuse and use that occurs in a busy kitchen.

Cast iron offers all these qualities. Easy to use and easy to care for, cast iron lasts practically forever, and you can use any cooking method to cook anything in it. And most cast-iron cooks will tell you that food cooked in cast iron tastes better than food cooked in anything else. But like any well-crafted cookware, cast iron does require some care, and what you cook in it can turn out better if you know a few tricks.

In this chapter, I introduce you to basic information about cooking in cast iron, explain its benefits, and tell you what you need to know to use it successfully.

Coming Down on the Side of Cast Iron

Most modern-day cooks have never cooked in cast iron, many have never (knowingly, anyway) tasted a cast-iron dish, and even fewer have probably ever cared for a cast-iron skillet — beyond hanging it on the kitchen wall and dusting it periodically. If you're one of these people, you may not realize the culinary wonder that cast iron can be.

Plain and simple, cast iron is a great cookware. In terms of heating properties, economy, usefulness, and health benefits (yes, even health benefits), cast iron has much to offer. And that list doesn't even begin to touch on the area of taste!

So what's so great about cooking in cast iron? Plenty. Cast iron, with the proper seasoning and care, offers all the same benefits — and then some — that more modern cookware offers, and it has a history and longevity that these others lack.

'Til death do us part

Cast iron isn't just a descriptive term. These pots and pans are actually made from *iron* that has been melted and formed in pan-shaped molds or *casts.* (If you're interested in the details of how cast-iron pans are made, see the sidebar "A pan is born.") Made from the same base material that's used in engine blocks and building girders, cast-iron pans can last forever. Well, maybe not forever, but pretty darn close.

Cast iron's longevity is one reason why it can be so easy to find and relatively inexpensive. You don't have to buy it new. Many people inherit their cast iron or buy it at garage and yard sales. Even old pans that have been abused can be reborn with a little work. (Chapter 4 tells you how to save a worn cast-iron pot.)

The essential utensil — until 1940

People have been using cast iron for more than cookware since the 1600s. They also used it to dip candles, dye fabric, make soap, and wash clothes. During the California Gold Rush, folks panned for gold using small cast-iron skillets. Keep reading for more cast-iron trivia tidbits:

✔ Many people credit Paul Revere with being the creator of the Dutch oven — a fact that the Dutch are none too happy about.

✔ George Washington's mother bequeathed her cast iron in her will. You can still see some of the selection on display in the National Museum in Washington, DC.

✔ Lewis and Clark listed their Dutch oven as one of the most important pieces of equipment that they took with them on their exploration of the Pacific Northwest in 1804.

✔ Cast-iron cookware remained popular in the United States until the 1940s, when lighter, shinier aluminum cookware was introduced. Boo. Hiss.

✔ Today, the Dutch oven is the official cookware of the states of Texas, Arkansas, and Utah.

If cared for properly, cast iron is extremely tough and can last generations. It won't scratch, chip, or melt. (Well, at least not below 2,500 degrees. And I'm guessing that you're dealing with temperatures slightly below that mark.) The handles don't fall off, and cooking in it won't kill your pet parakeet. (Believe it or not, some other nonstick pans actually release a fume that's deadly to birds; see the sidebar "Keeping Tweety safe" for details.)

In fact, few things can harm a cast-iron pan. The two biggest dangers to cast iron? Cold water on a hot pan and a trip through the dishwasher. Head to Chapter 4 for care instructions.

Growing old gracefully

If you've ever found yourself examining (and cursing) the bottom of a non-stick pan for scratches and peels, you may come to appreciate that cast iron doesn't wear out with age; it actually gets better. The reason is that every time you cook in the pan, you're actually *seasoning* it again, filling in the microscopic pores and valleys that are part of the cast-iron surface. The more you cook, the smoother the surface becomes until, lo and behold, you have a pan that's the envy of cast-iron cooks everywhere.

New cast iron is a gunmetal gray. This color darkens with the initial seasoning. (See Chapter 3 for seasoning instructions.) It grows darker with every use until you reach the *patina* (the dark color and slight shine cast iron develops over time) that's the mark of well-used and well-seasoned cast iron. (See Figure 1-1.)

Figure 1-1: New cast iron (front) is relatively light. Older cast iron (back) has a satiny patina.

Of course, not all old cast iron has been taken care of, and some old pans look their age. Your cast iron may have enough rust spots, cooked-on gunk, and pitted surfaces to earn a place on the junk pile.

Keep in mind, however, that looks can be deceiving. Many battered and beaten cast-iron pieces can be reclaimed, rejuvenated, and restored to life. (Chapter 4 provides details.) With a little work, you can restore most old cast iron to cooking condition. And many consider cast iron to be a collectible, so you could end up with a pan that has value beyond how well it bakes biscuits. (For a word or two about collectible cast iron, see Chapter 2.)

Making dollars and sense

Cast iron is rugged and heavy. It isn't fancy cookware, and it doesn't have a fancy porcelain surface or come in a variety colors that match your kitchen decor. Of course, it has other positive features: It's nonstick when seasoned and, as a rule, it costs much less than other types of nonstick cookware. Add the longevity of cast iron (explained in the preceding "Growing old gracefully" section), and the savings are even greater. Table 1-1 gives you an idea of the cost difference between new cast iron and other nonstick cookware. As you read this table, keep the following in mind:

- ✔ The prices are approximate. You may pay more or less, depending on whether you buy your cookware from a retailer, the manufacturer, or order it from a third party who's offering discounts.

- ✔ All the non-cast-iron items listed come from nonstick product lines. When seasoned properly, cast iron has a nonstick surface, so we've only included comparable surfaces.

If you're buying new cast iron, buy preseasoned if you can. Preseasoned pans are only slightly more expensive, and the preseasoning eliminates the need to season your pans before use.

Table 1-1	Cost of New Cast Iron versus Other Cookware	
	10-Inch Skillet	*12-Inch Skillet*
Cast Iron		
Natural finish	$10 (10.25 inch)	$18
Preseasoned*	$15 (10.25 inch)	$22

	10-Inch Skillet	*12-Inch Skillet*
Non-stick Cookware		
All Clad	$90	$115
Analon	$75	$95
Cuisinart	$70 (9.5 inch)	$100 (12.5 inch)
KitchenAid	$110	$140
Le Crueset	$50 (9.0 inch)	$60

* Lodge Manufacturing is the only domestic producer of cast iron in the United States, and the only cast-iron manufacturer that offers a preseasoned line of cookware.

As a rule, cast iron is inexpensive if you buy it new or as an antique. It's not uncommon to hear of someone buying a cast-iron dish from a rummage sale or farm auction for $1 or a set of cast iron pots or pans for $15. For information on what to look for, whether you buy new or used cast iron, head to Chapter 2.

TECHNICAL STUFF

A pan is born

The process used to make cast-iron cookware, *sand casting,* has existed for many centuries, and the basic technique is still pretty much the same as it's always been: Take a mold shaped in sand, pour in molten iron, let it cool, chip away the sand, and there you go.

Of course, the actual process is a little more complex than that. Lodge Manufacturing, the only domestic producer of cast-iron cookware in the United States, mixes and melts pig iron (basically iron ore) and scrap steel (the leftovers from the manufacture of electric plates — the cleanest scrap steel available) together in a 2,800-degree furnace. After slagging off the impurities, which rise to the top, Lodge tests the molten iron to make sure that it meets quality and safety standards.

Then the molten iron is poured into the *cast,* a sand-clay mold. After it cools, the mold is dumped onto a vibrating conveyor belt that shakes the sand mold loose from the cast-iron product. The cast-iron is then shot blasted with millions of tiny BB's to remove any crusted sand that remains. Rough or sharp edges left over from the molding process are ground by hand, and the pan is literally stone washed to remove any remaining dust and smooth the pan's surface.

Lastly, the pan is dipped in a food-grade, FDA-approved wax dip to protect it from rust during shipping. One final quality control check looks for imperfections or flaws, tossing out any cast-iron products that don't meet the standards before packaging and sending the product to destinations around the world.

Cast iron is economical in another way. Cooking with cast iron uses less heat. Cast iron absorbs and retains heat so efficiently that you use less fuel when you cook with it. If you cook daily in cast iron, over the course of the average life span, you may save enough to actually make up the cost of the $10 skillet you're using. Okay, so it's not a huge savings, but it's a savings nonetheless (well, less, actually). Chapter 5 explains the heating properties of cast iron and how these affect the way you cook in more detail.

Offering versatility and variety

As plain as it looks, cast iron offers plenty of variety regarding what you cook and how and where you cook it.

✔ **The selection is huge.** Cast iron comes in just about any kind of pan, pot, and cookware shape you can think of. In addition to fry pans and skillets, you can find cast-iron griddles, grill pans, serving pots, Dutch ovens, pizza pans, melting pots, kettles, casseroles, loaf pans, muffin pans, woks, and more. For information on selecting your cookware and specialty items, head to Chapter 2.

✔ **A single pan covers a multitude of dishes.** Just because you can find all sorts of different cast-iron products doesn't mean that you need to have them to have a well-stocked kitchen. You can use a single cast-iron skillet for just about any cooking task: Bake a cake (Chapter 13), sear a filet (Chapter 6), roast a chicken (Chapter 7), fry potatoes or stir-fry vegetables (Chapter 10) — one skillet is all you need. But if, like me, you discover that cast-iron cooking is loads of fun and makes the food you cook in it taste great, you're probably going to want more than a single skillet.

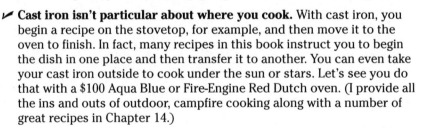

✔ **Cast iron isn't particular about where you cook.** With cast iron, you begin a recipe on the stovetop, for example, and then move it to the oven to finish. In fact, many recipes in this book instruct you to begin the dish in one place and then transfer it to another. You can even take your cast iron outside to cook under the sun or stars. Let's see you do that with a $100 Aqua Blue or Fire-Engine Red Dutch oven. (I provide all the ins and outs of outdoor, campfire cooking along with a number of great recipes in Chapter 14.)

This one probably goes without saying, but you *cannot* use cast iron in your microwave. If you do, you'll ruin your pan and your oven, and the fireworks display won't be worth the cleanup and replacement costs.

✔ **You can use it for most cooking tasks.** Cast iron is great for baking, simmering, braising, roasting, frying, grilling, and more. Really, the only thing that you don't want to do on a regular basis with your cast iron is boil water in it. (Water breaks down the seasoning and can cause your cast iron to rust; head to Chapter 4 for information on caring for your cast iron.)

✔ **You can cook almost anything in it.** Although cast iron made its reputation as the cookware to use for good, ol' fashioned cooking, don't let this reputation limit you as to how you use it. Because of its heating properties, its nonstick surface, its ability to withstand high temperatures, and the fact that you can use it both in the oven and on the stovetop, you can cook just about any food in it. Of course, some rules exist for what you can cook in cast iron and how you should cook it. Chapter 5 includes all the cooking tricks and techniques that are an important part of successful cast-iron cooking.

✔ **It's cookware and serving ware all rolled up in one.** Serving from a cast-iron dish has a presentation appeal all it's own (see Figure 1-2). You can't beat it for roasted meats, stews, chilis, pies, cobblers, and anything else that you want to look warm and appetizing. More importantly, cast iron holds heat, so your food stays warm throughout dinner, just the way you want it to for second helpings. One-dish meals, such as gumbo or jambalaya, are ideal candidates for serving straight from the pan. Chapter 9 has several recipes that you may want to try.

Figure 1-2:
Cast iron can go straight from the stove (or oven or campfire) to your table.

Experiencing Americana

The Pilgrims brought cast iron from the Old World to the New, and the pioneers took it westward. Heavy, dark, and rustic, cast iron has a nostalgic appeal that modern-day cookware lacks. It's the cookware of choice for countless outdoor enthusiasts, and no cattle drive would be complete — even today — without a cook, a cast-iron pot, and campfire.

Although you can cook just about any highbrow dish in cast iron, down-home favorites and comfort foods are what cast iron built its reputation on. These are also the foods that many modern cast-iron cooks still like to prepare in their black iron pans. And you'd be hard-pressed to find a better pan for many traditional favorites, such as cornbread, biscuits, and muffins. (Chapters 11 and 12 have several scrumptious recipes.)

This book contains several nontraditional cast-iron recipes, but if you like the old standards — the foods that your ancestors may have been inclined to make — head to Chapters 14 and 15, where you can find outdoor dishes and game recipes.

Here's to your good health

Cast iron gets a bad rep because it's often seen in the company of comfort foods and down-home country cookin' — the kind with plenty of fat and butter. And you can't beat it for frying eggs and potatoes — dishes that aren't the centerpiece of any heart-healthy diets that I've heard of.

True. All true. But it's not the whole story. Cooking in cast iron can actually be part of a healthy lifestyle.

Well-seasoned cast iron is virtually stick-free, requiring less or no oil — a characteristic of many heart-healthy recipes. You can cook any of the dishes that you would normally cook in any other nonstick pan in a cast-iron skillet. Cast iron isn't just good for heavy comfort foods; you can also use it to cook healthier, lighter fare. The trick is to keep your cast iron well seasoned. (Chapter 3 tells you how.)

Cooking in cast iron also boosts your iron intake. Trace amounts of iron get absorbed into the foods you cook.

Keeping Tweety safe

Rest assured that cooking in cast iron is safe for your feathered friends. Other nonstick cookware now must carry a warning that the fumes emitted during cooking can kill your pet bird. So you need to get rid of your nonstick cookware or move your bird from the room. Cast iron doesn't emit such fumes. However, you *can* kill a bird with a cast-iron skillet if you drop it on him.

The World Health Organization (WHO) considers iron deficiency to be the most prevalent nutritional disorder in the world. People at high risk of iron deficiency or anemia include women of childbearing age, pregnant women, older infants and toddlers, and teenage girls. Also at risk are those who suffer a significant or ongoing blood loss, due to a trauma or a disease. After you're diagnosed with an iron deficiency, you can't take in enough iron from the food that you eat to make up for the iron you lost.

Showing Special Consideration to Your Prized Possession

Cast iron can be great cookware. It's tough enough to withstand plenty of rough treatment. You don't have to worry about scratching it, so you can reach back into the far corners of your utensil drawer and grab hold of your long-forgotten metal whisk that would ruin the nonstick coating of your other pans. Now you're free to poke and prod your steaks at will with a meat fork or scrape the crispy fried potatoes from the bottom with a metal spatula. You can move the same pan from your stovetop into the oven and crank the temperature to broil to brown your shellfish or to warm the pan for fajitas. (Chapter 8 features fish and seafood recipes, and Chapter 16 has a great fajita recipe.) But despite how tough and versatile it is, keeping your cast iron in cooking trim does require some special care:

- ✔ **You have to season it.** Seasoning is the key to cooking in cast iron. Without the proper seasoning, food will stick and taste metallic, and your pan is more susceptible to rust. Seasoning isn't difficult, but it does take a little time. For information on how to season or reseason a pan, skip to Chapter 3.

- ✔ **The dark patina takes awhile to achieve.** Cooking with your pan frequently can help your pan along; washing and storing it as described in Chapter 4 also helps, but a new cast-iron pan takes a while to break in. After it's broken in, though, you're going to have a hard time finding another type of pan that beats it for usefulness and flavor.

If you can't stand the idea of seasoning a pan yourself or you want the instant gratification of a pan that's already been seasoned before you lay hands on it, consider wheedling Grandma out of her cast iron or buy preseasoned cast iron, which is now available.

- ✔ **To preserve your pan's seasoning, be careful when cooking certain types of foods.** Acidic foods, such as tomatoes or citrus products, can react to the iron and mess up your seasoning. So as a rule, avoid cooking these types of foods until your pan is well seasoned. Chapter 5 explains this and other cooking techniques that you need to know.

✔ **Cooking successfully in cast iron requires certain techniques that may be unfamiliar you.** Did you know, for example, that before you pour batter into a cast-iron pan, you should preheat the pan? You'd be surprised at the difference this little trick makes to the consistency and flavor of your foods. You can find other successful tips like this in Chapter 5.

✔ **You have to follow a few cleaning and storage rules.** These rules keep the seasoning intact and help you avoid rust. But don't worry, they aren't difficult to follow: Don't use soap; don't put it in the dishwasher; store the cookware in a cool, dry place, and so on, but they may be different from what you're used to. Head to Chapter 4 for cleaning and storage instructions.

✔ **Cast iron weighs a ton.** You can look at this as a good thing: Because of its weight, it's sturdy, and it'll help you stay buff. Or you can look at its heaviness as a negative: Heaven forbid that you should try to anchor it on the drywall in your kitchen.

Before you throw up your hands and proclaim that cast iron isn't worth the effort, try to keep a little perspective: These care instructions aren't much different from the instructions that come with fancier and more expensive cookware. Various manufacturers include the recommendation that you not wash their cookware in a dishwasher. (The detergent is too abrasive and can mar the surface.) And you're likely to find added warnings: Don't use high heat, or you void your warranty. Don't use metal utensils, or you run the risk of damaging the nonstick surface and ruining your pan.

If you don't follow the care and cleaning instructions with cast iron, what you run the risk of ruining isn't the pan; it's the seasoning. It's a hassle, but you can fix that.

Chapter 2

Selecting Cast-Iron Cookware

- -

- -

*I*f you're just starting to cook with cast iron, you're probably in the market to buy a piece or two. And even if you already have one, two, or a few cast-iron pieces, you may be looking to add to your set.

Fortunately, cast iron is easy to find; it's relatively inexpensive, and it comes in all sorts of shapes and sizes, from the traditional cast-iron skillets and camp ovens to specialty items, such as Bundt pans, loaf pans, and specially shaped cornbread or muffin pans. You can even find hibachi grills made of cast iron. And don't forget the accessories: grill presses, dinner bells, and sundry other items that you may decide you absolutely have to have.

To help you decide what you need (or want) and what you don't need and how to recognize quality pieces when you see them, this chapter explains the different cast-iron pieces and accessories available, and tells you what to look for when you're shopping for cast iron (quality matters, because you want cast iron that's safe, easy-to-use, and durable), whether you're buying it new or used. And for those just beginning their cast-iron cooking adventures, this chapter also gives advice on the cookware that's essential.

Ironing Out the Cast of Characters: Pots, Pans, and Specialty Items

You can find both new and used cast-iron cookware in a variety of shapes and sizes. The most popular pieces are the skillets and Dutch ovens, but you can find all sorts of other basic pans and pots, too, as well as specialty items. Keep reading for an explanation of the different kinds of cast-iron products and the types of food that you can cook in them.

When you talk about cast iron, you have to talk about *versatility*. Although some items are designed with a special purpose in mind (the camp oven, for example, is designed for use outside), you can use cast-iron cookware in a variety of ways and for several different purposes. Use it indoors or out. Put it on the stove or in the stove. Bake a pie in a Dutch oven or roast a chicken in a fry pan. I explain what these pans are *generally* used for. How *you* use them depends on your own cooking style, need, and imagination.

For information about where to go to buy cast iron and how to recognize well-made cast iron, head to the section "A Shopping We Will Go" later in this chapter.

Skillets

Cast-iron skillets (shown in Figure 2-1) come in a variety of sizes, from very small (approximately 6 inches in diameter, some less) to very large (over 15 inches in diameter). With average depths between 1¼ inches and 2½ inches (depending on the size of the pan), these pans are great for a number of cooking tasks, on the stove or in the oven:

✔ Baking

✔ Broiling

✔ Pan-frying

✔ Roasting

✔ Simmering

✔ Stir-frying

The size you need depends on how you plan to use your skillet and how many people that you need to feed. The smaller skillets are great for making great one- or two-serving meals and side dishes. The medium-size skillets (9 to 11 inches) are good for feeding average-size parties and baking cakes, breads, and biscuits. Reserve the larger pans for when you need to feed a crowd.

In addition to the standard, round skillets, square skillets are also available (see Figure 2-2), and you can use them in the same way that you use the round skillets. Some — particularly the smaller ones with shallow sides — can function as mini-griddles. (See the "Griddles and grill pans" section, later in this chapter.) These are ideal for grilled cheese sandwiches or pancakes if you want to make one or two at a time.

Photograph courtesy of Lodge Manufacturing Co.

Figure 2-1:
Cast-iron skillets are good, all-purpose cooking utensils.

Figure 2-2:
You can also find square skillets in different sizes.

Photograph courtesy of Lodge Manufacturing Co.

Two dishes that, hands down, are better when cooked in cast-iron skillet? Cornbread and Pineapple Upside-Down Cake. (See Chapter 11 for great cornbread recipes, if I do say so myself, and go to Chapter 13 for the cake recipe.) Many southern cooks, in fact, will tell you that they keep one skillet reserved solely for cornbread. Just as many will say that making Pineapple Upside-Down Cake in anything other than a cast-iron skillet is tantamount to heresy. Go to Chapter 18 for a list of other foods that are arguably better when cooked in cast iron.

Fry pans

Fry pans are similar to skillets except that the sides of fry pans are deeper (usually 3 inches or deeper) so that the grease doesn't splatter as much when you're frying. (See Figure 2-3.) You can perform many of the same cooking tasks in these pans that you can in the skillets. Because of the depth of the pan, you can also use fry pans to do the following:

✔ **Deep-frying:** When you deep-fry, you submerge the food completely in hot oil instead of cooking the food a side at a time as you do when pan-frying.

✔ **Simmering stews and soups:** Whereas shallower pans tend to expose too much of the soup's surface to evaporation, fry pans are deep enough to give you a nice slow simmer without drying out the broth.

✔ **Slow-cooking foods on the stovetop or in the oven:** If you have a lid or want to cover the top with aluminum foil, you can use a fry pan in the same way that you use a Dutch oven. See the section "Dutch ovens," later in this chapter.

Figure 2-3: The deeper sides of a fry pan mean less splattering and less mess.

Photograph courtesy of Lodge Manufacturing Co.

Griddles and grill pans

Griddles can be round, square, or rectangular (long enough to fit across two burners on your stovetop), and they come in various sizes. (See Figure 2-4.) The smooth surface and shallow sides (usually ½ inch or less) are perfect for making pancakes (see Chapter 12) and hot sandwiches; frying eggs, bacon, and anything else; roasting vegetables (Chapter 10); and making great foods of the hand-held variety, such as quesadillas, fajitas, and pizza (Chapter 16).

Figure 2-4:
A sampling
of griddles.

Photograph courtesy of Lodge Manufacturing Co.

Grill pans, shown in Figure 2-5, are exactly what they sound like: Pans that you use to grill food (vegetables, seafood, poultry, meat, and so on), either on the stovetop or over a campfire. The ribbed bottom keeps the food out of the drippings and leaves nice sear marks, much like you'd get from cooking on an outdoor grill.

Figure 2-5:
The ribbed
bottom of a
grill pan
keeps your
food up and
out of any
drippings.

Photograph courtesy of Lodge Manufacturing Co.

REMEMBER

Because of the ribbed bottom, grill pans aren't suitable for anything other than grilling. If you don't believe me, try stirring a stew or getting cornbread to pop out.

Dutch ovens

Dutch ovens are deep-sided pots with lids that you can use on the stovetop or inside the oven. They're the original slow cookers. Put in the food, slap on a lid, set the oven to a low or medium temperature and then come back a few hours later to a tender, delicious meal. But you can use your versatile Dutch oven for more than slow cooking. You can also use Dutch ovens for

- ✔ Baking
- ✔ Deep-frying
- ✔ Pan-frying
- ✔ Simmering

You name it; a Dutch oven can probably do it.

Staying inside or getting outdoors

If you go looking for a Dutch oven, keep in mind that they fall into two categories: those designed primarily for indoor cooking and those designed for outdoor cooking. (See Figure 2-6.) The differences between the two are as follows:

- ✔ **The lid:** An indoor oven has a domed lid. The lid of an outdoor oven is generally flatter and is *flanged* (has a lip around the rim) so that you can put coals on the top.

- ✔ **The bottom:** Indoor Dutch ovens have flat bottoms; outdoor Dutch ovens have three short legs to keep the oven above the heat source.

- ✔ **What they're called:** Indoor Dutch ovens are called *Dutch ovens.* Some people call them *bean pots.* Outdoor Dutch ovens are called *camp ovens* or, less frequently, *cowboy ovens.* You, however, may call yours anything you want.

For more information about cooking in the great outdoors (including camp oven info) and some recipes to go with it, head to Chapter 14.

Figure 2-6:
A Dutch oven for indoor use (left) and a camp oven, designed for cooking outdoors (right).

Photograph courtesy of Lodge Manufacturing Co.

Just because camp ovens are for outdoor use, don't assume that means that regular old Dutch ovens can't be used for outdoor cooking. They can. The outdoor ovens just have a few little amenities built right in to make outdoor cooking a little easier.

Size matters

Dutch and camp ovens come in all sorts of sizes. What size you get depends on how many people you're cooking for and what you're cooking. If you intend to cook breads and cakes, an oven with shallower sides works fine. If you cook mostly meats or stews and chilis, go for an oven with deeper sides.

Table 2-1 lists some common sizes of Dutch ovens and shows approximately how many people an oven of that size feeds. Most people do just fine with a Dutch oven in the 4- to 8-quart size range. (**Note:** A *deep* oven is one that simply has deeper sides than the regular ovens; for that reason, deep ovens can hold more food than regular ovens of the same size.)

Table 2-1	Dutch Oven Capacities	
Size	*Capacity in Quarts*	*Number of People Served*
8 inch	2 quarts	1 to 2
10 inch	4 quarts	4 to 7
12 inch	6 quarts	12 to 14
12 inch (deep)	8 quarts	16 to 20
14 inch	10 quarts	16 to 20
14 inch (deep)	12 quarts	22 to 28

Specialty items and accessories

The skillets, pots, and griddles that comprise the basic collection of many cast-iron cooks are the workhorses of the cast-iron world. However, specialty pans are available, too. Some are primarily fun; others are primarily functional. Are any of them absolutely mandatory? No. Not unless you just gotta have it.

Bakeware

You can find cast-iron muffin pans, loaf pans, biscuit pans, sectioned corn-bread skillets, corn-stick pans in various shapes, and cake pans (regular round and square and Bundt shaped). Figure 2-7 shows a sampling of the types of bakeware available.

Playing the Dutch-oven name game

A cast-iron pot by any other name would cook as well. Basically, what it's called doesn't make a lick of difference. Lodge Manufacturing, a cast-iron manufacturer, for example, uses the term *Dutch oven* to refer to the flat-bottomed ovens and *outdoors camp oven* to refer to the oven with legs. Wagner, another manufacturer of cast-iron cookware (who went out of business in 1999), preferred the term *cowboy oven* for the outdoor ovens. Some people use the term *camp oven* to refer to Dutch ovens that you use outside and *Dutch oven* to refer to those that you use inside. What you need to know is that, if you go looking for a camp oven, Dutch oven, cowboy oven, bean pot, or whatever it may be called in your neck of the woods, you may be at a linguistic disadvantage if the person

your talking to uses a different term. If that's the case, stick with *Dutch oven,* which seems to be the term that most people recognize and add any descriptors (with legs, that I can cook outdoors in, and so on) that you need to make yourself clear.

By the way, people can't even agree on why these devices are called *Dutch ovens* in the first place. Some claim the name was given to these pots because the sand-casting method was created in Holland (which may stun the Chinese who were making cast-iron products as early as 800 to 700 BC). Others claim that Dutch traders went around the United States selling wares and became famous for their cast-iron pots, which came to be referred to as *Dutch ovens.*

Figure 2-7:
Cast-iron
bakeware
serves a
variety of
purposes:
From left to
right, a
corn-stick
pan, a
muffin pan,
and a loaf
pan.

Photograph courtesy of Lodge Manufacturing Co.

Fry kits

A fry kit isn't anything other than a deep-sided cast-iron pot with a wire basket for lifting the food from the hot oil. As its name implies, a fry kit is used for deep-frying foods. The slightly sloped sides are deep enough to hold the amount of oil necessary to submerge foods and cut down on splattering.

You can buy these items as a kit (you may get a thermometer and a recipe or two to get you started), or you can assemble your own, using any deep-sided cast iron pot — even a Dutch oven. (See Figure 2-8.)

Figure 2-8:
A standard fry kit consists of a deep pan, a wire basket, and a thermo-meter (optional) for accuracy.

Photograph courtesy of Lodge Manufacturing Co.

Serving ware

Serving ware includes items such as casserole dishes, serving platters/griddles (like those used in restaurants), and single-serving soup dishes. These items let you take food directly from the oven and place it on your table. (Of course, you can do that with all cast iron.)

Other implements

You can find many other cooking implements and wares made from cast iron — casserole dishes, roasters, fish pans, hibachi-like grills, and so on. A plethora of accessories designed especially for cast-iron cooks is also available: meat racks, grill presses, tripods, tote bags, and even dinner bells, just to name a few.

What You Need to Get Started

One or two pans is really all you need to begin as a cast-iron cook, and you can't go wrong with a skillet with a lid. With a plain old 10-inch skillet, you can perform just about any cooking task that you want, and it's big enough for main-dish meals for most families. You can also cook cakes, breads, biscuits, cobblers, and a bunch of other edibles in it.

If your family is a little larger (say six or more), a 10-inch skillet may not be big enough for main dishes, such as casseroles or roasted meats with vegetables. In that case, you may want to add a 12-inch skillet, a fryer (which is like a skillet but with deeper sides), or a Dutch oven to your collection. But keep the 10-inch skillet, too, for other dishes.

What's *essential* depends on what you plan to cook. If you plan to spend every weekend outdoors cooking for friends and family, you're going to need a different pan than the person who only wants to make fried chicken the way her mother used to. Figure out what you want to do with your cast iron and then go from there.

A Shopping We Will Go

Cast iron is pretty easy to find. You can buy it new directly from the manufacturer or from retailers who carry that line of cookware. Hardware stores and recreational stores also sell cast-iron cookware (but their lines are usually limited to the outdoor supplies). If you're interested in used cast iron, you can find it at garage and rummage sales, farm auctions, or antique shops. You can even hit up Aunt Edna for her cast iron (but don't be surprised if she won't give it to you). You can also order cast iron from the Internet.

After you locate your cast-iron supplier, you need to do a little examination of the quality. Whether you're looking for cast iron that came straight from the foundry or has spent a few years (or several decades) in someone else's kitchen, you need to pay attention to the quality of the pan that you're buying.

Evaluating quality

Whether new or used, cast-iron pans are made from iron and steel formed in sand casts (or molds), hence the name, *cast iron.* The process itself and the materials used give cast iron the texture it has. If you're used to shiny, smooth aluminum or stainless steel, you may not realize that new cast iron is supposed to feel rough and be a dull, gray color like, well, metal.

When it comes to cast-iron quality, first off, it matters. The quality of the pan directly impacts how well it takes seasoning, how efficiently it heats, how long it lasts, and how safe it is to use. The quality of the material used, the mixture of the different metals (the *metallurgy*), and the quality of the mold determines the overall quality of the pan. When you shop for cast iron, look at the following:

✔ **Surface texture:** The cast iron should be uniformly rough (like a cat's tongue) and even. It shouldn't be jagged, pitted, chipped, cracked, or obviously scratched. Nor should you find areas that look "odd"— that is, not like the rest of the surface. When you run your hand along the interior, you shouldn't feel waves or dips.

Finer-grained cast iron is easier to cure or season. (See Chapter 3 for seasoning instructions.) Poorly made cast iron has a courser grain that's hard to season and that requires more attention and care after it's seasoned.

✔ **Width of sides:** To be an efficient and even conductor of heat (and thus avoid hot spots and warping), the thickness of the sides of the cast iron should be the same all the way around. Uneven sides also make the pan more prone to breaking. So if the sides seem thinner in some areas than in others, don't buy the pan unless you only want it for decoration in your kitchen.

✔ **Metallurgy:** The mixture of the metals matters. Much goes into the metallurgy of a cast-iron pan, and much of this, like the quality of the iron and steel used or the temperature at which it's heated, you can't judge just by looking. The metallurgy is as important to even heat conduction as is the mold tolerances that create a pan with uniform thicknesses. Either one can create hot spots or uneven heating — the bane of cooks everywhere. (See the sidebar "Mixing up the metal" in this chapter for info.) Occasionally, however, you may notice something is obviously wrong, like discolorations or blotchiness in the metal.

Steer clear of cast iron that has these flaws. Cast iron that has discolorations or blotchiness can be brittle and easy to break. Also stay away from cast iron that has other odd spots — areas that just don't look like the rest of the pan. If the material wasn't heated at a high enough temperature, you can have uneven distribution of the various metals (more steel in one place or more iron in another, for example), and that creates hot spots.

✔ **Where it's made:** American manufacturers have to meet government-mandated safety requirements regarding the product itself (and the materials that go into it) and the manufacturing process. These safeguards protect both consumers and employees. Manufacturers in other countries may or may not have to abide by similar requirements.

Although imported cast iron is often less expensive, make sure that your cast iron is made domestically, for both quality and safety reasons.

Mixing up the metal

Making a delicious cake requires that you mix certain ingredients in specific amounts into a batter and then cook the batter at a particular temperature. Making cast iron is essentially the same.

You gather your ingredients — pig iron, which is basically iron ore and steel. The steel has to be clean; it can't come from automotive parts (or worse, used automotive parts), and it shouldn't contain lead, cadmium (another metal), or any other substance that's toxic to humans.

You mix these metals (so much pig iron to so much steel). Instead of a blender, you use heat. When you heat up iron and steel at high temperatures (2,800 degrees), the substances mix automatically as their heated molecules perk up, begin to dance around, and then lose all control and start banging into each other. The temperature is important because, if the mixture isn't heated and poured at the proper temperature, the metal doesn't mix evenly, and you end up with more or less iron or steel in one spot or another.

Before the metal is poured into its mold, it should be tested with a *spectrometer* — a machine that can identify the amount and percentage of elements within a metal. Different spectrometers test for different elements. In a foundry that makes cast-iron cookware, the spectrometer should test to make sure that

✔ The percentage of iron to steel is what it should be. This test preserves the integrity and quality of the pan.

✔ That no problem metals (such as lead) are present. This test is performed for safety and health reasons.

Only when the mix is approved should the molds be poured.

Buying used cast iron

To find old cast iron, you can go to all sorts of places: estate sales, farm auctions, antique malls, rummage sales, and so on. The cost of used cast iron is generally quite a bit less than what you'd spend for new (which itself is relatively inexpensive). And, if the piece is still in cooking condition, the work (seasoning) has already been done for you.

Used cast iron — especially when it comes free from Grandma and includes a bunch of recipes to boot — is great. In fact, if you have a choice between a new cast-iron pan and an old one that's been well used and cared for, go for an old one.

You still need to evaluate the quality of the cast iron. When you buy used, pay attention to the following:

- ✔ **How well it's been cared for:** Although you can refurbish many abused pieces of cast iron (Chapter 4 tells you how), some pieces aren't worth salvaging. Avoid pieces that are warped, cracked, pitted, or have been chipped. Although fine for hanging as a wall decoration, these pans aren't suitable for cooking any more.

- ✔ **How much work restoring the piece will take:** Some old cast iron is ready to use as soon as you get it, provided of course, that you don't mind that the patina is the result of someone else's — a stranger's — cooking. (Absorbing the oil and fat of the foods that are cooked in the cast iron is the way that the cast iron is seasoned.) If you do mind, restoring the pan is fairly simple: You simply burn off the seasoning that's on it and reseason. (Go to Chapter 3 for instructions.) Some old pans, however, require much work because of rust, crusted on yuck, and other gunk that you have to remove. These pans can be reclaimed, but it'll take more work. Head to Chapter 4 for details on how to bring new life to an abused cast-iron pan.

- ✔ **Whether the item has any paint spots on it:** Dishonest dealers often repair holes and cracks with *epoxy resin* (an adhesive that hobbyists use in abundance when they build model airplanes and cars) and then paint over the repair to hide it.

Cast iron that looks like it's been used as a paint bucket isn't the issue; you can sand blast the paint off. The issue is black paint deliberately used on a black pan. Sure, black paint on a black pan may be as innocent as the bright yellow paint splashes and drips on another pan, but you can't be sure until you remove the black paint. If it's epoxy, you don't want to use the pan. Epoxy resin is a great adhesive: strong, durable, long-lasting . . . but it's also poisonous if swallowed, can damage skin on contact, can irritate eyes, and needs to be used in a well-ventilated area.

If you stumble across a cast-iron pan with the *Griswold* logo on it, and it's going for a couple of bucks, snatch it up. Griswold cast-iron cookware is a collector's item. Many pieces fetch upwards of several hundred dollars. For more info on collectible cast iron, hop to the sidebar titled — what else? — "Collecting cast iron."

Collecting cast iron

Cast-iron cookware is becoming a collector's item. As you shop for used cast iron — particularly if you're browsing through an antique store — you may come across some pieces that are priced in the hundreds of dollars. If you're just looking for a biscuit pan, you probably don't want to spend what these people are asking. Still, in case you're interested, the cast iron from two companies (now out of business) are fetching a pretty penny:

✔ **Griswold Manufacturing Company of Erie, PA:** Griswold was in business between 1865 and 1957. Family controlled until 1947, the company fell into decline during its last years; the Wagner Manufacturing Company of Sydney, Ohio, eventually bought the Griswold molds. Much sought after pieces of Griswold cast iron go for around $1,000; many sell for $400 to $600. The Griswold logo is on the bottom of its pans. Before you buy, though, keep in mind that some Griswold pans aren't valued as much as others. I'm referring to the pans made during the declining years and the ones that Wagner made and put the Griswold logo on. (Wagner also bought the Griswold logo in addition to the molds.)

✔ **Wagner Manufacturing Company of Sydney, OH:** Incorporated in 1891, Wagner Manufacturing was another family business; brothers Bernard, Milton, Louis, and William Wagner owned and controlled it. The company remained in business until 1999 and, until its closure, was the oldest continuously operating manufacturer of cookware in the United States. Many Wagner pieces sell for between $50 and $200 dollars.

If you're interested in collecting cast-iron pieces, several resources are at your disposal. First, head to the Web. In your Internet search engine, type in **heirloom cast iron** or **collectible cast iron.** You'll generate a whole list of sites for cookware and other cast-iron collectibles, such as toys. Before you buy anything, be sure to research its worth in books devoted to the topic. Some to get you started:

✔ *The Book of Wagner and Griswold, Martin, Lodge, Vollrath, Excelsior,* by David G. Smith (Schiffer Publishing, 2000)

✔ *Collectors Guide to Wagner Ware and Other Companies with Prices* (LW Publishing & Book Sales, 1995)

✔ *300 Years of Kitchen Collectibles,* 5th edition, by Linda Campbell Franklin (Krause Publications, 2003)

Features to look for (or avoid)

A pan may just be a pan, but many cast-iron pieces have little extras that make cooking in them, carrying them, and otherwise using them easier. So look for the following when you buy:

✔ **Support handles:** Cast iron is just plain heavy. Add the weight of dinner to an already heavy skillet, and carrying the loaded cast iron to the table *without* a support handle opposite the usual handle requires a clear path, a mad dash, and a little luck.

✔ **Heat-resistant bails:** The *bail* is the arched metal handle that you often see on kettles. If you're using a Dutch oven in the oven or over a campfire, a heat-resistant bail comes in mighty handy.

✔ **Flanged lids:** You can use any cast-iron pan outdoors; the key is to have a *flanged lid* (a lid with a rim around it). The flange lets you put coals right on top of the lid without worrying that they'll roll off. (For more on the ins and outs of outdoor cooking, see Chapter 14.)

✔ **Lids that can serve double duty:** Some Dutch oven lids, when turned upside down, serve as griddles. If you have a choice between a regular lid and one of these, why not go with the lid that gives you added flexibility? ***Note:*** Cast iron lids fit multiple, same-size pots and pans. If, for example, you have a 10-inch lid, you can use it on any 10-inch skillet, deep fryer, Dutch oven, and so on.

Some cast-iron pans have wooden handles. Don't buy them. Sure, maybe they look pretty, and people may try to tell you that the handle stays cool, but that's only true if you use the pan on the stovetop. These handles reduce the functionality and life of your pan. You can't use the pans over the campfire, and the bolts that hold the handles on eventually loosen.

Other Items You Need If You Use Cast Iron

You really don't need much to have a well-stocked cast-iron kitchen: one or two pans, a few good recipes (or the creativity to make your own), and the following:

✔ **Hot pads — and good ones:** Cast iron gets hot, and it's unforgiving. All cast-iron cooks, sooner or later, grab a hot handle and then spend a few painful seconds trying to shake away the sting from their palms while cursing for being so careless. And you're not the only one to get burned. Think about your tabletop, too. Hot pads are the answers. (Kitchen towels and tablecloths generally don't have enough heft.) You can even find hot pads made just for the skillet handle, which you can slide on and off.

✔ **Stiff-bristled brush:** You need a stiff-bristled brush to clean your cast iron.

Don't mistake a stiff-bristled brush for a wire brush. Wire brushes are too abrasive. They can scratch right through your seasoning; then you'll have to reseason your pan.

For the indoor cook, that's about it. Nothing fancy. And certainly not enough to break the bank.

If you're cooking outdoors, you'll probably want to add a number of other items to your laundry list to make the experience easier and safer. I discuss lid lifters, spyders, charcoal chimney starters and a number of other outdoor accessories in Chapter 14. That chapter also features general outdoor-cooking information and a number of campfire recipes.

Chapter 3

This Little Pan of Mine, I'm Gonna Make It Shine: Seasoning Cast Iron

- -

In This Chapter

▶ Getting a new pan ready for seasoning

▶ Seasoning a pan, step by step

▶ Recognizing the signs that tell you to reseason

▶ Preparing a preseasoned pan plan

- -

*T*he key to cast-iron cooking is the seasoning, and I'm not talking about spices and herbs. Because of the natural characteristics of cast iron — the rough, porous surface — you have to season new cookware before you use it, and you have to reseason old cast iron periodically.

How well your pan is seasoned determines how well it cooks, how stick-free the surface is, and, frankly, how happy you'll be with the whole cast-iron cooking experience.

The idea of seasoning cast iron often strikes terror in the hearts of otherwise brave kitchen dwellers. But I'm here to tell you that the seasoning process suffers from an undeserved, bad reputation: It's actually quite simple, and reseasoning is even easier. This chapter tells you everything that you need to know to season, reseason, and preserve the seasoning you have. If you have preseasoned cast iron, you can also find information on what you have to do to it before you cook.

Preseasoned cast iron — cast iron that's been seasoned at the foundry — is pretty much ready to use as soon as you take it from the box. Only slightly more expensive than cast iron that has a natural finish, the preseasoned variety is definitely worth the money. For information about preseasoned cast iron or to order some, visit the Web site of Lodge Manufacturing Co. (the company that created the process and currently the only one that sells pre-seasoned cast iron) at www.lodgemfg.com. (Of course, if you don't want to buy new cast iron, another option is to get cast iron that's been preseasoned the old fashioned way, through cooking. Buy it used — or talk a relative or old family friend into giving up her cast iron.)

Seasoning a New Pan

Because of the materials that make up a cast-iron pan and the casting process, new cast iron is porous. It has a slightly rough texture and microscopic pores that you have to fill before you can use the pan. *Seasoning* (which is also called *curing*), is the process of filling these pores and smoothing the rough texture with oil, thus creating a smooth, nonstick surface. (Basically, you're cooking the oil into the pan.) Seasoning also serves a purpose: It protects your iron pan from rust.

If you try to cook in cast iron that hasn't been seasoned, you're going to end up with a burned, sticky mess. The pores in your hot pan (which expand slightly when you cook) will absorb whatever it is that you put in it. Hamburger? Eggs? You name it. It'll get cooked into the pores, and then your task to make the pan useable becomes a tad more time consuming. Head to Chapter 4 for information on how to restore an abused pan.

What you need: Supplies and a little time

It doesn't take much to season a pan. You just need the following:

- **Oven:** Any old oven will do — gas, electric, convection, or standard all work fine. Some people even cure their cast-iron in an outdoor grill, which is fine as long as it has a lid, and you can control the heat.

- **Shortening:** Any good quality solid vegetable shortening (melted) or vegetable oil will do; I like Crisco. Some people say that you can season a pan with lard, bacon grease, butter (or margarine) or other animal products, but I don't recommend it. If you don't use your cast iron regularly, these seasonings can turn rancid — ugh; then you're left with the job of cleaning the seasoning off yourself and reapplying it. Fun, fun, fun.

- **Paper towel, sponge, or dish cloth:** To spread the melted shortening over the pan, I like using a clean old dish cloth that doesn't lint or tear, but you can use anything you want — even a brand new dish cloth that matches your dish towels and apron if that's what you're into. Just keep in mind that whatever you use will turn gray or black from being rubbed over the new pan.

- **Aluminum foil or baking sheet:** You use this to catch any dripping oil.

> ✔ **Time:** You cook the piece in the oven for about an hour. While it's in the oven, you want to stay nearby, simply because you should never leave a hot oven unattended. After the oven's off and the pan's cooling inside, you're off the hook.

To save time, season multiple pieces at the same time. If your pan has a lid, season the lid when you season the pan. The only limit is the amount of cast iron that you can fit into your oven. Keep reading for an explanation of how to season a pan, but the instructions are the same for seasoning multiple pieces, too.

Step 1: Preparing the new pan for seasoning

Cast-iron pans that aren't preseasoned come from the factory with a protective coating. Cast iron made in the United States uses a food-grade, FDA approved wax. Imported cast iron uses a water-soluble shellac. Either way, you have to remove this preservative first before you can begin seasoning.

Don't wash the protective coating off your cast iron unless you're sure that you have time to season it. Without the coating, your pan may rust; then before you can season it, you have the hassle of removing the rust. For tips on getting rid of rust, head to Chapter 4.

To get rid of the protective coating on new cast iron, follow these steps:

1. **Scrub the pan using the hottest water that you can stand, a mild dish detergent or soap, and a stiff-bristled (not wire) brush or a scouring pad (not steel wool).**

   Rather than fill a sink with water, which has a tendency to cool fairly quickly, I boil about 2 cups of water in the microwave and pour this directly into the bottom of my pan. Then I add a little dish detergent and scrub away with my brush. (And I'll admit it; I wear rubber gloves to protect my hands from the hot water.)

   Be sure to scrub all surfaces of the pan: the bottom, the handle, inside and out. *Note:* This is the only time that you'll ever use soap or a scouring pad on your cast iron — unless, that is, you're reseasoning it because of some disaster, culinary or otherwise.

2. **Dry the pan thoroughly.**

   Use a paper towel or dish towel. If the water was hot enough, most of it evaporates by itself. You can also put the pan on a burner and let it warm up until all the moisture is gone.

When the pan is clean and dry, you're ready to season.

Step 2: Seasoning your new cast iron

After your pan is clean, you're ready to season it. Follow these steps:

1. **Place aluminum foil on the bottom rack in your oven and preheat your oven to 350 degrees.**

   Make sure that you cover the area underneath your cast iron. The foil catches any excess shortening that may drip off. If you prefer, you can use a baking sheet. Just place the cast iron directly on the baking sheet.

2. **Place the cast-iron pan on a stovetop burner and melt about a table-spoon of shortening in it.**

   If you don't melt the shortening, you run the risk of getting too much on the pan, which isn't a huge problem — it'll just be more to drip and smoke in your oven.

3. **Using a paper towel or sponge, wipe the entire surface of the pan with the melted shortening.**

   Be sure to get all the surfaces: tops, bottoms, handles, and legs, too, that is, if you're seasoning an outdoor oven. You only need to cover the pan in a thin layer of oil. If your oil is pooling or dripping you've got too much on there. Wipe the excess away.

4. **Place the cookware upside down in the oven.**

   You place the pan upside down so that any excess shortening drips off instead of pooling inside the pan and carbonizing.

5. **Bake for 1 hour.**

   As the cast iron cooks, you may notice a slight smell and perhaps some smoke. That's normal, and nothing to call the fire department about. The more shortening you use, the more pronounced the smoke and the smell will be. Fortunately, the smell and smoke dissipate pretty quickly. If you can't stand it, open a window to air out your kitchen a bit.

6. **When the hour's up, turn the oven off and leave the cookware in the oven until the oven cools down.**

   The cast iron is still baking while the oven cools, so you achieve a deeper cure.

7. **When the cast iron is cool, remove it from the oven.**

   Admire your handiwork. If anyone else is around the house, have him admire it, too. Or go door to door through the neighborhood, shouting, "I'm one mean seasoning machine." It's up to you.

Didn't get the shiny black surface that you were expecting? Don't worry. The black, shiny surface comes as you use your pan. What you've just done is the *initial* cure. Every time you cook with your cast iron, the cure will deepen, and in a few months time, you'll have the deep black and satiny patina that you want.

8. **Put your cast iron away (see Chapter 4 for storage info) or start cooking!**

If you're in the mood to cook, have never cooked in cast iron before, and just want to try your hand at it, try a dessert. They're always fun to make and eat. Head to Chapter 13 for recipes. Of course, if you're the practical type, head to Chapter 10; that's where the vegetables are.

Protecting your seasoning

Now that your pan is seasoned, keep the following in mind to protect and deepen the seasoning:

- The first few times — say, six or seven — you cook in your cast iron, use it to cook foods that have plenty of fat. Doing so deepens the seasoning more quickly and gives you the nonstick surface that you're aiming for. Fry hamburgers, fry chicken, make bacon, bake pies, and so on.

- Initially (the first 6 or 7 times that you use the pan), avoid cooking acidic foods (such as tomato-based dishes) and alkaline foods (such as beans), because the acid and alkali react with the iron and mess up the seasoning.

- Use your cast iron frequently. First, if you're new to cast-iron cooking, this gives you practice. Second, every time you cook with your cast iron, you're essentially reseasoning it.

- After you clean your cast iron (without soap, by the way; Chapter 4 has instructions), wipe a small amount of vegetable oil around the pan. This puts back any seasoning that was lost during cleaning.

Before you know it, your cast-iron pan will have the shine that you want. And who knows? Maybe someday, your kid will be pestering you to give him your old pan.

Reseasoning a Pan

First things first. The best way to reseason a pan is to cook frequently in it. Every time you cook, the oils from the food are absorbed into the pan and deepen the seasoning. And when the meal is over and you're done cleaning the pan, wipe a little vegetable oil around its surface. Just doing these two things — cooking in it and wiping it with a very thin layer of oil before you put it away — will keep your pan nicely seasoned.

Occasionally, however, your seasoning may break down. If you don't use your pan for a long period of time, if you cook food with liquid (steaming vegetables or deglazing the pan with wine, for example), or if you cook acidic foods, such as tomatoes, in it, you may have to reseason your pan.

The following signs let you know that you need to reseason your cast iron:

- Rust forms.
- Foods begin to stick to the pan.
- Your food tastes like metal — and you didn't intend for it too.

If you notice these signs, first get rid of any rust or whatever's burned on (see Chapter 4), and then follow the steps in the "Step 2: Seasoning your new cast iron" section, earlier in this chapter.

What to Do with a Preseasoned Pan

Preseasoned cast iron, true to its name, has already been seasoned. You can skip the seasoning step entirely and do a little victory dance to boot. All you need to do is clean it.

Natural-finished cast iron comes from the foundry with a protective wax coating. (See the "Step 1: Preparing the new pan for seasoning" section, earlier in this chapter, for details.) Preseasoned cast iron doesn't have this coating, because it doesn't need it. The *seasoning* is the protection.

Follow these instructions to get preseasoned cast iron ready to use:

1. **Using hot water and a stiff-bristled brush, wash the cast iron.**

Don't use soap. You need to treat a preseasoned pan the way that you'd treat a seasoned pan, and soap is a no-no. If you use soap, you're just going to have to reseason it, and then what's the point of buying it preseasoned? (If you're concerned about bacteria, rinse the pan with boiling water. Of course, if the only way that you can feel comfortable using cast iron is to clean it in soapy water, go ahead, but remember that you need to reseason it more frequently.)

2. **Dry the pan completely.**

After you wipe the water off, put the pan in a warm oven or on a warm burner to get rid of any remaining moisture.

3. **Wipe the cooking surface with a light coating of vegetable oil.**

You can also use cooking spray, if you prefer. Just spray it on the cooking surface and wipe away the excess. There you go. Easy as pie.

Chapter 4

Caring for Cast Iron

· ·

In This Chapter

▶ Following a few easy cleaning rules

▶ Instructions for everyday cleaning

▶ Cleaning second-hand cast iron

▶ Carting your cast iron around safely

· ·

Ah, the joy of cooking meets the chore of caring for your cookware. Fortunately, taking care of cast iron isn't that difficult. In fact, it's not difficult at all. Yes, you do need to follow a few simple rules to keep your seasoning intact. (Head to Chapter 3 if you're not sure what seasoning is.) But it's nothing that requires Herculean efforts.

This chapter tells you just what you need to know about cleaning and storing cast iron. And because even the best of cooks has a catastrophe every once in a while, this chapter also provides tips for how to get rid of stubborn stuck-on food that you burned into the pan's very core. This information is also helpful to anyone who's bought or been given an old piece of cast iron that needs a little extra attention, before it's ready for seasoning. Finally, because cast iron really is perfect campfire cookware, I explain how to transport your pots and pans safely from here to wherever there is.

How your cast iron fares depends not only on how you clean and store it but how you use it, too. For information on caring for your cast iron while you cook, go to Chapter 5.

Cleaning Tips and Tricks

When you clean cast iron, you're aim is two-fold: Clean off whatever remains of dinner and do so without destroying your pan's seasoning. (If your cleaning task is more dire than this and you want to get down to the bare metal so that you can start over, skip ahead to the section "Super-Cleaning for Old — or Abused — Cast Iron.")

When your task is just basic cleaning and you want preserve your pan's seasoning, keep these rules in mind:

✔ **Don't use soap.** Soap effectively cuts through oil and grease, and if you consider that *that's* what your seasoning is — oil and grease baked into your pan through possibly years of cooking — you can understand why soap is verboten.

If you absolutely, positively can't give up the dish soap, be prepared to reseason your pan more frequently, possibly after every cleaning. Go to Chapter 3 for seasoning instructions.

✔ **Don't use a wire brush or a steel-wool scouring pad.** These aren't necessary; other less abrasive ways are available for getting off stubborn bits of food, explained in the "Getting stuck-on food off" section, later in this chapter.

The reason you season the pan in the first place is to fill in the pores and valleys that are just part and parcel of cast iron's structure. By using a wire-bristled brush, you're just adding more little voids to fill.

✔ **Don't let your cast iron soak or let water sit in it. For that matter, don't let it air dry, either.** When you clean cast iron, your goal is to use as little water as possible in the shortest amount of time.

✔ **Never** *ever* **wash cast iron in an electric dishwasher.** Dishwasher detergent strips the seasoning you've lovingly applied, the rinse cycle throws water on the newly stripped pans, and then the pans are left to essentially drip dry during the dry cycle.

✔ **Don't pour cold water into hot cast iron.** Doing so can cause your pan to break. When you clean your cast iron, you want to use hot water on a hot pan.

Now that I've told you all that you *don't* want to do, I'm ready to take a positive outlook on life. How about getting ready to clean your cast iron?

Rub-a-dub-dub, Removing the Grub

Cleaning cast iron doesn't require anything more than hot water and elbow grease. To clean your cast iron after use, follow these steps:

1. **Remove any stuck-on bits of food.**

   In a well-seasoned pan, this task usually requires nothing more than scraping the sides and bottom with a spoon — the same task that you do to get the last bit out for leftovers. If your stuck-on bits are a bit more stuck on, hop to the section "Getting stuck-on food off," later in this chapter, for suggestions.

2. **Using hot water and a scrub (nonwire) brush, scrub the cooking surface.**

   Let the hot water flow over the pan as you scrub with a natural-bristled or stiff plastic brush. (You want the bristles to be about as stiff as the bristles on a medium or hard toothbrush.)

   If not using soap makes you worry about what sort of germs may be lingering, pour boiling water into and over the pan after you're done brushing it.

3. **Immediately and thoroughly dry the cast iron with a towel.**

   Never *ever* let cast iron drip-dry. And don't leave it sitting on top of anything or touching anything — like the towel you dried it with — that has moisture. ***Remember:*** Any remaining moisture — whether it's on your pan or on the item that your pan is sitting on — will cause your cast iron to rust. And then you have to remove the rust and reseason it all over again.

   Put the cast iron on a burner or in a heated oven for a few minutes to make sure that all the moisture is gone.

4. **Coat the cast iron with a thin layer of vegetable oil while it's still warm and wipe it dry with a paper towel.**

   Doing so helps preserve the seasoning and replaces any that was removed during the cleaning.

5. **After you wash, dry, and re-oil your cast iron, put it away.**

   For storage instructions, see the section "Storing Your Cast Iron," later in this chapter.

Getting stuck-on food off

Sometimes, high-tech approaches, such as picking at the food with your fingernails or poking at it with a table knife aren't enough to get the stuck-on bits off. In those cases, try these suggestions to remove the stragglers and then clean and dry the pan as usual:

✔ Before you go at it again, heat the pan to a temperature that's still safe to touch. Doing this opens the pores and makes it easier to clean.

✔ Instead of just water, try a mixture of vinegar and water. Keep in mind however, that you'll probably have to reseason your pan. The acidity of the vinegar helps release stuck on food, but it also may take off the seasoning, too.

✔ Scrub the problem spots with table salt moistened with either oil or water.

✔ Use really hot, almost boiling, water (be sure to use rubber gloves) and scrub the spot with crumpled up aluminum foil. Experienced foil users say that the foil breaks down before it can harm the pan's surface.

When you can skip cleaning altogether

When you use your cast iron to cook bakery-type foods — such as breads, biscuits, and cakes — you don't really have to clean it at all. Simply turn the bread or cake out of the pan to cool, wipe the surface with a clean paper towel, and then apply a light layer of vegetable oil. You're pan is good to go for your next round of cooking.

Super-Cleaning for Old — or Abused — Cast Iron

Many people get their cast iron from garage sales, farm auctions, antique stores, and so on. These items can have all manner of substances stuck or cooked on them — substances that you'll want to remove before you use the pan yourself. (The remnants of someone's 20-year-old cornbread just aren't that appetizing.) Figure 4-1 shows an abused pan that needs a little — or a lot — of care before it's in cooking trim again.

Figure 4-1:
A mildly (believe it or not) abused cast-iron pan.

To super clean a pan in order to get it ready for reseasoning, do the following:

1. **Remove the rust.**

   Most old pans (and some newer pans that haven't been cared for) have some rust on them that you have to get rid of before you can do anything else.

2. **Remove any gunk that seems to be permanently attached to the pan's surface.**

   This can be the old seasoning, bits of food from ages past, or any number of other pieces of gunk that you don't want.

Keep reading to find out about cleaning methods that are more drastic. When you have a pan that needs serious cleaning, you're going to ruin the seasoning. Sometimes, such as when you need to remove rust, you may be focusing on one or two spots. At other times, you're goal is to clean the whole darn pan, bringing it back to its natural, unseasoned state. In either case, you're going to end up reseasoning the whole enchilada. Head to Chapter 3 for details.

Removing rust

Several techniques exist for removing rust from a cast-iron pan. Which technique you use depends on how extensive the rust damage is and how many rusty pans you have.

If the rust is relatively minor, try the following:

- ✔ **Sandpaper and elbow grease:** Be sure that your sandpaper has a medium to fine grit; otherwise, you may leave big scratches on the surface of the pan.

- ✔ **Raw potato, cut in half, and scouring powder:** Use the potato as your scouring pad and scrub until the rust is gone.

- ✔ **Steel wool:** Scour the rusty area until the rust is gone.

- ✔ **Rust eraser:** These gadgets do exactly as their name implies. You can find them in hardware stores, woodworking shops, bike shops, and many other places that sell items that are susceptible to rust.

If the rust that you're dealing with is extensive or you don't have the heart to spend an afternoon (or longer) hand-sanding your cookware, you may want to give these suggestions a try:

- ✔ **Use a drill or grinder and a wire brush:** This method can definitely get rid of the rust, but a wire brush whirling around at several hundred rpm (revolutions per minute) can change the look of your cast iron, possibly leaving it polished, which is a bad thing because a polished pan doesn't accept seasoning well — the seasoning wipes right off. If you use a drill or grinder be careful not to get carried away and start sanding valleys into your pan's surface.

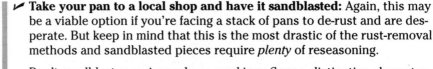

✔ **Take your pan to a local shop and have it sandblasted:** Again, this may be a viable option if you're facing a stack of pans to de-rust and are desperate. But keep in mind that this is the most drastic of the rust-removal methods and sandblasted pieces require *plenty* of reseasoning.

Don't sandblast any piece whose markings (logos, distinctive characteristics, and so on) you want to preserve. This would include special family heirloom pieces, collector's pieces, and any other cast iron that you're particularly fond of for whatever reason. Sandblasting strips these markings right off — or ruins them. If the pan is worth a bit of money (as some collectible cast iron is) or it's special to you, hand sanding it may be worth the time and trouble.

Removing old seasoning, leftover gunk, and mysterious chunks

When the rust is gone, you're ready to remove the old seasoning and whatever else may be lingering on your pans. Basically, you can turn the heat way up or go the chemical route:

✔ Put the cast iron in a hot fire (outdoors obviously) until the fire dies down and the embers are cool. Everything that's on the pan — old, stuck-on food, burned lard, and all the old seasoning — should be gone.

✔ Put the cast iron in your self-cleaning oven and turn that feature on. Essentially, it's like putting the cast iron in the hot outdoor fire: You're burning off the old crud at really high temperatures. When your self-cleaning oven unlocks itself, your pan should be free from its old seasoning.

✔ Spray the pan with oven cleaner and put it in a plastic bag for a couple of days. When you remove the pan from the bag, scrub off the cleaner, and wash the pan in soap and water. Then rinse thoroughly. And then rinse it again to make sure that you've taken all the oven cleaner off.

If you use this method, be sure to wear plastic gloves and be careful. The chemicals (notably lye) in oven cleaner is super caustic and can hurt you if you get it on your skin or in your eyes.

If anything that you don't want remains (such as paint), you're free to use pretty much whatever can remove it: putty knife, wire-bristled brush, non-toxic stain or paint remover, or trained elephants with sledge hammers.

After the old seasoning is burned off and you've removed anything else that was left, basically, you have a new cast-iron pan. Your next step is to scrub it in hot soapy water and reseason it. See Chapter 3 for details on seasoning a pan.

Storing Your Cast Iron

Cast iron is pretty easy going. You can stack it in a cabinet or hang it from a hook or pan rack. If you take your only cast iron with you on camping trips, leave it in the box that it came in. Wherever you plan to keep (or arrange) your cast iron, follow these suggestions:

- **Make sure that you store your cast iron in a cool, dry place.** Remember, moisture is the enemy.

- **Store your cast iron with the lid off or ajar.** Cast-iron lids fit fairly tightly, and if any moisture is in the pan, a closed lid won't let it escape. The result is a rusty pan. This advice is especially important if you live in a humid environment.

  If you want to leave the lid on, place a folded-up paper towel between the lid and the pan and place a crumbled up paper towel inside the pan to absorb any moisture.

- **If you hang your cast iron from the wall, be sure that the hook or nail is anchored in a stud and that it can bear the weight of your pan(s).** The same goes if you're hanging it from the ceiling. And never hang cast iron — even just decorative cast iron — over a doorway unless you're really, *really* sure it won't fall.

Hitting the Road with Your Cast Iron

Many people never take their cast iron anywhere other than potluck dinners, family reunions, or Thanksgiving get-togethers, and then they have a tendency to transport it on their lap, between their feet, or safely surrounded by towels in the trunk of their car. Not to protect the cast iron, mind you, but to protect whatever delectable dish is inside it.

Many other people, those who take their kitchens outdoors, consider their cast iron a transportable tool, something that they pack with the rest of their gear.

If you're one of the latter group and plan to take your cast iron with you when you head out for an adventure in the great outdoors, the trick is to keep the pan from bouncing and banging around too much. Put it in the box it came in, wrap it in a towel or burlap sack, or wedge it securely against the skis or other paraphernalia. If you're feeling particularly protective, you, too, can cradle cast iron in your lap — but you don't need to. If cast iron could survive being carted thousands of miles west in covered wagons, it can probably survive your trip into the next county for a cook-off.

Chapter 5

Cast-Iron Cooking Techniques

In This Chapter

▶ Discovering cast iron's heating properties

▶ Cast-iron cooking know-how

▶ What utensils to use and what to avoid

Making good food in a cast-iron skillet or pot isn't rocket science. All you need is a well-seasoned pan (seasoning details and instructions are in Chapter 3) and a few simple cooking techniques. And because cast iron is such an efficient conductor of heat, knowing how to control the temperature and to take advantage of its heating properties is vital when you cook with cast iron. This chapter tells you everything that you need to know.

Of course, having a few recipes doesn't hurt either. You can find those in Chapters 6 through 16.

Out of the Frying Pan and into the Fire: Heat and Temperature Control

Cast iron is a great heat conductor. It absorbs heat quickly, and it distributes it evenly. The advantages of this are

✔ **You can use less heat.** Often, when you cook with cast iron, you find yourself turning the heat down from its original setting, not up.

✔ **Food cooks uniformly.** If you set something to simmer in a cast iron, for example, *all* the food in the pan simmers, not just the part that's directly over the burner.

✔ **You're less likely to get hot spots that'll scorch or burn your food.** As a general rule, heavier pots and pans of any kind are less likely than lighter pots and pans of the same kind to have hot spots.

✔ **Your food stays warm longer.** Even after you remove your cast iron from the heat source, the heavy metal of the pan keeps the food warm, without cooking.

Still, if you're not used to cooking with cast iron, the heating properties that make it such a good cookware may be exactly what trips you up. Keep reading to find out what you may struggle with until you're accustomed to your cast-iron pans.

Getting the temperature right

Because you use less heat, your temperature setting may need to be lower than what's specified in recipes not geared toward cast-iron cookware. Generally, you simply have to set the temperature as the recipe indicates and then adjust it downward as needed. If you notice, for example, that your stew's soft simmer is actually more of a pre-boil, simply turn the heat setting down until you get the result that you want. Eventually, you'll know what setting to use to get the appropriate cooking temperature.

Because cast iron absorbs and retains heat so well, you don't need to use temperatures as high as you may need for your other pans. Use the following general guidelines for the temperature settings for stovetop cooking. Keep in mind that these are simply guidelines; your stove and oven's heat settings may differ:

Cooking Method	Heat Setting
Braising	Medium-low to Medium
Frying	Medium-high to brown, Medium-low to Medium to cook
Sautéing	Medium
Searing	Medium to Medium-high
Simmering	Medium-low to Medium
Warming	Low

As you cook a single dish, you can move your cast iron from one heat source to another. Many recipes in this book, for example, instruct you to begin the recipe on the stovetop and then place it in the oven to finish.

Is it done yet?

Because cooking times aren't exact, always check for doneness. The following signs indicate that your food is done:

✔ **Cakes and quick breads:** A toothpick or cake tester inserted in the center comes out clean. Another sign is that the sides of the cake or bread begin to pull away from the pan.

✔ **Yeast breads:** The top is light- to dark-golden brown, and the bread sounds hollow when you tap on the crust.

✔ **Poultry:** The legs feel loose (they begin to separate from the rest of the bird), and the juices run clear. The internal temperature is between 170 and 185 degrees.

✔ **Fresh pork:** Juices run clear, meat is white, or the internal temperature is 170.

✔ **Beef:** Internal temperature is between 140 degrees (rare) and 170 degrees (well done).

You can find more information about testing for doneness in Parts II and III of this book.

Getting the cooking time right

The actual cooking times on many recipes may be slightly less when you cook in cast iron. (*Note:* The recipes in this book are based on cast-iron cooking, so this isn't an issue that you need to worry about.)

A recipe's cooking time is an approximation — a pretty accurate approximation, true, but an approximation nonetheless. Just because most 3½-pound fryers are done roasting in a 325 degree oven in 1½ hours doesn't mean that yours will be. All sorts of factors can affect cooking times: the type of oven you have (convection or non-convection), the accuracy of your appliance's temperature gauge, the actual size (diameter, thickness, weight, and so forth) of what you're cooking, and your altitude, the alignment of the stars, or whatever. The type of cookware is just another variable to add to this list.

Warming up to the advantages of preheating

Cast iron works best when the heat source is the same size as the bottom of the pan, but burners on modern electric and gas ranges are usually smaller than that. To eliminate this problem, you simply have to preheat the pan when you're going to cook on top of the stove.

You can preheat your cast iron on the stovetop or in the oven. Follow these guidelines:

- **On the stovetop:** Set your burner on low and let the cast iron warm up slowly. After the entire pan is warm, turn the heat up to the temperature you want.

- **In the oven:** Set your cast iron in a warm oven set to low (225–250 degrees). When it's heated, take your cast iron out of the oven, put it on the stovetop, and turn the burner to the appropriate temperature.

CAUTION! Unlike a pan that's preheated on the stovetop, where the heat works its way from the burner surface outward, a pan that's preheated in the oven is surrounded by heat — which means that the handles get as hot as the pan's cooking surface. Remember to always use hot pads or oven mitts when you remove a preheated pan from the oven.

Unless the recipe indicates otherwise, you don't need to preheat your cast iron when roasting in the oven, because the oven heats the cast iron evenly. If you do need to preheat the cast iron, simply put the cool iron in the cool oven and let it warm up as your oven does.

 Many cast-iron recipes include preheating instructions. Non-cast-iron specific recipes may or may not include such instructions. If you're using a recipe that doesn't include preheating instructions for your cookware, use this rule as your guide: You almost always preheat your cast iron when you're making foods that you want to be crispy on the outside and tender or moist on the inside. These foods include the following:

- **Cornbreads:** Good cornbread has a slightly crispy crust and is moist. Bad cornbread is gritty and dry. The difference between the two (aside from variations in recipes and the different types of cornmeal used) is often the preheating. Baking or frying your cornbread in a preheated pan is more likely to give you the consistency that you want. Head to Chapter 11 for cornbread recipes.

- **Muffins and quick breads:** Often you preheat the pan to the same temperature as the oven. So if the recipe cooks at 350 degrees, you simply stick your cornbread skillet or muffin pan into the oven as it preheats and pull it out when it reaches temperature. You can find muffin and quick bread recipes in Chapter 12.

- **Pancakes:** Preheating to the right temperature gives you pancakes that rise nicely, are light and fluffy on the inside, and have a slightly crispy edge. Your pan or griddle is hot enough if a bead of water skips across the surface. Head to Chapter 12 for pancake recipes.

✔ **Any seared dishes:** Searing browns the outside of your meat, poultry, or seafood, and holds the moisture inside. You can find recipes that require searing in Chapter 6 (Pan-Seared Fillets of Beef with Peppercorn Sauce and Perfect Pot Roast) and Chapter 8 (Skillet Salmon).

For cowboy cooks and campfire folks

When you cook outdoors over an open fire or hot coals, the rules for controlling your cooking temperatures are quite a bit different than those for indoor cooking. For outdoor cooking, you basically control your temperatures by the placement and number of coals. More coals closer to the pan mean higher temperatures; fewer coals farther from the pan mean lower temperatures.

Getting and maintaining the right temperature when you cook outside is a little more complicated than simply counting coals. You also have to adjust for the weather: air temperature, humidity level, wind speed, and so on. Chapter 14 explains all about outdoor cast-iron cooking and includes several easy and delicious recipes for the outdoor cook.

Tuning in to the Tricks and Traps

If your cast iron is well seasoned and you can adequately control the cooking temperature, there really isn't anything you can't make in a cast-iron pan. Seasoning and temperature control, more than anything else, can determine whether you become a fan or a foe of cast iron. To nudge you farther over to the fan side, keep reading to get some other cooking tips to keep in mind.

Brand spankin' new cast iron

Following these simple suggestions when your cast-iron is new ensures that your initial journey into the world of cast-iron cooking will be successful:

✔ **Before you cook anything, season your cast iron.** Seasoning cast iron is simply baking oil or some other fat into the pores of the cast iron, thus creating a smooth, nonstick surface. Chapter 3 has seasoning instructions.

✔ **The first six or seven times that you cook in your cast iron, cook foods that are rich in natural fat or oils.** Cook bacon, hamburgers — not the lean kind — and sausage; fry chicken; or make fried potatoes. Doing so deepens the seasoning and enhances the pan's nonstick surface.

✔ **Wait until the pan is well seasoned before you cook some foods.** These foods include acidic foods (such as tomato-based dishes, or dishes that require citrus juice or mustard), alkaline foods (such as beans), or anything with a high-moisture content (such as soups or stews). Initially avoiding these types of foods preserves your new pan's seasoning.

If you can't wait until the seasoning builds and just have to cook your grandfather's favorite soup beans, go ahead and enjoy yourself. Just keep in mind that you may need to reseason your pan after you use it. See Chapter 3 for signs that your cast iron needs reseasoning and instructions. After your cast iron is broken in really well, you can cook just about anything in it.

Other dos and don'ts

The following list offers a few random recommendations to keep in mind as you cook and serve in cast iron:

✔ **Never put cold pan on a hot burner, pour cold liquid into a hot pan, and so forth.** If you do, you run the risk of shocking your cast iron to the breaking point, literally. Let your pan heat up as the burner heats up, and if you have to add water to a hot pan, make sure that the water is warm or hot. (The same rule applies when you clean cast iron. Head to Chapter 4 for cleaning instructions.)

All metal cookware is susceptible to *thermal shock,* a drastic and quick change in temperature. Cast iron, being the most brittle of all metal cookware, is more likely to break; aluminum cookware is more likely to warp. Whether the result of thermal shock is a broken or warped pan, the outcome is the same: a pan that's no good for cooking anymore.

✔ **Don't store food in cast iron.** The acid in the food breaks down the seasoning, and the food will take on a metallic taste. When you're done serving the food, transfer what's left to another container.

✔ **Although you shouldn't use your cast iron to store your food, you can use it to serve food.** Follow these suggestions:

• Keep the food simmering until you're ready to sit down to eat.

• Be sure to put a hot pad or trivet under the pan. Cast iron stays hot for a long time, and it could burn or mar your tabletop.

• To keep food warm for second helpings, cover the pan while you eat.

• As soon as your meal is over, put the food in another container for storage and then wash up. (See Chapter 4 for details about cleaning your cast iron.)

✔ **Move your cast iron off an electric burner after you turn the burner off if you want the dish to stop cooking.** Unlike a gas flame, which goes out as soon as you turn the burner off, an electric burner takes a while to cool off. Because cast iron retains heat in proportion to that emitted by the heat source, a dish left over a cooling burner will still cook. This may not present a problem when you're fixing a stew (and a little extra simmer time is not an issue), but it could be a problem if you're thickening a sauce and don't want it to caramelize.

✔ **Before you cook with cast-iron cake pans, corn-stick pans, muffin pans, and other bakeware, oil them or spray them with nonstick cooking spray.** Even the fat-free kind can do the trick. Although these pans should be nonstick if they're properly seasoned, why take a chance if you're going for presentation in addition to taste?

Ending the Exile of Your Metal Utensils

Although cast iron does require some care, it isn't particularly persnickety about the type of utensils you use. You can use wooden utensils, plastic utensils, or (believe it or not) the frequently banned pariah of a Teflon-coated kitchen — metal utensils! That's right: Dust off your wire whisk and polish up that metal spoon. They're back in business, baby.

In fact, if you find yourself facing a chunk of food that seems to have permanently attached itself to your cast-iron cookware, you can even scrape it with a (hopefully clean) putty knife to pick it off. If you're so inclined — or so desperate — just remember that you may have to reseason the spot you scratched at.

I don't recommend scrubbing your pan clean with a wire brush. First, it isn't necessary. You can usually get even the most stubborn stuck-on food off in less abrasive ways. (See Chapter 4 for ideas.) Second, although this type of brush won't hurt the iron, it will scrub off your seasoning, and then you'll have to start over again.

Part II

Main-Dish Cast-Iron Recipes

The 5th Wave By Rich Tennant

"Gee, Mark - look at this pot. It's obviously quite old, but in very good condition, and I would imagine, wonderfully seasoned."

In this part . . .

Every meal has a main course, the dish around which all others are planned, and this is the part where you can find main-dish recipes to whip up in your cast iron. Whether you're in the mood for meat, poultry, seafood, soups, or one-dish meals, you can find the recipe that you're looking for right here.

Chapter 6

It's Meat for Dinner Tonight

In This Chapter

▶ Enhancing the flavor and tenderness of beef and pork

▶ Understanding the USDA grading system

▶ Selecting the right cut of meat

▶ Carving instructions

Although more and more people are eating more and more poultry, seafood, and vegetable-heavy dishes (see Chapters 7, 8, and 10 respectively), meat is still the mainstay of most diets. Beef and pork are particularly popular, and for good reason. They're affordable, widely available, and versatile.

More importantly, however, they taste great. Whether you want a down-home meal to fill hungry stomachs, a more sophisticated dish to wow your friends, or a dinner that your kids will love, chances are, pork or beef will be featured prominently on your menu. And wouldn't you know it, cast iron is a near-perfect cookware for the methods you use to cook meat. Braising, searing, broiling — you name it, and you can do it in your cast iron.

This chapter includes several great beef and pork recipes. I also provide some pointers, tips, and tricks for choosing a cut of meat and cooking the cuts you choose for maximum taste and tenderness. You can also find a corn dog recipe here, too, just for the kids. Most hot dogs are, after all, made of beef or pork or a combination of the two. (I know. It's a stretch.)

Beef Tips

Beef's beef: It all comes from a cow. I'm not splitting atoms here. But where the cut of beef comes from makes all the difference in terms of the amount of fat and how tender (or tough) it is. Check out Figure 6-1, which maps out where the different cuts come from.

Figure 6-1: Cutting up, down on the farm.

In general, if you start at the front of the cow and work your way back, the tenderness of the meat progresses from least to most tender and then back again. Meat that comes from the shoulder is tougher than the meat that comes from the rib, which is tougher than the meat that comes from the loin, where the tenderest meat of the cow is. Then the meat begins to get less tender as you move toward the rear legs. But wait, there's more: The meat from the belly of the cow (the brisket, plate, and flank portions) produces the toughest, fattiest cuts. If you're not sure where the cut you want comes from, simply ask the butcher, "Does this come off the front or the hind end?"

Butchers can carve a cow just about any way they want to. As a result, what a particular cut of meat may be called at your grocery store depends, in large part, on the butcher and the decisions he makes when he cuts the meat. If, for example, he sees that the meat from the flank portion is lean, he may chop it into stew meat; if the meat can be removed whole, he may cube it (run it through a machine that scores the meat in order to break up the tough fibers) and call it a cube steak. If you don't have any idea what a particular piece of meat is or how best to cook it, simply ask. A knowledgeable butcher can be one of your best friends in the kitchen.

When you buy beef, use the USDA (United States Department of Agriculture) grading system to evaluate the quality of your beef. One of the factors that determines the grade is the amount of *marbling* (the distribution of fat and lean) the cut contains. More marbling generally means that the meat is more moist and tender than cuts with less marbling.

> ✔ **Prime:** Beef that falls into this grade has the most marbling. Beef in this category is also the most flavorful and the most tender. Not surprisingly, it costs more, too.

> ✔ **Choice:** Meat of this grade is the biggest seller, simply because, by applying a few tricks (which are explained in the "Holy Cow! Cooking Beef" section that follows) you can make it as flavorful and tender as prime cuts of meat but at a fraction of the cost.

> ✔ **Select:** This is the leanest cut. It has the least marbling and isn't as flavorful or as tender as the other two grades. It's also the least expensive.

So how do you use this grading system? Good question. If you want to cook a steak, for example, choose Choice or Prime. If you're planning a dish that requires slow cooking the meat (braising it, for example), Select is the better choice. Slow-cooking methods tenderizes the meat, so you don't need to spend the extra money for an already tender piece of beef that will become tough if cooked too long.

Holy Cow! Cooking Beef

Cooking methods impact how flavorful and tender your beef is. Use the wrong cooking method, and what had been a nice tender cut of beef will be leathery tough. Use the right cooking method, and even a tough piece of meat will be tender.

Any cut of beef — even the toughest — can be a "good" cut. What makes a cut good depends on what you want and how you plan to cook it. If you want to grill a melt-in-your mouth, juicy steak, for example, a good cut is a ribeye (which comes from the rib area) or a T-bone or Porterhouse (from the short loin area). A bad cut is a flank steak or chuck steak. Similarly, using a porterhouse to make beef stew is just a waste of money. Stew meat works better.

When all else fails, just keep this simple rule in mind: Cook beef with liquid (braising and boiling) when dealing with tougher cuts. Hold the liquid (roasting, grilling broiling, pan-frying, and so on) for tender cuts. The following list runs down the beef cuts used in this section, including the best cooking method:

- ✔ **Pot roasts** come from the shoulder or chuck. There are two kinds of pot roasts: chuck roasts and arm roasts. You can use either in a recipe that calls for pot roast. Because pot roasts tend toward toughness, you cook them slowly in liquid, as shown in the Perfect Pot Roast recipe.

- ✔ **Sirloin steak** comes from the sirloin. Although not as tender as meat from the short loin area, meat from the sirloin area is still really tender. Prepare sirloin as you would any other steak or you can cut it into cubes, as I do with the Beef Stroganoff recipe and cook it in liquid.

- ✔ **Flank steak,** a less-expensive alternative to sirloin in the Beef Stroganoff recipe, comes from the flank area, on the underside of the cow. Flank steak is generally pretty tough, and many butchers either score it (make shallow cuts against the grain to break up the tough sinew) or run it through a cuber (a machine that scores the meat) to tenderize it.

- ✔ **Brisket** comes from the cow's breast and, if not cooked properly, is notoriously tough. The only way to cook brisket so that it isn't tough is to slow cook it for a really long time. The recipes in this chapter — Corned Beef and Cabbage and Slow Brisket of Beef — simmer and braise the brisket for hours. Cooked properly, you'd never suspect that the meat you started out with was less than melt-in-your-mouth tender.

- ✔ **Round steak** comes from the hindquarter of the cow, the section behind the sirloin area. Round steak is a nice cut of meat, but you need to do a little work to make it tender. To broil or grill it as a steak, use a tenderizer. In the Chisholm Trail Swiss Steak recipe, you pound it with a meat mallet to tenderize and simmer it in liquid for a couple of hours.

- ✔ The **tenderloin,** the most tender part of the whole beef, comes from the muscle on each side of the cow's spine, around the short loin area. This meat is naturally tender; filets sliced from here don't require Herculean efforts to soften them up. The simplest cooking methods (broiling or pan-searing) are best, as shown in the Pepper-Crusted Filets of Beef Tenderloin and Pan-Seared Filets of Beef with Peppercorn Sauce recipes.

Making tougher cuts tender

Some cuts of meat are simply less tender than other cuts of meat. Chuck roasts, round steaks, briskets, and stew meat fall into this category, and they probably show up on your dinner table often. These cuts are common to many tables because they're affordable. Keep in mind, however, that these meats can be as delicious, as mouth-watering, and, yes, *as tender,* as their more tender-from-the-get-go brethren, but you need to use the right cooking method. With tougher cuts, the best cooking method is a slow one over a low temperature that requires some liquid. Think braising or boiling.

Perfect Pot Roast

Pot roast gets a bad rap as being tough, dry, and stringy. What's the secret to a tender, fall-apart-at-the-touch-of-a-fork pot roast? First, select a roast that has consistent marbling. Second, braise it for a long time (several hours) at a *low* temperature (325 degrees max). Cooked this way, the meat attains a high internal temperature, which effectively melts the fat and the connective tissue into the flesh, providing both taste and tenderness.

Preparation time: *30 minutes*

Cooking time: *3 to 3½ hours*

Yield: *8 to 10 servings*

5 to 6 pound shoulder roast or chuck roast	*1 rib celery without top, cut into 2-inch pieces*
Salt and pepper	*1 bay leaf*
Garlic salt	*1 tablespoon chopped fresh parsley*
1 to 2 tablespoons vegetable oil	*4 carrots, peeled and cut into 2-inch pieces*
2 to 3 beef bouillon cubes	*5 to 6 medium potatoes, peeled and halved*
2 medium onions, quartered	

1 Rub the roast with salt, pepper, and garlic salt.

2 Heat the oil in 5- or 7-quart cast-iron Dutch oven on medium high or high. Sear the roast on all sides until its very brown. Reduce the heat to medium, add enough water to almost cover roast and add bouillon cubes.

3 Add 1 of the quartered onions, all of the celery, the bay leaf, and the parsley. Bring to a boil, then cover, reduce heat, and simmer for 2 or 2½ hours.

4 Add the carrots and the remainder of onions. Bring to a boil, then reduce heat and simmer for 30 more minutes.

5 Add the potatoes, bring to a boil, reduce heat and simmer until potatoes are fork tender, about 30 minutes. Salt to taste during last 20 minutes. (More salt will be required due to addition of vegetables.)

6 Use spatulas to remove the roast to a large serving platter. (It will be so tender that it may fall apart.) Pile the vegetables on and around roast. Strain the broth and reserve for making gravy or freezing for later use. For tips on carving a pot roast, see the "Carving Like a Pro" section, later in this chapter.

Vary It! *Take the oven route. After searing the roast, add all remaining ingredients and place in a 275-degree oven for 4 hours, or until fork tender. Salt to taste during last 30 minutes. For additional flavor, add 1 cup red wine when adding liquid to almost cover in Step 3.*

Per serving: *Calories 351 (From Fat 102); Fat 11g (Saturated 4g); Cholesterol 119mg; Sodium 357mg; Carbohydrate 19g (Dietary Fiber 3g); Protein 41g.*

Beef Stroganoff

For this recipe, you can use sirloin steak or flank steak cut into 1-inch cubes. Flank steak (sometimes, already cut into cubes as stew beef) is less expensive. It's also less tender, but the length of the cooking time is sufficient to soften it up. For more tender meat, use the sirloin.

Preparation time: *20 minutes*

Cooking time: *2 hours*

Yield: *6 servings*

3 pounds flank or sirloin steak	*½ pound mushrooms, sliced*
Salt and pepper	*1 cup tomato juice*
1 cup all-purpose flour	*¾ cup cooking sherry*
¾ cup butter	*1 cup sour cream*
3 medium onions, sliced	*6 cups hot noodles*

1 Cut the steak into strips about 1-inch wide. Lay the strips onto wax paper and sprinkle salt and pepper on both sides of meat. Dredge in the flour.

2 Heat the butter in 5-quart cast-iron Dutch oven on medium or medium-high heat. Cook onions, mushrooms, and steak slices in butter until the onions and mushrooms are soft and the steak is browned.

3 Add the tomato juice, sherry, and 2¼ cups water. Bring to a boil, reduce heat, cover, and simmer for 2 hours.

4 Add the sour cream and heat through without allowing to boil. Serve over noodles.

Per serving: Calories 711 (From Fat 255); Fat 28g (Saturated 13g); Cholesterol 166mg; Sodium 372mg; Carbohydrate 60g (Dietary Fiber 3g); Protein 50g.

Corned beef that grays gracefully

If you're accustomed to thinking of any meat that *isn't* pink as past it's prime, you may turn up your nose at gray corned beef brisket. But don't be so hasty: Gray doesn't always mean old with this cut of beef. The reason why some corned beef is gray and other corned beef is pink (almost red) has to do with how the meat was preserved. Gray corned beef has been preserved with brine that contains salt and water only. The pink (or regular) corned beef uses a brine that has sodium nitrate (saltpeter) in it. The sodium nitrate helps the meat retain its red color.

By the way, if you want gray corned beef, you have to travel to New England (where the folks prefer the gray). You probably won't have much luck finding it anywhere else.

Corned Beef and Cabbage

Also called New England Boiled Dinner, this dish — or the beef used in it — doesn't have anything to do with corn, the vegetable. *Corning* means to salt with brine (salt water) as a way of preserving the meat. You can buy brisket that's already been corned (the easier option), or you can buy fresh brisket and corn it yourself. The process is fairly easy (rubbing the meat with salt and other spices, wrapping it securely, pressing it down with weights, and letting it sit in your refrigerator for five days), but it takes so long that I recommend buying it ready to go.

Preparation time: *20 minutes*

Cooking time: *3 to 4 hours*

Yield: *8 to 10 servings*

4 pound corned beef brisket	*1 medium onion, quartered*
2 teaspoons sugar	*8 medium potatoes, peeled and halved*
1 tablespoon whole black peppercorn	*1 cabbage, cored and cut into 6 wedges*
3 to 4 sprigs fresh parsley	*Salt*
6 carrots, peeled and quartered	

1 Place the brisket in a 7-quart cast-iron Dutch oven and cover with water.

2 Add the sugar, peppercorn, and parsley and bring to a boil. Cover, reduce heat, and simmer for 2¾ hours. Check the water level once and hour throughout, and add additional water, if necessary, to cover brisket.

3 Add the carrots, onion, and potatoes. Cover and simmer for 30 minutes.

4 Add the cabbage; cover and simmer for 15 minutes, or until the cabbage is tender. Salt to taste. Place the corned beef in the middle of a serving platter and surround with vegetables.

Vary It! *You can use other root vegetables in addition to or in place of the carrots, onion, and potatoes. Try turnips, brussels sprouts, parsnips, or rutabagas.*

Per serving: *Calories 494 (From Fat 237); Fat 26g (Saturated 9g); Cholesterol 133mg; Sodium 1,594mg; Carbohydrate 35g (Dietary Fiber 6g); Protein 29g.*

Slow Brisket of Beef

A whole brisket, which comes from the front part of the cow's breast, is usually cut into two pieces: the flat cut and the point cut. The flat cut is leaner and, as a result, lacks some of the flavor that the fattier point cut has. Nevertheless, you can use either for any beef brisket recipe.

Preparation time: *10 minutes*

Cooking time: *3 to 3½ hours*

Yield: *8 servings*

4 pound beef brisket	*1 teaspoon garlic powder*	*1 teaspoon pepper*
3 tablespoons Canola oil	*¾ teaspoon chili powder*	*1 teaspoon paprika*
⅓ cup firmly packed light brown sugar	*2 teaspoons salt*	*½ teaspoon ground cayenne pepper*

1 Preheat the oven to 300 degrees. Place the Canola oil in bottom of 7-quart cast-iron Dutch oven and warm it in the preheating oven so that the oil coats the entire bottom surface of Dutch oven.

2 Make a dry rub by combining the brown sugar, garlic powder, chili powder, salt, pepper, paprika, and cayenne pepper in a small bowl and stir until the spices are well blended. Rub the dry rub into all sides of the brisket.

3 Place the brisket into the Dutch oven. Add 1½ cups water to the bottom of the Dutch oven, being careful not to disturb the dry rub. Bake the brisket, covered, at 300 degrees for 2 hours

4 Increase the oven temperature to 350 degrees. and continue cooking for another 1 to 1½ hours, checking the brisket every 15 to 20 minutes. Another ½ cup warm water can be added if necessary to prevent the brisket from burning.

5 Remove the brisket from the oven when it's very tender, but not falling apart. To serve, cut the brisket diagonally across the grain into ¼-inch slices and drizzle with pan juices. For tips on carving brisket, see the "Carving Like a Pro" section, later in this chapter.

Vary It! *Use beer or beef broth in place of the water for added flavor.*

Per serving: Calories 310 (From Fat 137); Fat 15g (Saturated 4g); Cholesterol 97mg; Sodium 652mg; Carbohydrate 10g (Dietary Fiber 0g); Protein 32g.

Chisholm Trail Swiss Steak

Swiss steak is a round steak that has flour pounded into both sides and is then browned in fat and smothered with vegetables and seasonings. All this work is necessary because, on its own, a round steak tends to be tough. If you don't have a round steak on hand for this recipe, you can substitute an arm roast (from the chuck portion of the cow), but keep in mind that the arm may have a little more fat.

Preparation time: *15 minutes*

Cooking time: *1½ hours*

Yield: *8 to 10 servings*

3 pounds boneless round steak, cut into servings

¾ cup all-purpose flou

2 teaspoons salt

2 teaspoons pepper

½ teaspoon garlic salt

3 tablespoons vegetable oil

1 cup chopped onions

½ cup chopped celery

½ cup chopped bell pepper

2 tablespoons garlic, diced

1 can (28 ounces) diced tomatoes

1 cup beef broth

1 tablespoon soy sauce

2 tablespoons all-purpose flour

1 Using a meat mallet, pound the round steak between two pieces of wax paper until tender.

2 In large bowl, combine the flour, salt, pepper, and garlic salt. Dredge the steak in the flour mixture and continue to pound the flour into the grain of the meat.

3 In a 13-inch cast-iron skillet, heat the oil over medium-high heat. Cook steak until golden brown on both sides. Remove the steak from the pan.

4 Add the onions, celery, bell pepper, and garlic. Cook until vegetables are wilted, about 5 minutes. Return the meat to the skillet.

5 Add the tomatoes, broth, and soy sauce. Bring mixture to a boil, reduce heat, cover and simmer for 1½ hours, or until meat is tender. Remove the steak and vegetables from the Dutch oven to a serving platter.

6 In a measuring cup, combine ¼ cup of cold water and with the flour until flour is thoroughly dissolved. Pour flour/water mixture into the sauce and stir until thickened.

7 Adjust seasonings if necessary. Pour the sauce over the meat and vegetables on the platter.

Per serving: Calories 302 (From Fat 105); Fat 12g (Saturated 3g); Cholesterol 77mg; Sodium 894mg; Carbohydrate 15g (Dietary Fiber 2g); Protein 33g.

Making the most of good cuts

Almost any cut of beef can be quality depending on what you what to use it for and how you prepare it, but some cuts are "good" in the sense that they're naturally tender and flavorful and retain these qualities when cooked simply. Cuts of meat that fit this description include meat from the rib and loin areas (refer to Figure 6-1). Your challenge with these cuts is not making them tough. The best cooking methods include grilling, pan-frying, and broiling.

Good cuts of meat are too expensive to ruin while cooking. Overcook the meat, and your previously tender, mouthwatering cut is dry and tough. Here are some tips for keeping your meat moist:

- ✔ **Sear the meat first.** When you sear meat, you essentially quick-cook the outside over intense heat (usually medium-high on your stovetop) to form a crust and seal in the juices.

- ✔ **Use tongs, not a meat fork, to turn the meat.** Every time you prick the meat with the fork, you're letting juice seep out.

Cooking slowly is a way to make dryer, tougher cuts moist. (See the "Making tougher cuts tender" section, earlier in this chapter, for details on the proper cooking methods for these cuts.) Slow cooking isn't the best cooking method for already tender meat; in fact, it's often a waste of time and money. First, the longer you cook already-tender meat, the drier it gets, and second, if you're going to take the time to tenderize a piece of meat, why not spend that time on a cheaper cut that could actually benefit from it?

Auroch on the loose!

When you think of cows, *ferocious, wild,* or *awesome* probably doesn't spring to mind. But the *auroch,* the ancient wild ancestor from which domestic cattle come, was, it seems, a pretty impressive and intimidating animal.

Aurochs were large, long-horned wild oxen that lived in German forests. They became extinct during the 17th century. The theory is that they died from embarrassment when they realized how wimpy their descendants turned out.

Veal with Mushroom Sauce

Veal, known for its tenderness and subtle flavor, comes from a young calf. Whereas beef traditionally has been the meat of choice in the United States, veal is favored in many European countries. This recipe combines the techniques of other famous veal dishes. Inspiration for the flour dredging and frying steps comes from veal scaloppini; similarities to osso buco can be seen in the seasoned stock that you simmer this dish in.

Preparation time: *5 minutes*

Cooking time: *30 minutes*

Yield: *3 to 4 servings*

1 to 1½ pound veal cutlets	*2 cups mushrooms, sliced*
Salt and pepper	*2 cloves garlic, minced*
All-purpose flour for dredging	*⅔ cup beef broth*
¼ cup butter	*½ cup sherry*
¼ cup vegetable oil	

1 Lay the veal on wax paper and season both sides with salt and pepper to taste. Dredge in the flour and pat.

2 Heat the butter and oil in a 10-inch cast-iron skillet over medium heat. Add the garlic and mushrooms and cook about 10 minutes. Remove the mushrooms from the skillet.

3 Add the veal to the skillet and brown it on both sides. When the veal is browned, add the broth and sherry, scraping any brown bits from the skillet bottom.

4 Turn heat to medium-high and reduce liquid by one third (that is, let ⅓ of the broth steam away).

5 Add the mushrooms, cooking for 2 or 3 minutes or until the mushrooms are heated through. Remove the veal to a platter and pour the pan juices over the veal.

Per serving: *Calories 425 (From Fat 326); Fat 36g (Saturated 12g); Cholesterol 104mg; Sodium 366mg; Carbohydrate 4g (Dietary Fiber 1g); Protein 21g.*

Pan-Seared Filets of Beef with Peppercorn Sauce

Sear your filets to seal in the juices and finish them in the broiler, and you have a melt-in-your-mouth meal. The peppercorn sauce is, to mix courses, the icing on the cake.

Preparation time: *5 minutes*

Cooking time: *10 to 12 minutes*

Yield: *2 servings*

2 filets of beef tenderloin, about 2 inches thick

2 tablespoons clarified butter, or vegetable oil

¾ cup white wine or vermouth

1 tablespoon green peppercorns

1½ tablespoons salted butter

1 Preheat oven to 500 degrees.

2 Heat a 10-inch cast-iron skillet on a burner over medium-high or high heat, depending on stove performance.

3 Heat the clarified butter in the skillet, without burning. Add the steaks (they should make a hissing sound) and sear for slightly over 1 minute.

4 When the fillets are brown, turn them over using tongs or a spatula to avoid piercing the fillets. Sear for another minute. Remove the skillet and fillets from burner.

5 Place the skillet containing the fillets in the oven for about 5 minutes, depending on preferred result. When the filets have reached desired doneness, carefully remove the hot pan from the oven and place the filets on serving plates.

6 To the pan juices, add wine and peppercorns. Reduce the wine mixture over medium-high heat by one third. Add the butter, heat for 30 seconds, and pour over filets. Serve immediately.

Per serving: Calories 588 (From Fat 379); Fat 42g (Saturated 21g); Cholesterol 197mg; Sodium 210mg; Carbohydrate 1g (Dietary Fiber 0g); Protein 48g.

Pepper-Crusted Filets of Beef Tenderloin

A tenderloin filet, the cut that's famously used in Filet Mignon, is one of the most tender (and most expensive) pieces of meat you can buy. To cook your filet without drying it out, sear the meat first to hold in the moisture, and then finish it in the oven.

Preparation time: *5 minutes*

Cooking time: *10 minutes*

Yield: *4 servings*

4 beef tenderloin filets (10 to 12 ounces, each), about 2 inches thick	*Kosher salt*
⅓ cup cracked black peppercorns	*3 tablespoons Canola oil*
	4 teaspoons butter

1 Preheat oven to 500 degrees.

2 Rub the filets with the pepper, pushing the pepper into filets. Rub salt over both sides of the filets.

3 In a cast-iron skillet large enough to hold the filets, heat the oil over medium-high to high heat until a drop of water sizzles when dropped in the oil.

4 Sear the filets for about 3 minutes on each side. Move to the oven and bake about 3 minutes for medium-rare.

5 Top each filet with butter before serving.

Per serving: Calories 537 (From Fat 318); Fat 35g (Saturated 11g); Cholesterol 151mg; Sodium 228mg; Carbohydrate 5g (Dietary Fiber 2g); Protein 48g.

Pigging Out

Because it's so versatile — coming fresh, smoked, pickled, and in sausage form — pork is popular. Many of the people who eat pork consider it the richest and most flavorful of the meats. This impression is due in part to the fact that pork has an abundance of high-quality fat running through it, which helps the meat avoid becoming too dry during cooking. Even with today's leaner pork, the right cooking method can yield the tender, tasty meat people rave about. (To find out why pork is leaner today than it was a few years ago, see the sidebar "Pigs used to be fatter — believe it or not" for details.)

You can prepare pork in any number of ways. How you cook it depends on the cut and the preparation method. Smoked (or cured) pork, for example, requires different cooking techniques and times than does fresh pork.

Where the meat comes from

As with beef and cows, where the pork comes from on the pig gives you some sort of indication about how tender or flavorful it is and what cooking method is best. Figure 6-2 shows where on the pig the various cuts come from, and the following sections explain the cuts you get from these areas.

Figure 6-2: Where pork cuts come from.

Pigs used to be fatter — believe it or not

Pigs used to be valued for their fat almost as much as for their meat. Up until World War II, a pig with a hefty layer of exterior fat was prized for the amount of lard it would give. But then along came vegetable shortening and information about how bad animal fat was for you, and the fat that had once been so valuable became a liability. The result? Pigs that were genetically engineered to be leaner. An unfortunate (for taste at least) side effect of cutting down on the exterior fat was that the interior fat was reduced, too. With less marbling, pork is leaner, true, but it also tends to be dryer and tougher if you don't cook it carefully.

TECHNICAL STUFF

A pig by any other name

Although most people use the terms *pig* and *hog* synonymously, a *pig* doesn't technically become a *hog* until it weighs more than 50 kilograms (a little over 110 pounds). A *piglet* is a baby who becomes a *shoat* once it's weaned. A *gilt* is a female who turns into a *sow* after she matures. A *barrow,* alas, is a castrated male who will never become a *boar.* A *swine* can be any pig of any age or either gender. Whatever this beast may be technically called, you probably simply call it dinner.

Boston butt

Contrary to what you may have assumed, the Boston butt doesn't come from Massachusetts or the neighborhood that a pig's tail occupies. No, this cut comes from the shoulder, hence the other common name for this cut — Boston shoulder. When cut into slices, the Boston butt yields pork steaks. You can cook pork steaks the same way that you cook a steak or the way you cook a pork chop. When it's not sliced, you cook it as a roast.

When you're figuring out how much to buy, remember that meat from the shoulder has quite a bit of fat, so think larger portions.

Picnic ham

The picnic ham, also called a *picnic shoulder,* isn't a ham at all. (Ham comes from the leg portion of the pig.) The picnic ham is a tough piece of meat. One popular way to prepare a picnic ham is to make barbecue (often called *pulled pork*). To do this, you slow cook the meat to make it tender, pull it apart, and mix and serve it with barbecue sauce. You also get ham hocks from here, which you can braise or cook in liquid. They're great for flavoring soup beans.

Loin

Just as on a piece of beef, the loin on a pig is where the most tender meat is. A pork loin is a long strip of meat that, when cut or sliced, yields these pieces:

- **Roast loin of pork:** This piece of meat used to be called *backstrip tenderloin* because it's on top of the backbone and ribs. If you buy this piece whole, it's often rolled and tied into a roast. The roast loin of pork is also the *Canadian back* because, when smoked and sliced, it's Canadian bacon.

- **Tenderloin:** The tenderloin, also called *catfish tenderloin* because it resembles a catfish, is under the backbone. It's the most-tender piece in the whole pig.

✔ **Baby back ribs:** After you remove the meat from the top of the back-bone (the pork loin roast) and the meat underneath it (the tenderloin), you're left with the ribs.

✔ **Loin chop:** If you leave the roast loin of pork and the tenderloin on the bone, and slice it, you get loin chops. Slices of meat from the tenderloin are boneless loin chops.

✔ **Country style ribs:** This is simply yet another cut from the loin area of a pig.

What piece of meat you get depends on what the butcher cuts. Pork chops, for example, come from the loin area, too.

Belly

From the top part of the belly, you get bacon (unsmoked bacon is *fat back, salt pork,* or *fresh side*). After you remove the strip of bacon, you're left with a cut of pork ribs and breastbone, popularly known as spareribs.

Leg

The leg is also known as the ham. Hams come smoked and fresh, whole and half (or any other portion), with and without the bone.

A smoked ham can come either fully cooked or partially cooked. The distinction is important because you simply need to warm up a fully cooked smoked ham; an internal temperature of 140 is fine. A smoked ham that hasn't been fully cooked (or a fresh ham, which hasn't been cooked or smoked at all) should be cooked long enough to attain an internal temperature of 160.

Other parts

Just about every single part of the pig is used as food. Some of the more popular remaining pieces include:

✔ **Pig's feet:** As the name implies, these cuts come from the hindfoot and forefoot of the pig. These can be pickled, braised, or cooked in liquid.

✔ **Jowl:** The jowl is the pig's jaw. From here, you get jowl bacon (a less expensive cut of bacon).

Cooking methods

Like beef, you can cook pork either with liquid (braise or boil, for example) or without (roast, pan-fry, and broil). The cut of meat you have determines the cooking method.

Because of the fear of *trichinosis* (a parasite that lives in pork that people can ingest and the basis for your grandmother's admonition, "You'll get worms!"), people for a long time considered pork done and the trichinosis dead when the meat had an internal temperature of 170 degrees. With the leaner cuts of today's pork, however, a 170-degree internal temperature means your meat is pretty dry and tough. Fortunately, trichinosis dies at around 140 degrees, so you can safely cook your pork without steaming every last bit of juice and flavor out of it. Today, many people cook pork until it has an internal temperature of between 155 and 160 degrees.

Dutch-Oven Thyme Pork Roast

What's a pork roast? Just about any unsliced (and unsmoked) cut from the hog. You can use a fresh ham, a rib end roast, a loin end roast, a crown roast, a Boston shoulder, a fresh picnic — you name it. For this recipe, I recommend a loin end roast. If you prefer a boneless cut, use center cut pork roast. *Here's a little tip:* You can sometimes find boneless loin roasts on sale in your grocer's case. It's a large piece of meat, enough to yield a nice combination of roasts and pork steaks. Your butcher will slice it for you for free.

Preparation time: *10 minutes*

Cooking time: *About 3 hours*

Yield: *12 servings*

5 pound pork roast	½ tablespoon pepper	½ cup cider vinegar
3 cloves garlic, sliced	3 bay leaves	1 teaspoon dried thyme
2 teaspoons salt		

1 Preheat the oven to 325 degrees.

2 With a small knife, pierce the top of the roast and force garlic slices into the cuts. Rub the roast with salt and pepper.

3 Place bay leaves in the bottom of a cast-iron Dutch oven and set the roast on top of the bay leaves, fat side up.

4 Mix the vinegar and thyme in a small bowl or measuring cup and pour over the top of the roast.

5 Bake the roast for 3 hours, or until an internal temperature of 150 to 155 degrees is reached. Baste the roast with the drippings frequently during cooking.

6 Let the roast rest for 10 minutes before slicing.

Per serving: *Calories 217 (From Fat 89); Fat 10g (Saturated 4g); Cholesterol 83mg; Sodium 447mg; Carbohydrate 1g (Dietary Fiber 0g); Protein 29g.*

Good Ol' Green Beans and Pork Chops

When you choose your pork chops, you can select either center cut chops or rib chops. A center cut chop is a little more expensive and has a bone running down the center, with meat on both sides. Some of this meat comes from the tenderloin, one of the most tender parts of the pork loin. A rib chop, which is slightly less expensive, has a bone running down side of the chop and meat on the other side.

Preparation time: *10 minutes*

Cooking time: *1 hour*

Yield: *5 servings*

2 pounds fresh pole green beans, such as Kentucky Wonders

1 tablespoon butter

4 or 5 thick pork chops

1 medium onion, quartered

4 medium potatoes

Salt and pepper

1 Prepare fresh green beans by washing, stringing, and breaking the bean pieces, discarding ends.

2 Place the butter in a 5-quart cast-iron Dutch oven and set burner to medium high. Lightly brown both sides of the pork chops, a few chops at a time, in butter. Only brown a few chops at a time so as not to crowd them, causing them to steam instead of brown.

3 Add 2 cups water, the beans, and the onion. Reduce the heat and simmer for 45 minutes. Salt and pepper to taste.

4 Peel and quarter potatoes. Place the potatoes on top of beans. Cover and simmer until potatoes are tender, adding more water if necessary to keep water level 1-inch deep. Adjust seasoning with salt and pepper due to addition of potatoes.

Per serving: Calories 479 (From Fat 178); Fat 20g (Saturated 8g); Cholesterol 108mg; Sodium 183mg; Carbohydrate 34g (Dietary Fiber 9g); Protein 39g.

Head cheese: It's a no-brainer

Pigs are amazing in that just about every part of them is used in some way as a food. Head cheese is an example. Inside a pig's head are all sorts of bits and pieces of meat that the butcher (or slaughterhouse) collects. When enough has been gathered, the meat is cooked and mixed in a gelatin that solidifies into a sort of meat mold, which can then be sliced and sold.

Apricot-Ginger Glazed Pork Rib Roast with Fruit Stuffing

A 7-bone pork rib roast is simply a pork roast (from the loin) that has 7 bones attached. For carving tips, see the "Carving Like a Pro" section, later in this chapter.

Preparation time: *20 minutes*

Cooking time: *2½ hours*

Yield: *7 servings*

7-bone pork rib roast	1 teaspoon salt
2 tablespoons butter	½ teaspoon pepper
1 cup chopped onion	1 teaspoon dried thyme
1 cup chopped celery	9-ounce jar apricot preserves
1 box pork stuffing mix	1 tablespoon soy sauce
½ cup dried apricot halves	1 tablespoon lemon juice
⅓ cup dried cranberries	½ teaspoon ground ginger
¼ cup chopped fresh parsley	

1 Preheat the oven to 325 degrees.

2 In a 7-quart cast-iron Dutch oven, melt the butter over medium-high heat. Cook the onion and celery until tender, stirring occasionally. Remove the cooked onions and celery and place in a large bowl. Add the stuffing mix, apricots, cranberries, and parsley to the onions and celery.

3 Rub all sides of the pork roast with salt, pepper, and thyme. With heavy string, tie a loop around the end of the bones and pull until the roast fans out. Place the roast in a Dutch oven. Add ¾ cup water, cover and place in the oven.

4 Meanwhile, in a small metal bowl, make the glaze by combining the apricot preserves, soy sauce, lemon juice, and ginger and heating over low heat. Baste the pork roast with the glaze at 15-minute intervals for 1 hour.

5 Take the roast from the oven and remove the pan drippings into a small bowl, being careful to not disturb the roast. Skim fat from drippings and discard fat. Mix pan drippings into stuffing mixture, adding more water if too dry. Spoon the stuffing into the slits and around the roast.

6 Return the roast to the oven and cook, covered, for another 1½ hours or until a thermometer inserted into the thickest part of the meat registers 160 degrees. Let the roast stand 15 minutes before slicing. Heat the remaining glaze and serve over the meat.

Per serving: Calories 698 (From Fat 241); Fat 27g (Saturated 11g); Cholesterol 151mg; Sodium 1,024mg; Carbohydrate 50g (Dietary Fiber 3g); Protein 62g.

The illustrious history of the pig in America

You can thank Christopher Columbus for bringing pigs to North America. He carried eight of them with him on his second voyage, and these eight multiplied like crazy on the Caribbean island of Hispaniola and then went wild — literally. A few of the descendents of these eight were rounded up in 1539 and brought to the southeastern United States (of course, it wasn't called that back then) with Hernando de Soto. More pigs arrived later from England, coming with John Smith and his group of guys to Jamestown in 1607. Some people believe that the razorbacks that exist today in the southern United States are the direct descendents of de Soto's pigs.

A recipe no cast-iron cookbook should be without

Country Ham and Red-Eye Gravy is a traditional part of a Southern breakfast, often served with biscuits and grits. Where the name came from is a matter of conjecture. The two most popular theories are as follows:

- ✔ Andrew Jackson (the seventh president of the United States) asked his hung-over cook (who had been imbibing whiskey the night before) to make some ham with gravy as red as the cook's eyes.
- ✔ A circle of fat with a slightly reddish cast (the eye) appears as the gravy thickens.

However it was named, the recipe is a favorite of many.

Country Ham and Red-Eye Gravy

You can use water instead of coffee in this recipe. Keep in mind, however, that it won't have that distinctive taste that's made it a favorite breakfast food for over a hundred years.

Preparation time: *5 minutes*

Cooking time: *10 minutes*

Yield: *2 to 3 servings*

½ tablespoon bacon drippings

3 slices country ham

Pinch or two of sugar

⅓ cup brewed black coffee

½ cup water

Hot biscuits or grits, for serving

1 Heat the bacon drippings in a 12-inch cast-iron skillet over medium heat.

2 Add the ham slices and fry until brown, about 3 to 4 minutes on each side. Remove to platter and keep warm.

3 Add the sugar and coffee to skillet to deglaze, stirring and scraping any brown bits from the skillet.

4 Increase the heat to medium-high, add ½ cup water, bring the mixture to a boil, and cook for about 3 to 5 minutes to reduce. Ladle over hot biscuits or grits.

Per serving: Calories 396 (From Fat 168); Fat 19g (Saturated 6g); Cholesterol 63mg; Sodium 2,671mg; Carbohydrate 27g (Dietary Fiber 1g); Protein 28g.

Something for the Kids

Kids love hot dogs. Cast iron hates water. So how do you cook hot dogs with cast iron? You could broil them or cook them on a griddle, but as any parent of a young child knows, that leaves "marks" or "bubbly things," both of which are grounds for adamant declarations that the hot dog is burned. And then you're back to peanut butter and jelly. The solution is corn dogs. Kids love food that comes on a stick, and your cast iron is great for deep-frying.

Corn Dogs

Cook the hot dogs before you dip them in the batter. You can boil or microwave them. (I recommend microwaving because it doesn't dirty another pan.) The batter will stick better, and you don't have to worry about getting the hot dog done. Also, use wooden skewers made especially for corndogs or popsicle sticks: You can find either in your grocery store.

Preparation: *10 minutes*

Cooking time: *5 to 10 minutes*

Yield: *10 corn dogs*

Oil for frying	*2 tablespoons sugar (optional)*
1 package wieners	*⅔ cup cornmeal*
1 cup all-purpose flour	*2 tablespoons melted butter*
1½ teaspoons baking powder	*¾ cup milk (or buttermilk)*
1 teaspoon salt	*1 egg*

1 Preheat oil in your cast-iron deep fryer to 350 degrees.

2 While the oil is preheating, cook the hot dogs. (If you boil them, wipe them dry.)

3 To prepare the batter, mix the flour, baking powder, salt, sugar, if desired, and cornmeal in medium bowl. In another bowl, combine the butter, milk, and egg; stir the milk mixture into flour mixture. Set the batter aside and re-stir before coating hot dogs.

4 Insert skewers in the hot dogs. If you don't have skewers, serve the finished product on a plate. Coat each hot dog well with batter.

5 Carefully place hot dogs in oil and fry until golden brown. Drain on paper towel. Serve while hot.

Per serving: Calories 304 (From Fat 189); Fat 21g (Saturated 6g); Cholesterol 68mg; Sodium 832mg; Carbohydrate 20g (Dietary Fiber 1g); Protein 8g.

Carving Like a Pro

With so many ready-to-serve portions available at the grocery store, carving is practically a dying art. That's too bad, for the following reasons:

✔ **You get more meat, especially with bone-in cuts.** Too many people ignore the bones or hack around them. The result is a lot of wasted meat. Knowing how to carve around a bone or remove it entirely yields more meat.

✔ **How you carve has a direct impact on how chewy — or not — your meat is.** Even a tender cut of meat becomes chewy if carved incorrectly. All meat is essentially muscle, and muscle has grain. Cut *with* the grain, and your meat is chewy and stringing. Cut across the grain, as shown in the carving illustrations I include this section, and the meat practically falls apart in your mouth.

✔ **When you stand at the head of the table, holding a steel in one hand and a blade in the other, you look *very* in-charge.**

The following sections and illustrations show you how to carve some the cuts of meat prepared in this chapter.

Carving a brisket

Figure 6-3 provides step-by-step (by step) directions for carving brisket. Follow these guidelines, and you'll be on your way to the Meat Cutters Hall of Fame. The most important thing to remember about the brisket is to *cut across the grain,* rather than with it. Fortunately, the grain is very pronounced in a brisket.

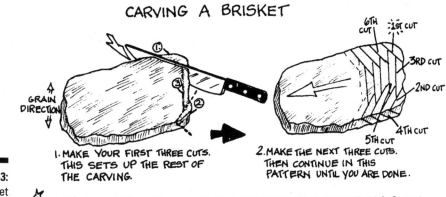

CARVING A BRISKET

GRAIN DIRECTION

1. MAKE YOUR FIRST THREE CUTS. THIS SETS UP THE REST OF THE CARVING.

6TH CUT — 1ST CUT
3RD CUT
2ND CUT
4TH CUT
5TH CUT

2. MAKE THE NEXT THREE CUTS. THEN CONTINUE IN THIS PATTERN UNTIL YOU ARE DONE.

★ DON'T CARVE STRAIGHT DOWN. MAKE SURE YOU HAVE YOUR BLADE AT A SLIGHT ANGLE SO THAT YOU GO ACROSS THE GRAIN, NOT WITH IT !

Figure 6-3:
Beef Brisket
101.

Carving a pot roast

When you carve a pot roast, you follow the same basic guidelines, regardless of the cut. Figure 6-4 shows a seven-bone pot roast (so called because the bone looks like the number 7).

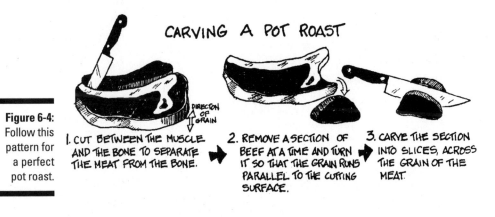

CARVING A POT ROAST

1. CUT BETWEEN THE MUSCLE AND THE BONE TO SEPARATE THE MEAT FROM THE BONE.

2. REMOVE A SECTION OF BEEF AT A TIME AND TURN IT SO THAT THE GRAIN RUNS PARALLEL TO THE CUTTING SURFACE.

3. CARVE THE SECTION INTO SLICES, ACROSS THE GRAIN OF THE MEAT.

Figure 6-4: Follow this pattern for a perfect pot roast.

Carving a pork roast

Several pieces of meat qualify as a pork roast. The steps in Figure 6-5 explain how to cut a loin roast. (*Note:* This piece of meat is also sometimes called a crown roast, because you can tie the ribs together to make a crown, as I have you do in the Apricot-Ginger Glazed Pork Rib Roast with Fruit Stuffing recipe in this chapter.)

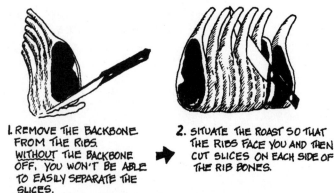

CARVING A PORK ROAST

1. REMOVE THE BACKBONE FROM THE RIBS. WITHOUT THE BACKBONE OFF, YOU WON'T BE ABLE TO EASILY SEPARATE THE SLICES.

2. SITUATE THE ROAST SO THAT THE RIBS FACE YOU AND THEN CUT SLICES ON EACH SIDE OF THE RIB BONES.

☆ EVERY OTHER PIECE OF MEAT WILL HAVE A RIB BONE IN IT.

Figure 6-5: Boning up on pork rib roast.

Chapter 7

Tastes Like Chicken (and Turkey)

. . . .

In This Chapter

▶ Getting familiar with different types of chicken

▶ Facing the roasting challenge

▶ Following time-proven tricks to great fried chicken

▶ Carving 101

. . . .

Many birds qualify as *poultry,* domesticated birds that are kept for both their eggs and for their meat: chickens, turkeys, ducks, geese, guinea fowl, peafowl, pigeons, and others. Chicken, of course, is one of the favorite birds, hands (or wings) down. Turkey, that holiday staple, comes in second. Poultry is great tasting, but it also owes much of its increasing popularity to the fact that it's generally healthier than red meat. (See Chapter 6 for beef and pork recipes.)

But even before people were drawn to poultry as an alternative to fattier meats, it's always been a versatile staple of American diets: baked, roasted, fried, stir-fried, sautéed, broiled, barbecued, fricasseed, stewed, and more — and that's even before you get to the leftovers.

In this chapter, I offer ideas and instructions for choosing the right bird, preparing it for cooking, and carving it when it's done. You can find safety information here, too. And, although eating duck and goose is also relatively common in America — and you can probably find a peacock to eat somewhere — this chapter focuses on chicken and throws in a turkey recipe or two for good measure. To find a good duck recipe, head to Chapter 15.

Chicken Basics

When you go to the grocery store, you'll find plenty of chicken options. Basically the difference is in the size and the amount of meat. Table 7-1 lists the types of chicken and the cooking methods.

Table 7-1	Types of Chicken and Cooking Methods	
Bird	*Weight*	*Cooking Methods*
Game hens (Rock Cornish hens)	1½ pounds or less	Stuffed and roasted or split and broiled
Fryers (broiler-fryers)	1½ to 3 pounds	Broiled, fried, roasted, or stewed
Hens (stewing chickens)	2½ to 5 pounds	Stewed, fricasseed, or used in soup
Roasters	More than 4 pounds	Roasted
Capons (castrated roosters)	4½ to 7 pounds	Roasted

When you buy a chicken, plan on a ½ pound of chicken per serving — less, if the chicken is boneless. If you're serving game hen, plan on ½ to 1 bird per person.

You can buy whole chickens, quartered chickens, or chickens that have been cut up into individual pieces. You can also buy particular pieces: a package of drumsticks, for example, or thighs. Buying pieces is a good choice if you like (or your recipe calls for) particular pieces, or if you just don't want to take the time to cut up a whole chicken yourself. Buying whole chickens, on the other hand, is usually less expensive than buying pieces, and when they go on sale, they're cheaper yet.

If you run across a sale on whole chickens, buy a few. Leave some whole or quarter them for roasting; cut the others into individual pieces for other chicken dishes. (Figure 7-1 demonstrates one technique for cutting a whole chicken into parts.) Chickens store well in the freezer. Simply remove the giblets, wash the chicken and pat it dry, and then wrap it tightly in freezer wrap. It can stay in the freezer for up to 9 months at 0 degrees. You can freeze giblets for up to 3 months.

Don't throw the giblets away! They make great gravy, they're good fried, and you can cut them up and use them in any dish that calls for cut-up chicken.

CUTTING A CHICKEN INTO PARTS

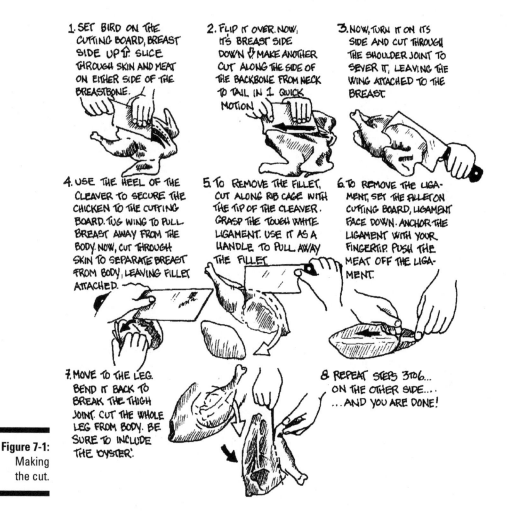

1. SET BIRD ON THE CUTTING BOARD, BREAST SIDE UP. SLICE THROUGH SKIN AND MEAT ON EITHER SIDE OF THE BREASTBONE.

2. FLIP IT OVER. NOW, IT'S BREAST SIDE DOWN & MAKE ANOTHER CUT ALONG THE SIDE OF THE BACKBONE FROM NECK TO TAIL IN 1 QUICK MOTION.

3. NOW, TURN IT ON ITS SIDE AND CUT THROUGH THE SHOULDER JOINT TO SEVER IT, LEAVING THE WING ATTACHED TO THE BREAST.

4. USE THE HEEL OF THE CLEAVER TO SECURE THE CHICKEN TO THE CUTTING BOARD. TUG WING TO PULL BREAST AWAY FROM THE BODY. NOW, CUT THROUGH SKIN TO SEPARATE BREAST FROM BODY, LEAVING FILLET ATTACHED.

5. TO REMOVE THE FILLET, CUT ALONG RIB CAGE WITH THE TIP OF THE CLEAVER. GRASP THE TOUGH WHITE LIGAMENT. USE IT AS A HANDLE TO PULL AWAY THE FILLET.

6. TO REMOVE THE LIGAMENT, SET THE FILLET ON CUTTING BOARD, LIGAMENT FACE DOWN. ANCHOR THE LIGAMENT WITH YOUR FINGERTIP. PUSH THE MEAT OFF THE LIGAMENT.

7. MOVE TO THE LEG. BEND IT BACK TO BREAK THE THIGH JOINT. CUT THE WHOLE LEG FROM BODY. BE SURE TO INCLUDE THE 'OYSTER'.

8. REPEAT STEPS 3 TO 6... ON THE OTHER SIDE.... ...AND YOU ARE DONE!

Figure 7-1: Making the cut.

Roasting Guidelines

Cast iron is great for roasting because it holds and distributes heat evenly. Although you can buy cast-iron roasters, which have ridges cast into the bottom of the pan to hold your meat out of its juices, you don't need a roaster to roast in cast iron. Any skillet or Dutch oven big enough to hold your bird will do. To keep the cooking meat out of its juices, use a standard roasting V rack, just as you would in any pan, or a cast-iron trivet.

For as simple as roasting is — basically you just put the meat in a pan and stick it in a 325- or 350-degree oven until it's done — much can go wrong, especially with a chicken. Unlike roasting beef and pork roasts, which are pretty symmetrical and cook evenly, roasting a chicken forces you to accommodate all its parts, many of which could benefit from different cooking times and, frankly, different cooking temperatures.

The breast meat is lean and prone to drying out. This liability is only made worse by the fact that, to brown nicely, you situate the bird in the roasting pan so that the breast is on top and closer to the oven's heat source. The dark meat of the thigh and drumstick, however, has more fat and connective tissue and therefore requires longer cooking times before it's done.

The end result of all this? If you cook a chicken until the legs are nicely done, the breast is bone dry. If you cook until the breast is nicely done, the leg meat is still bloody near the bone. Yummy.

Various cooks swear by the following tricks to produce a roast chicken that's done and still moist:

- ✔ **They don't truss the bird.** When you truss a chicken for roasting, you bind its legs and wings tightly to the body. The idea is that this helps the chicken cook more evenly by slowing down how quickly the breast cooks. People who don't truss the bird disagree. They claim that, trussing the bird actually slows down how quickly the *legs* cook, specifically the inner part of the thigh. And since the legs require *more* cooking time, trussing exacerbates the original problem: The legs are still too raw to eat when the breast reaches its optimum temperature.

- ✔ **They turn the bird while it cooks.** Turning a roasting chicken or turkey is gaining popularity, precisely because of the problem of getting the parts of the bird to cook evenly. Basically, the goal is to move different parts of the bird close to the oven's heating element as a way to even out the meat's exposure to the highest heat. Some start the bird on its belly and then flip it to its back; others start the bird on one side, turn it to the other, and then finish it, breast up.

  If you decide to turn your chicken during roasting, make sure that the bird is breast-side up for the last half of the cooking time.

Chicken can harbor *salmonella,* bacteria that causes food poisoning. The bacteria die when exposed to temperatures of 160 degrees and higher. Therefore, according to the U.S. Department of Agriculture, you need to cook chicken until it reaches an internal temperature of 165 degrees. A stuffed chicken is done when the thigh has an internal thigh temperature of 180 to 185 degrees. When the thigh is at this temperature, the stuffing is at 165 degrees (considered safe) and the breast at 170 (also safe).

Dutch Oven Chicken

You can use a large fryer, which generally weighs between 1½ to 3 pounds, or a small hen, also called a *stewing chicken,* which tends to weigh between 2½ to 5 pounds and has more meat. Whichever bird you choose to roast, use the trivet or roasting rack. It keeps the slow-cooking chicken out of its own juices and drippings.

Preparation time: *15 minutes*

Cooking time: *1½ to 2 hours*

Yield: *4 servings*

3 or 4 pound whole fryer or hen	*1 tablespoon chopped fresh parsley*
Salt and pepper	*½ teaspoon dill or rosemary (optional)*
Juice of one lemon	*1 onion, quartered*
2 tablespoons olive oil	*2 ribs of celery with tops*

1 Preheat your oven to 325 degrees. Remove the neck and giblets from your chicken and freeze for later use. Thoroughly rinse the chicken inside and out. Pat dry. Salt and pepper the cavity.

2 Combine the lemon juice and olive oil and rub all over the chicken. Rub the salt, pepper, parsley, and dill or rosemary, if desired, over the chicken.

3 Put a few pieces of onion and celery in the cavity. Place the remaining onion and celery around the chicken. Place the chicken on the trivet or roasting rack in a 10-inch Dutch oven and cover.

4 Cover and bake until fork tender or until a meat thermometer inserted in the fleshy part of a thigh registers 180, about 1½ to 2 hours. Let the chicken stand for 10 minutes before carving.

Per serving: *Calories 453 (From Fat 260); Fat 29g (Saturated 7g); Cholesterol 178mg; Sodium 278mg; Carbohydrate 1g (Dietary Fiber 0g); Protein 45g.*

Southern Fried Chicken: The Ultimate in Comfort Food

People who make great fried chicken swear by their own unique recipes. If you don't yet have a tried, trusted, and true — not to mention knock-your-socks-off — recipe that you swear by, try experimenting with some of the following variations to see what suits your particular taste (or just check out the award-winning technique from the Southern Fried Chicken recipe in this chapter):

 ✔ **Coating:** Apply different coatings and coating techniques. Try dipping the chicken in milk, then flour, then milk, and then the flour again. Some cast-iron cooks dip it in a milk-egg mixture and then dredge it in flour. Some don't use flour at all and cover it with cracker crumbs, potato flakes, or cornmeal.

 After you coat your chicken, let it air-dry. Air-drying your chicken for 20 minutes to a half hour after it's been coated lets the coating toughen and produces a crispier crust.

 ✔ **Seasoning:** Use plain old salt and pepper or create special seasoning mixes. You may want to season the flour that you dredge the chicken through; you can also season the chicken itself. Some people swear that paprika enhances the flavor; others claim it's just there for color.

 ✔ **Other prep:** Cook the chicken straight from the package (after washing and patting dry, of course); or let it soak in brine or buttermilk for a half-hour to make it juicier.

The real secret to Southern Fried Chicken, however, isn't in the recipe; it's in the cooking. Properly pan-fried chicken is tender and moist (not greasy) on the inside and golden brown and crispy on the outside. Follow this advice:

 ✔ **Keep your oil very hot.** To make sure that your chicken doesn't get greasy, you want the oil hot enough (375 degrees) that the water in the chicken stays above the boiling point during frying. The force of the steam leaving the chicken keeps the oil from being absorbed. The hot oil also makes the outside wonderfully crispy. Some tips for keeping the oil at the temperature you want are as follows:

  • Use peanut oil, which has a hotter smoke point than vegetable oils or shortenings.

  • Allow the chicken to come almost to room temperature before you cook it so that when you put it into the hot oil, it doesn't reduce the oil temperature as much as really cold chicken would.

- • Don't overcrowd the chicken in the pan. Putting too many pieces in the pan causes the temperature to drop and takes it longer to heat up again.

- • Use a deep-sided cast-iron skillet or Dutch oven and an iron cover. Cast iron is the cook's best friend when pan-frying. It absorbs heat evenly, eliminating hot spots, and its ability to retain heat keeps the temperature of the oil as even as possible.

✔ **Brown the chicken quickly to seal in the juices.** After the initial browning, reduce the heat to allow the chicken to cook through without drying. Then return the heat to medium-high to re-crisp it before you remove it from the pan.

✔ **Use tongs to turn and move the chicken.** Tongs won't pierce the chicken and let the juice escape.

✔ **Drain fried chicken on a paper towel and then place it on a metal wire cooling rack in a warm oven.** This simple step keeps your cooked chicken crisp and warm. After all, what good's a crispier crust if it just gets soggy and cold while sitting in a puddle of oil?

The Century of the Chicken

Most people today wouldn't think of a chicken as particularly pleasing to the eye. They certainly wouldn't think of the buggers as show animals. But before chickens became popular as food, they were quite the lookers, it seems:

✔ In Japan and other East Asian countries, chickens were used for decoration — live decoration, that is.

✔ As exotic animals in places such as India, chickens were part of royal menageries.

✔ During the 19th century, chickens were bred for show, with the emphasis on feather coloring and combs.

Chickens aren't just good-lookin', though. They were also hard workers and held down a couple other jobs. In particular, they were used for divination and religious rituals and entertainment — cock-fighting.

Chickens fascinated so many people that they even have their own century, The Century of the Chicken, which began in the early 19th century when Europe, and later the United States, was first introduced to new, ornamental (think pet) chickens from Asia. The introduction of these new birds fascinated the public, and huge numbers of people started breeding and raising the birds.

Southern Fried Chicken

This recipe is simple, delicious, and easy to make. Just be sure to make enough for dinner and still have a few pieces leftover — as delicious as fried chicken is straight from the pan, it's even better cold the next day.

Preparation time: *30 minutes*

Cooking time: *About 35 minutes*

Yield: *4 servings (2 pieces each)*

3 pounds chicken pieces

1½ cups buttermilk or milk

Salt and pepper

Paprika

About 1 cup all-purpose flour for dredging

Peanut oil or shortening to fill skillet 1-inch deep

1 Wash the chicken pieces and pat dry.

2 Dip the chicken pieces in milk and then lay them on wax paper. Sprinkle both sides of the pieces with salt, pepper, and paprika and then dredge them in the flour. Let the chicken stand for 20 minutes and dredge in flour again.

3 While the chicken is resting, heat the oil or shortening in a deep cast-iron skillet or a Dutch oven on medium-high heat to 375 degrees. (The oil will be hot but not smoking.) Use an instant read thermometer to test the temperature now and throughout cooking.

4 Add 4 to 5 pieces of chicken to the skillet, browning both sides. Be careful not to add so much chicken at one time that the oil temperature drops significantly. Turn and move the chicken as necessary to ensure even browning. (Use tongs so that you don't pierce the meat.)

5 Move the chicken to a platter to allow room for the next 4 or 5 pieces. Add the next 4 to 5 pieces of chicken and cook until all are brown.

6 When the second batch of chicken is about brown, return all chicken to the skillet, reduce the heat to low or medium-low and cover. At this point, stacking the chicken in the skillet may be necessary. Cook slowly and gently for about 20 minutes, or until fork tender. Check several times and turn or move the pieces as necessary to keep all the chicken browned evenly.

7 Remove the cover and return the heat to medium-high to re-crisp the chicken, about 5 minutes after the skillet is hot again. While re-crisping, watch the chicken carefully and turn the pieces so that all sides are crisp, taking care not to burn the bottom pieces of chicken.

8 Drain and move to a serving platter or place on a rack in the oven to keep warm.

Per serving: *Calories 664 (From Fat 332); Fat 37g (Saturated 9g); Cholesterol 182mg; Sodium 1,392mg; Carbohydrate 29g (Dietary Fiber 1g); Protein 51g.*

Down Home Favorites

Barbecued chicken. Chicken and gravy. Chicken potpie. Some foods just reach out and grab you as good, old-fashioned, comfort foods. This section shares these and other recipes that have withstood the test of time.

Honey Barbecued Broilers

In this recipe title, *broiler* refers to the chicken (the broiler-fryer, as explained in the "Chicken Basics" section, earlier in this chapter), not the cooking method. The same with the term *barbecued*. Instead of being cooked on a grill, this chicken is slow-cooked in the oven. For traditional barbecues, the sauce must be brushed on during the last couple of minutes of cooking to avoid burning. But the barbecue in this recipe is the basting liquid, infusing the meat with flavor.

Preparation time: *10 minutes*

Cooking time: *About 1½ hours*

Yield: *6 servings*

¾ cup butter, melted	*2 teaspoons salt*
⅓ cup vinegar	*½ teaspoon dry mustard*
¼ cup honey	*¼ teaspoon pepper*
½ teaspoon crushed marjoram	*¼ pound sliced bacon*
2 garlic cloves, minced	*6 chicken quarters*

1 Preheat your oven to 350 degrees.

2 In a small bowl, combine the butter, vinegar, honey, marjoram, garlic, salt, dry mustard, and pepper, mix well, and set aside.

3 Fry the bacon in 7-quart cast-iron Dutch oven. Remove the bacon and set aside, leaving the drippings in the skillet. Add the chicken pieces to the skillet and brown on all sides, about 7 minutes per side.

4 Reduce the heat to low and baste the chicken with about ⅛ of the sauce.

5 Cover and place in a 350-degree oven. Bake for about 1¼ hours, turning the chicken and basting with the sauce every 10 or 15 minutes until fork tender. Add the bacon back into the Dutch oven and serve.

*****Per serving:*** *Calories 682 (From Fat 437); Fat 49g (Saturated 22g); Cholesterol 249mg; Sodium 1,013mg; Carbohydrate 12g (Dietary Fiber 0g); Protein 48g.*

Smothered Chicken

Paprika is a main ingredient in this recipe, and if you're of the "it only adds color" school, you may wonder why. Paprika is actually a cousin of cayenne pepper. Made from dried red peppers, it comes sweet, spicy, and hot. Some of the best paprika comes from Hungary. You can use any combination of chicken pieces for this recipe, but legs and thighs remain juicier than white-meat breasts through all the cooking. The spiciness of this dish goes well with plain mashed potatoes or rice.

Preparation time: 10 minutes

Cooking time: 1½ to 2 hours

Yield: 4 servings

3 pounds chicken pieces	*4 tablespoons butter*
Salt and pepper	*2 tablespoons vegetable oil*
Paprika	*3 to 4 tablespoons all-purpose flour*

1 Preheat oven to 300 degrees. Wash chicken pieces and pat dry. Lay them on wax paper and salt, pepper, and paprika both sides of chicken.

2 Melt butter and oil in cast-iron chicken fryer or Dutch oven over medium-high heat.

3 Brown the chicken on both sides; reduce heat to medium. Continue browning the chicken, turning it several times until the chicken is almost too brown. As the chicken pieces are brown, remove them from the skillet.

3 Pour excess grease from the skillet and place the chicken pieces back into the skillet.

4 Generously shake more paprika on the chicken and add ½ cup water. (The paprika and the browning of the chicken will produce a richly colored broth.) Cover tightly with the iron lid and cook in a 300-degree oven for about 1½ hours, or until the chicken is so tender that it can be cut with a fork.

5 Remove the chicken from the Dutch oven and keep warm. Place the Dutch oven on a burner on medium to heat drippings. While the drippings are heating use a spatula to scrape any brown pieces from the bottom.

6 In a cup, combine the flour and ¼ cup water, adding more water if necessary, to allow it to pour but still be as thick as possible. When the pan juices are hot (bubbling but not fast), add the flour mixture by pouring it through a strainer and stirring constantly to avoid lumps. Simmer until gravy thickens, about 3 minutes.

Vary It! *To "stretch" your pan juices, add 1 cup chicken broth to the drippings.*

Per serving: Calories 561 (From Fat 365); Fat 41g (Saturated 14g); Cholesterol 209mg; Sodium 279mg; Carbohydrate 2g (Dietary Fiber 0g); Protein 45g.

Country Captain

This recipe came from the late Mrs. W. L. Bullard of Columbus, Georgia. She once served it to a distinguished guest, Franklin Roosevelt, and it soon became a specialty of the house. Another fan of the dish was General George Patton. On leaving for Europe with the Second Armored Division, he wired a message to Mrs. Bullard's daughter to please meet him at the train with a whole bucket of Country Captain.

Preparation time: *15 minutes*

Cooking time: *10 to 12 minutes per piece of chicken; 45 minutes in oven*

Yield: *8 to 10 servings*

4 pounds your favorite chicken pieces, skinned

Salt and pepper

2 cups all-purpose flour

Shortening or peanut oil to fill skillet 1-inch deep

2 medium onions, finely chopped

1 clove garlic, minced

1 bell pepper, seeded and finely chopped

2 teaspoons curry powder

1½ teaspoon salt

½ teaspoon pepper

1 can (28 ounces) whole tomatoes with liquid

1 can (14 ounces) diced tomatoes with liquid

2 tablespoon chopped fresh parsley

½ teaspoon dried thyme

8 cups hot cooked rice

¼ cup currants

½ pound sliced almonds, toasted

1 Preheat your oven to 350 degrees. Wash the chicken and pat dry. Lay the pieces on wax paper; salt and pepper both sides of the chicken. Dredge the pieces in flour until all sides are well coated with flour.

2 Meanwhile, heat 1-inch of shortening or peanut oil in a 12-inch cast-iron skillet over medium-high heat.

3 Fry the chicken pieces a few at a time, in the skillet turning over until golden brown on both sides. You may need to reduce the heat as chicken cooks, but also raise it when adding uncooked chicken pieces. As the chicken pieces are cooked (about 10 to 12 minutes per piece), remove them to a 5-quart cast-iron Dutch oven.

4 Drain most of the oil from the skillet, leaving 2 tablespoons behind. Add the onions, garlic, and bell pepper to the skillet. Cook until tender. Add the curry powder, salt, pepper, tomatoes, 1 tablespoon parsley, and thyme and bring to a boil. Pour the mixture over the chicken in the Dutch oven. Bake in the oven for about 45 minutes.

5 Place the chicken pieces around the rim of a large serving platter and mound rice in the center. Stir the currants and half of the almonds into the sauce and immediately pour the sauce over the rice. Garnish with remaining almonds and parsley.

Per serving: Calories 592 (From Fat 224); Fat 25g (Saturated 4g); Cholesterol 60mg; Sodium 651mg; Carbohydrate 63g (Dietary Fiber 7g); Protein 31g.

Chicken Potpie

Many people think chicken potpie is difficult to make or it takes too long to cook. But if you use leftover chicken and an already-made pie crust, you have about 15 minutes in prep time before it goes into the oven. If you want to make your own pie crust, see the sidebar "A quick, easy crust" in this chapter and add about 10 minutes to your prep.

Preparation time: *15 minutes*

Cooking time: *45 minutes*

Yield: *8 to 10 servings, depending on size of slices*

½ cup butter

⅓ cup all-purpose flour plus more to dust

⅓ chopped onion

Salt and pepper

1¾ cup chicken broth

⅔ cup milk

16-ounce package of frozen vegetables (any combination of corn, green beans, carrots, and peas)

2 cups cut up, cooked chicken (preferably leftovers)

Already-made pie crust for a 2-crust pie

1 Preheat your oven to 425 degrees.

2 Over low heat, melt the butter in a saucepan. Add the ⅓ cup flour, onion, and salt and pepper, and cook until mixture is smooth and bubbly, about 3 to 5 minutes. Remove from heat.

3 Slowly add broth and milk to flour mixture, stirring constantly to avoid lumps.

4 Return to the burner, turn the heat to medium-high, and heat to boiling, stirring constantly, until the mixture begins to thicken and fat bubbles roll to the surface. Boil and stir for a couple minutes more. Remove from heat and mix in frozen vegetables and chicken.

5 Line the bottom of a 10-inch cast-iron skillet or chicken fryer with one pie crust. Sprinkle flour on the crust to cover lightly. Pour the chicken mixture into the crust. Top with the second pie crust, dust with flour, and crimp edges. Cut slits in the top.

6 Place the pie in the center of the oven and bake for 45 minutes or until the crust is golden and the insides bubbling. (If you're not making this in a Dutch oven or deep skillet, you may want to put a pie plate or oven liner on the lower rack to catch any drips.)

Vary It! *Use cut up turkey instead of chicken. For a more savory pie, add 1 teaspoon of thyme or rosemary or ½ teaspoon sage to the milk sauce. Or flavor the pie crust with sesame seed or celery seed.*

Per serving: *Calories 481 (From Fat 266); Fat 30g (Saturated 14g); Cholesterol 71mg; Sodium 556mg; Carbohydrate 40g (Dietary Fiber 3g); Protein 14g.*

Chicken Dishes for the Uptown Crowd

Who says the only chicken dishes that you can cook in cast iron are the down-home favorites? Not me. You can cook *any* chicken recipe in a cast-iron pan, even more sophisticated ones, and this section includes dishes to prove it to you. For more recipes from around the world, hop on over to Chapter 16.

Chicken Marsala

Marsala is a dark-colored, sweet wine made in Marsala, Sicily. (Of course, wines that look like the Sicilian Marsala but are made in other places are also called marsala.) In Chicken Marsala, this wine is a key ingredient in the sauce.

Preparation time: *10 minutes*

Cooking time: *10 minutes*

Yield: *4 servings*

4 skinless, boneless chicken breast halves	*½ cup Marsala wine*
4 tablespoons butter	*½ cup chicken broth*
½ teaspoon salt	*½ pound mushrooms, sliced*
Pepper	*Fresh parsley for garnish (optional)*
1 tablespoon fresh lemon juice	

1 Pound the chicken pieces between two pieces of wax paper until ¼-inch thick.

2 Melt the butter in a 12-inch cast-iron skillet over medium heat. Cook the chicken for about 5 minutes on each side or until golden brown. Remove to platter and keep warm.

3 Increase heat to medium-high. Add the salt, pepper, lemon juice, wine, and chicken broth to the skillet and blend. Cook the wine mixture for a few minutes and then add the mushrooms and cook until tender.

4 Pour the sauce over the chicken and garnish with parsley, if desired.

Per serving: *Calories 267 (From Fat 136); Fat 15g (Saturated 8g); Cholesterol 104mg; Sodium 483mg; Carbohydrate 3g (Dietary Fiber 1g); Protein 29g.*

Chicken Picata

Chicken Picata is simply chicken cooked in a sauce. You can find various Picata recipes that differ in their specifics: for example, whether the chicken breast should be halved, sliced, or, as in this recipe, pounded thin, and whether wine or broth should be used. The basic cooking method, however, is the same: sautéing the chicken in butter or oil (usually olive oil), adding the other ingredients, and cooking until the liquid is reduced to a nice sauce. The result is a simple but elegant dish that you can serve alone or over pasta.

Preparation time: *10 minutes*

Cooking time: *20 minutes*

Yield: *5 to 6 servings*

4 or 5 skinless, boneless chicken breast halves

Salt and pepper

½ cup all-purpose flour

3 to 4 tablespoons butter

¼ cup white wine, or vermouth

⅓ cup chicken broth

Juice of ½ lemon

Lemon slices (optional)

Parsley sprigs (optional)

1 Between two pieces of wax or parchment paper, pound the breast until flat. Sprinkle with salt and pepper on both sides of the chicken. Dredge in the flour.

2 In a 12-inch cast-iron skillet on medium-high heat, sauté breasts in butter. When both sides are brown, about 5 minutes, remove from the skillet and keep warm.

3 Reduce the heat and add the wine and chicken stock to the skillet. Simmer for a few minutes and then add the lemon juice.

4 Place the chicken on serving plates, pour the pan juices over the chicken.

5 Garnish with lemon slice and parsley sprig, if desired.

Vary It! *Make Veal Picata simply by substituting veal for the chicken in the recipe.*

Per serving: *Calories 280 (From Fat 109); Fat 12g (Saturated 6g); Cholesterol 97mg; Sodium 293mg; Carbohydrate 13g (Dietary Fiber 1g); Protein 29g.*

Chicken Stir-Fry

The key to a good stir-fry is a hot wok (or skillet), a little oil, and speed. When you stir-fry, make sure that all your ingredients are chopped, sliced, and otherwise ready to go, because after you're cooking, you'll be cookin'.

Preparation time: *20 minutes*

Cooking time: *7 to 10 minutes*

Yield: *4 servings*

½ cup chicken broth

3 tablespoons soy sauce

2 teaspoons sugar

2 teaspoons dry sherry

¼ teaspoon salt

1 pound boneless, skinless chicken breasts, cut into 1-inch strips

3 tablespoons cornstarch

2 scallions, chopped

1 teaspoon freshly grated ginger root

2 cloves garlic, minced

4 tablespoons oil

1 onion, sliced into ¼-inch pieces

½ red bell pepper, sliced into ¼-inch pieces

½ green bell pepper, sliced into ¼-inch pieces

8 to 10 mushrooms, sliced

2 tablespoons hoisin sauce

¼ cup cashew nuts

4 cups hot cooked rice

1 In a small bowl, combine the chicken broth, soy sauce, sugar, sherry, salt, and 1 tablespoon cornstarch. Set aside. In a large bowl, combine the chicken, 2 tablespoons cornstarch, scallions, ginger, and garlic.

2 Heat 2 tablespoons of oil in a cast-iron wok over medium-high heat until hot but not smoking. Add the chicken mixture to the hot wok and stir to separate the pieces. Cook the chicken, stirring constantly, until it turns white, about 2 minutes. Remove the chicken from the wok and set it aside.

3 Add the remaining oil to the wok and the onion, bell peppers, and mushrooms. Cook, stirring constantly, about 3 minutes or until vegetables are crisp tender.

4 Return the chicken to the wok to warm. Add the chicken broth mixture and stir until thickened, about 2 minutes more.

5 Add the hoisin sauce and cashews. Serve over hot rice.

Per serving: *Calories 592 (From Fat 198); Fat 22g (Saturated 3g); Cholesterol 64mg; Sodium 1,175mg; Carbohydrate 65g (Dietary Fiber 3g); Protein 32g.*

Talking Turkey

Whereas chicken makes a popular weekday meal, turkey is usually reserved for the holidays. Part of the reason, surely, is tradition. How many preschool and kindergarten Thanksgiving celebrations *don't* include kids' handprints made into construction-paper turkeys? The other reason is the turkey's size. Even the size of a small turkey is enough to make most people think, at the very least, Sunday dinner.

Which is a shame, really. Like chicken, turkey is a healthy alternative to meats that have more fat. You can cook and use it in much the same way you do chicken. And the leftovers make great sandwiches, pies, chilis, and a bunch of other fun edibles. And who says that you have to buy a whole turkey? You can buy turkey breasts to roast. They're great for both traditional turkey recipes, like the Orange Honey Ginger Turkey Breast recipe included in this chapter, or for those times when you just want a nice, warm turkey sandwich.

Like chicken, turkeys can harbor salmonella. When you cook a stuffed turkey, it's not done until the internal thigh temperature reaches 180 to 185 degrees. When the thigh is at this temperature, the other parts of the bird are also at safe temperatures: the stuffing at 165 and the breast at 170. An unstuffed turkey or turkey portion, such as a breast, is safe when its internal temperature is 165 degrees.

A quick, easy crust

An easy pie crust recipe that you can use for any pie is as follows:

Ingredients:

- 2 cups all-purpose flour
- 1 teaspoon salt
- ⅓ cup plus 2 tablespoons shortening
- ⅓ cup butter

Steps:

1. Cut the flour and salt into the shortening and butter until the mixture resembles course crumbs.

2. Add 4 to 5 tablespoons cold water, one tablespoon at a time until the mixture holds together.

3. Divide the dough in two, form into balls, and roll out on a floured surface.

For detailed information on how to make a flaky crust and alternative crust recipes, head to Chapter 13.

Orange Honey Ginger Turkey Breast

Placing orange slices under the skin is easier than it sounds. Simply find an edge and pull the skin up, using a knife blade to separate the skin from the breast as needed. Then slide the orange slices in and pull the skin back over oranges to cover. As the turkey cooks, the juice and flavor of the trapped oranges will infuse the meat.

Preparation time: *15 minutes*

Cooking time: *2½ hours*

Yield: *8 servings*

1 can (6 ounces) orange juice concentrate	*1 teaspoon ground pepper*
1 can (12 ounces) Fresca or Squirt	*5 to 6 pound turkey breast*
1 cup honey	*1 orange, thinly sliced*
½ teaspoon paprika	*2 tablespoons Canola oil*
½ teaspoon tarragon	*¼ cup wild rice*
1 teaspoon onion powder	*¾ cup long-grain rice*
1 teaspoon ground ginger	*Fresh pea pods for garnish (optional)*

1 Preheat your oven to 325 degrees. Put the 7-quart cast-iron Dutch oven in the oven to warm while the oven is preheating.

2 In a bowl, mix the orange juice, Fresca, honey, paprika, tarragon, onion powder, ginger, and pepper. Reserve 1 cup of the mixture.

3 Brush the turkey breast inside and out with the mixture. Place the orange slices under the turkey skin.

4 Place the turkey in the warm cast-iron Dutch oven. Add the remaining honey mixture, except for the reserve. Cover and cook at 325 degrees for about 2½ hours. Baste with the honey mixture several times while cooking.

5 About 40 minutes before the turkey is finished, heat Canola oil in a 10-inch cast-iron skillet. Sauté and stir both rices until toasted (about 7 minutes over medium heat). Stir in ¾ cup water and ¾ cup of the reserve honey mixture.

6 Cover and cook until the liquid disappears, and the rice is soft and flaky, about 25 to 30 minutes. Steam pea pods, if desired, on top of the rice for about 5 minutes.

7 About 10 minutes before the turkey is finished, remove the orange slices and the skin from the turkey.

8 When the turkey is done, place it on bed of rice and garnish with pea pods.

Per serving: Calories 671 (From Fat 169); Fat 19g (Saturated 5g); Cholesterol 137mg; Sodium 121mg; Carbohydrate 67g (Dietary Fiber 1g); Protein 58g.

Dutch Oven Turkey

This succulent turkey will tempt you to dive right in as soon as it's on the platter, but be patient. A turkey is easier to carve if you let it sit for 20 minutes first.

Preparation time: *15 minutes*

Cooking time: *About 1½ hours*

Yield: *6 to 8 servings*

1 whole turkey breast (5 to 7 pounds) or whole chicken (giblets removed)	1 stick butter
	1 jar (16 ounces) honey
2 whole garlic bulbs, plus 10 garlic cloves, thinly sliced	2 cans (14 ounces, each) chicken broth
	½ cup orange juice
1 large onion, chopped	3 tablespoons cornstarch

1 Make sure that your bird fits into either a 7- quart or 9-quart Dutch oven. If the turkey is touching the underside of the lid, break the breastbone to flatten the turkey. Prepare the turkey by rinsing and patting dry. Place 2 whole garlic cloves in the turkey cavity. Set aside.

2 Preheat the oven to 350 degrees.

3 Sauté the remaining garlic slices and the onion in the butter in the Dutch oven over medium-high heat. Add the honey, 1 can of the chicken stock, and orange juice. Stir until blended; remove from heat.

4 Carefully place the turkey in the Dutch oven and cover with a lid. If the turkey is touching the lid, spray some cooking spray on the underside of the lid to keep the turkey from sticking. Or, use foil to "tent" the Dutch oven and don't use the lid.

5 Bake for 1 hour to 1 hour and 20 minutes, depending on size of the bird, basting the bird every 15 minutes with pan juices. Add the other can of chicken stock sparingly as needed to keep liquid at about the same level in the oven. When the turkey has reached 165 degrees on the meat thermometer in the thickest part of the breast, remove from the oven. Remove to a platter and let rest 10 minutes before carving.

6 For delicious gravy, strain and defat the pan juices, reserving the solids. Return the juices to the Dutch oven. Dissolve the cornstarch into ½ cup of water and add to the pan juices. Simmer for about 3 minutes, scraping up any browned bits, until the mixture thickens. Add the reserved solids, if desired.

Per serving: Calories 696 (From Fat 246); Fat 27g (Saturated 12g); Cholesterol 169mg; Sodium 327mg; Carbohydrate 57g (Dietary Fiber 1g); Protein 57g.

Carving Made Easy

Roasting whole chickens and turkeys is one of the easiest and most popular cooking methods for poultry. But when your beautifully roasted whole bird is done, your task is to get the meat off the bone.

You have a few options. You can pick up a knife and plunge right into the closest part. When the breast is gone (you'll probably target it first; most people who use this method do), use a table fork to pry and scrape whatever other meat you can see around the bird's legs and wings. Or you could dispense with the knife altogether and let people pull meat from the bone with their fingers. No kidding. I actually saw this done once at a Thanksgiving buffet.

Or you could carve the bird. With a sharp kitchen knife and a little know-how, you can get nice, even-size servings, more meat, and more control. And as an added bonus, you can ask the question "Light meat or dark?" without panicking that someone will actually state a preference.

Can you guess which method I recommend? Carving: It's simple, it's methodical, and it yields the most meat. Figure 7-2 provides easy, step-by-step instructions for carving poultry.

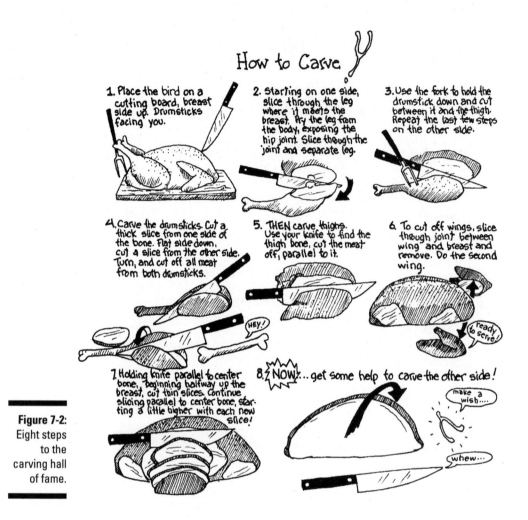

Figure 7-2:
Eight steps
to the
carving hall
of fame.

Chapter 8

Fish, Shellfish, and One Amphibian

Sure, fish is good for you. You can find all sorts of information on the health benefits of diets rich in fish and shellfish. But if you only eat fish for the good it does you, you may be missing out on the simple pleasure that a fresh fish dinner can give. Cooked in cast iron, fish is a feast for the senses. Picture this: A lazy river, a setting sun, a rock to lean against, a slow-rolling campfire, and the sizzle and smell of freshly caught trout being sautéed in a cast-iron skillet.

No lazy river, you say? And no rock to rest against? Forget the setting sun because you have to get your kids fed before soccer practice? No problem. Take out your cast-iron skillet, and try out the recipes in this chapter. Most of them are fast and easy, and they're all bound to please. And if you close your eyes and concentrate real hard, you may just be able to hear that river after all.

Gone Fishin'

Sure, you can buy frozen fish — whole or in fillets. But the best-tasting fish is fresh fish, and the best way to get the freshest fish is to know your neighborhood fishmonger (for folks who are lucky enough to still have small fresh-fish shops) or the person behind the fish counter at the grocery store.

When you buy whole, fresh fish, look for the following:

- ✔ **Bright, clear, bulging eyes:** Sunken, cloudy eyes indicate that the fish is past its prime.

- ✔ **Firm flesh:** If you have the opportunity to touch it, the flesh should spring back slightly when you put a little pressure on it. If it feels mushy or soft, don't buy it.

- ✔ **Gills that have a reddish tint and bright-colored scales close to the skin:** The longer the fish sits in your grocer's case, the duller it becomes. The scales begin to loosen, too.

- ✔ **Smell:** Some people say fresh fish smells like the ocean; older fish smells like a tidal pool. I suppose that, if you know the difference between an ocean smell and the smell of a tidal pool, this description is probably all you need. However, if you're a landlubber, I suggest that you simply avoid fish that smells too fishy or that has an overpowering odor.

If you're buying fresh fillets, the same guidelines apply, with the obvious exceptions of the eyes and gills, which a fillet *shouldn't* have. But then, of course, you probably already know that.

When you buy frozen fish, make sure that it's frozen solid, that the flesh isn't discolored, and that the wrapping is tight, with little or no air between fish and wrapping.

How much fish you buy depends on whether the fish is boneless and whether you're cooking a *fish steak* (a thick, cross-section cut) or a *fish fillet* (the meat off of one side of the fish). If the fish is boneless, you need to buy less; if the bones are still in it, you need to buy more. In general, you also need more fish per serving for steaks and less for fillets. Table 8-1 gives you general serving guidelines; adjust them for the appetites at your table.

Table 8-1	Serving Sizes for Fish
Type of Fish	*Amount Needed for a Serving*
Whole fish	1 pound per serving
Whole fish (cleaned but not boned)	¾ pound per serving
Fish steaks	½ pound per serving
Fillets	¼ pound per serving

The first fisheries

Give credit to the Chinese for creating aquatic farming, which they may have done as far back as the Shang Dynasty (1765–1123 B.C.). Oracle bones from this period have been found that include marks believed to refer to fish farming.

No one knows for sure why fish farming started in China, but fish have been symbolically important to the Chinese culture. Carp, for example, symbolize fortune, and the Chinese bestow carp as gifts. The Chinese also include fish in their ornamental ponds — having a daily food supply close at hand is beneficial.

The Chinese weren't the only ones in the ancient world to farm fish, though. Other groups also took up aquatic farming: the Egyptians, the Sumerians, the Babylonians, and the Romans. By the Middle Ages, the Europeans and Polynesians had taken the leap into aquatic farming, too.

Basic cooking and handling techniques

Fish can be steamed, poached, fried, boiled, broiled, and baked. Broiling and baking is best for fatty fish, such as mackerel, salmon, and trout. Lean fish, such as cod, flounder, haddock, tuna, and ocean perch, can be steamed and poached, because they'll stay firm and moist. You can fry both fatty and lean fish.

When you cook fish in cast iron, the best cooking methods are frying, broiling, pan-frying, and baking — basically, the cooking methods that don't require water. You want to avoid water-based cooking in cast iron.

The trick to cooking fish is knowing when it's done. Undercook it, and it'll feel chewy, and the flavor won't be developed. Overcook it, and you'll think you're eating chalk. Most fish is done when it flakes — that is, if the meat comes apart when you pick at it with a fork. Of course, how long it takes to reach the "flake stage" depends on the type of fish and the cooking method. In general, though, you can use these clues as guidelines to doneness:

- Most fish, as it cooks, weeps a white liquid. So remember: No more crying; no more frying.
- As it cooks, the color of the flesh doesn't usually change, but its opacity does. Uncooked white fish, for example, is less opaque than cooked white fish. If the flesh still seems shiny or translucent, it isn't done.

Check out the following tips and recommendations for more on handling and preparing fish:

- ✔ **Cutting:** Slightly frozen fish is easier to cut. If you want to cut a block of frozen fish, for example, do so before it's completely thawed. Your cuts will be cleaner, and the process won't be nearly as messy.

- ✔ **Thawing:** Leave the fish in the refrigerator to thaw. *Don't* thaw fish at room temperature. If you have to speed up the thawing, place the fish in a waterproof bag and immerse it in cold water or hold it under running water.

  Never refreeze thawed fish. Use it immediately after you thaw it. If something interrupts your cooking plans, you can store the thawed fish in the coldest part of your refrigerator for no more than a day.

- ✔ **Turning:** Use a spatula to turn fish: Fish is too delicate to be turned with a meat fork. If you use a fork, you'll end up with a pile of fish pieces instead of a nice whole piece of meat. If you're grilling outdoors, use a basket made especially for grilling fish so that you don't have to touch the fish at all to turn it. You simply turn the basket.

- ✔ **Storing:** Wrap fresh fish loosely and store it in the coldest part of your refrigerator. Be sure to use it within a day or two. If you need to store it for longer than that, freeze it. You can store cooked fish in the refrigerator for three days, or in the freezer for up to three months.

Fish, mercury, and pregnancy

Nearly all fish contain at least trace amounts of mercury, more specifically *methylmercury*, a by-product of industrial pollution that accumulates in living organisms, such as fish, and is easily passed on to people.

Mercury is dangerous for pregnant women, because it can harm the developing child. So does that mean you should swear off all fish if you're pregnant? No.

The U.S. Food and Drug Administration (FDA) recommends the following: If you're pregnant or may become pregnant, you should avoid eating shark, swordfish, king mackerel, and tilefish, which are known to contain higher levels of methylmercury.

Why avoid these fish and not salmon or cod, for example? Salmon and cod, as well as haddock, pollock, and sole, have shorter life spans. The longer that a fish lives, then the longer that it's exposed to mercury, and the more mercury it absorbs. For that reason, large predatory fish that live longer, such as shark or swordfish, accumulate the highest amounts of mercury and pose the largest threat to people who eat them regularly. Most shellfish contain relatively low levels of methylmercury.

If you're pregnant or trying to get pregnant and are concerned about this issue, talk to your doctor.

Blackened Redfish

Redfish can be any of several fish, such as blueback salmon, that have a reddish color. For this recipe however, channel bass or sea bass are the way to go. Both channel bass and sea bass are *drum fish* — so called because they make a noise that sounds like a drum. If bass isn't available, you can use red snapper — also called *red rockfish,* because it lives among rocks or along the rocky ocean bottom — or tilefish.

Note: Cook this recipe outdoors, because it produces plenty of smoke (too much smoke for most home ventilation systems). Also keep a lid nearby, just in case you get a flame.

Preparation time: *5 minutes*

Cooking time: *5 minutes per batch*

Yield: *6 servings*

12 tablespoons unsalted butter, melted	*6 redfish fillets*
Cajun seasoning	

1 Outdoors on a propane cooker, heat your 14-inch cast-iron skillet until it smokes.

2 Coat each fillet well in the melted butter; then sprinkle the Cajun seasoning generously over the entire fillet, patting it in.

3 Place 2 or 3 fillets in a hot skillet and carefully spoon 1 teaspoon of the melted butter on top of each fillet, being careful not to cause a flame.

4 Cook about 2 minutes until cooking surface of fillets look charred. Turn the fish over, carefully spoon 1 teaspoon of the melted butter on the fish, and cook until the fish is done, about 2 more minutes.

5 Continue until all the fillets are cooked. Immediately turn off the flame.

Per serving: Calories 328 (From Fat 228); Fat 25g (Saturated 15g); Cholesterol 115mg; Sodium 168mg; Carbohydrate 0g (Dietary Fiber 0g); Protein 24g.

Warming up to salmon

Because of its huge health benefits, salmon has grown in popularity, and you can find fresh salmon (in fillet and steak form) in most grocery stores. Of course, you can still find canned salmon, too. Whether you buy a side of salmon, canned salmon, or salmon fillets depends on the recipe. The Skillet

Salmon recipe in this chapter, for example, calls for salmon fillets. But, because the only difference between a salmon fillet and a salmon steak is the cut (fillets come from the sides of the fish; steaks come from the cross sections), you can substitute one for the other in many recipes. Just remember to adjust the cooking time as necessary (particularly because salmon steaks can be cut to varying thicknesses).

Keep reading for an explanation of how to prepare salmon fillets and a side of salmon for cooking. For good measure, I even throw in some tips on preparing canned salmon too, if you have a salmon-cake recipe you want to try or you just want to toss some salmon over a salad and call it dinner.

Preparing a side of salmon

At most grocery stores, you can buy a side of salmon, which is exactly what it sounds like: the meat stripped from one side of the fish. To prepare a side of salmon before cooking, follow these steps:

1. **Remove the pinbones (the small, sharp bones that are embedded in the flesh).**

   To do this, gently run your fingers over the surface. You'll feel the pinbones. Simply remove them with tweezers.

2. **Cut away the fatty portion of the belly (the whitish membrane).**

   Do this by holding a sharp knife at a slight downward angle and cutting just beneath this membrane. (***Note:*** If you hold the knife at too steep an angle, you'll cut away the fish. It won't hurt anything, but it's a waste of perfectly good — and probably fairly expensive — salmon.)

Preparing canned salmon

Got a salmon cake recipe that you want to try with your cast iron? I don't blame you. Cast iron makes a great little salmon cake. It makes great tuna and crab cakes, too, for that matter. Just be sure to put a couple of tablespoons of oil in the bottom of the pan and let it warm up to cooking temperature before you add your cakes. Also remember to add oil between batches so that the cakes don't stick.

Of course, if you make salmon cakes, you need canned salmon. Check out how I prepare canned salmon:

1. **Dump the contents of the can into a strainer.**

2. **Sift through the contents with your fingers until you've removed all the small bones, pieces of cartilage, and skin.**

   You can leave the small bones if you want. They're edible (soft enough to be chewed) and a good source of calcium.

Honestly, this job is pretty ugly. If the task is too much for you, you can buy canned salmon that's packaged like tuna: just chunks of meat without all the yucky stuff. Or, in some recipes, such as many salmon cake recipes, you can substitute canned tuna for the canned salmon.

Preparing a salmon fillet

If your salmon fillet comes already skinned, you don't have to do anything to prepare it for cooking. You're ready to go. If it isn't skinned, however, you can remove the skin. To do so, simply run a sharp knife along the edge between the flesh and the skin and pull the skin away as you cut. Alternatively, leave the skin on the fish while cooking and then remove it afterward.

Skillet Salmon

The biggest challenge when you cook fish is getting the cooking time right. The difference between undercooked salmon that has a gummy and chewy texture, salmon that's cooked just right, and overcooked salmon that's dry and chalky is often a matter of a few minutes. Salmon is done when the flesh is flaky and mostly opaque, and the center is slightly translucent.

Preparation time: *35 minutes*

Cooking time: *5 minutes*

Yield: *2 servings*

Salmon fillets for two (6 to 8 ounces per serving)	Fresh dill, chopped
	2 tablespoons butter
Juice of 1 lemon	2 lemon halves
Salt and pepper	Fresh dill sprig (optional)

1 Squeeze the lemon juice over both sides of the salmon. Sprinkle the salt, pepper, and dill on both sides of the fish. Place the fillets in the refrigerator and let stand about 30 minutes.

2 Place your 10-inch cast-iron skillet on a burner and heat over medium-high heat.

3 Heat the butter in the skillet but don't let it burn. Place the salmon in the skillet, skin side down, and sear for 2 minutes. Turn the fish with a spatula and sear for 2 to 3 minutes, or slightly longer depending on thickness, until salmon is just cooked through.

4 Serve with the lemon halves and top with a sprig of fresh dill, if desired.

Per serving: Calories 322 (From Fat 160); Fat 18g (Saturated 8g); Cholesterol 128mg; Sodium 417mg; Carbohydrate 2g (Dietary Fiber 0g); Protein 37g.

Are you vulnerable to Vibrio vulnificus?

Eating raw oysters does have some risk associated with it. The concern centers around *Vibrio vulnificus,* bacteria found in seafood, such as oysters, that can be passed on to people who eat raw or partially cooked seafood. Usually appearing within 16 hours of ingesting the bacteria, symptoms include nausea, chills, vomiting, diarrhea, confusion, weakness, and enlarged blood-filled or clear blisters, usually on the legs.

Although most people don't have to worry about developing the infection, for people with the following high-risk medical conditions, it can be serious and potentially fatal:

✔ Chronic kidney or stomach disease

✔ Diabetes

✔ Immune disorders, including HIV infection and AIDS

✔ Liver disease

✔ Lymphoma, leukemia, Hodgkin's disease

People taking anti-cancer drugs, radiation treatment, or steroids (for conditions such as asthma, arthritis, and so on) should also avoid raw oysters. Pregnant women should avoid raw oysters, too. The reason isn't that pregnant women fall into the high-risk category — they're no more likely than others to contract the disease. But should a pregnant woman contract the disease, she can't take advantage of the standard treatment (tetracycline) that doctors administer to lighten the symptoms and shorten the duration of illness. Besides, when you're pregnant, you want to avoid any illness — especially a preventable one.

If you fall into one of the at-risk categories — or simply don't want to have to worry about this infection at all — all you have to do is make sure that the oysters you eat are fully cooked.

Pan-frying fish

You can pan-fry just about any fish: cod, trout, perch, catfish, and so on. The combination of flaky, tender flesh and golden-brown, crispy crust is a real treat, provided, of course, that the fish is fresh and the cook knows what he's doing. (For tips on buying fresh fish, head to the "Gone Fishin'" section, earlier in this chapter.) Cast iron is ideal for pan-frying. The even heating and higher temperatures help you attain the nice crispy crust that makes pan-fried food worth the effort.

Breading options

If you ask me, a great piece of pan-fried fish starts with the best breading. When you're whipping up a breading, remember to try any of the breading combinations that follow when you pan-fry:

- **Plain cornmeal:** Season both sides of the fish before you dredge it in the cornmeal. This simple coating is the lightest of the breading options in this list, but it's also most prone to falling away during frying. (***Note:*** Flour alone usually isn't substantial enough to serve as breading; it gets absorbed right into the fish.)

- **Egg and flour or cornmeal:** Dip your fish in egg that's been slightly beaten and diluted with water, shake off the excess, and then dredge in flour or cornmeal. Season the flour or cornmeal instead of the fillets, because the egg bath rinses off your seasoning. This breading offers the lightness of the plain cornmeal breading, but the egg helps the cornmeal adhere during frying.

- **Milk and flour or cornmeal:** Dip the fish in milk, shake off the excess, and then dredge in seasoned flour. With this breading, season the flour instead of the fillets. Like the egg and flour or cornmeal breading, this breading is also light.

- **Flour, milk, and cornmeal:** This is called *bound breading,* or *three-stage breading,* because you dredge the fillet in flour, dip it in egg, and then dredge it in cornmeal, and it's the most substantial of the breadings. It also stays crisp the longest.

- **Any other concoction or combination your heart desires:** Why not invent your own method? Use other liquids and experiment with other breadings — cracker crumbs, breadcrumbs, potato flakes — you name it.

Health benefits of fish

Fish and shellfish are near-perfect foods for the human body. Overall, they provide the benefit of protein without the saturated fat. Of course, different species have different nutritional composition. Freshwater fish are generally lower in fat than are marine fish, for example. But the fact is still the same: Fish is an important part of a healthy diet.

For a long time, scientists have known that fish or fish oil provides some protection against heart disease: Many have long touted the health benefits of omega-3 fats (found in fish), and studies have recently found that people whose diets include plenty of fish have lower levels of *leptin,* a fat-regulating hormone that, when elevated, is linked to obesity and cardiovascular disease.

Of course, people have been eating fish for thousands of years, and it probably hasn't been due to the health benefits. Even if you disregard the healthy reasons why fish should figure into your diet, you can still find a couple of reasons to eat more fish: It tastes good, and most fish dishes are easy to prepare. Try a few of the recipes in this chapter, and I think you'll agree.

So what seasonings do you use? Really anything that you want to use is fair game. Salt and pepper are obvious choices. Cayenne pepper is another popular option. You can also try any sort of seasoned pepper (such as lemon pepper) or seasoning mix (Cajun seasoning, for example). Just keep in mind that it's easy to overdo the seasoning and lose the flavor of the fish. So start light and increase the amount to suit your own tastes.

Tips and techniques

Pan-frying differs from deep-frying in that, when you deep-fry, you submerge the food entirely in hot oil. When you pan-fry, you cook the food, one side at a time, in oil that only goes partially up the side of the food. For most fish fries, a half-inch of oil is sufficient for pan-frying. Some suggestions for pan-frying are as follows:

- **Start at a high heat to brown the coating on each side and then reduce the heat slightly to finish.** Some people swear by higher heat and shorter cooking times; others swear by lower heat and longer cooking times. What matters is that you balance the two so that the breading doesn't burn before the fish gets done.

- **Cut the fish into equal-size pieces.** Doing so helps even out the cooking time. Pieces that are around four to six ounces are easy to bread and fry.

- **Keep the cooked fish warm while you cook the rest of the fish.** The best way to do this is to drain the fish on a paper towel and then transfer it to a wire rack in a warm oven.

- **Serve the fish immediately.** Pan-fried fish (or pan-fried anything, for that matter) doesn't keep well. Have everyone at the table or within easy shouting distance when you're finishing up the last batch. Honestly, though, collecting people won't be much a problem: Most of the crowd will be hanging around hoping for a nibble anyway.

Tartar sauce

I suggest serving tartar sauce often in this chapter. You can easily whip up a batch with this recipe. Mix all of the following ingredients together and refrigerate until you're ready to serve.

- 1 cup mayonnaise

- 1½ tablespoon finely chopped cornichons, plus 1 teaspoon cornichon juice

- 1 tablespoon finely chopped green onions — only the green part

- 1 tablespoon Dijon mustard

- ½ to 1 teaspoon minced garlic

Note: Cornichons are tart pickles make from tiny little gherkin cucumbers. If you can't find cornichons, you can substitute the same amount of any other pickle you like.

Pan-Fried Catfish

Once considered a "junk" fish, catfish has gained popularity recently. You can now find it served in many restaurants. When you prepare your catfish fillets, remove any skin and the dark fatty tissue that's directly underneath it. This tissue has a strong fishy taste.

Preparation time: *25 minutes*

Cooking time: *5 minutes*

Yield: *4 servings*

4 catfish fillets (about 1½ pounds)	*Cajun seasoning*
1 cup buttermilk, or enough to cover the fillets	*1 cup cornmeal*
Salt and pepper	*Canola oil to fill skillet ¼-inch deep*

1 In a flat dish, soak the fish fillets in the buttermilk for about 20 minutes.

2 Lay the fish on wax paper. Discard the buttermilk. Season both sides of the fish with the salt, pepper, and Cajun seasoning. Dredge in the cornmeal.

3 Heat the oil in a 12-inch cast-iron skillet over slightly higher than medium-heat. Place fillets in the skillet and brown on both sides, about 2 minutes on each side, turning carefully with a spatula.

4 After the fish browns, reduce the heat to medium or lower to finish cooking if your filets are thick.

Per serving: *Calories 427 (From Fat 196); Fat 22g (Saturated 4g); Cholesterol 78mg; Sodium 348mg; Carbohydrate 30g (Dietary Fiber 3g); Protein 31g.*

Shellfish Galore: Shrimp, Scallops, Oysters, and More

Shellfish goes hand in hand with fish as part of a healthy diet. Keep reading to find out what to look for when you buy shellfish, how to store it safely, and how to prepare it so that it remains tender and flavorful.

In addition, because most shellfish requires some sort of preparation before you can use it in recipes, you'll want to find out how to clean, shuck, devein, and otherwise get your shellfish ready to cook.

If you've never cleaned shellfish in your life, you may be a bit grossed out at the process, but keep the following in mind: Getting shellfish that requires cleaning is one way to maintain freshness. This alone may outweigh any potential queasiness that you may suffer when you clean it yourself.

However, if that doesn't work for you, and you still can't stand the idea of cleaning shellfish yourself, you can usually buy it already prepared. This route may cost more, but if cleaning the food yourself makes it impossible for you to enjoy your meal, it's probably worth it.

Shrimp-ly amazing

You can't judge a book by its cover, and you can't judge a shrimp by its color. Raw shrimp can be white (more like gray, actually), brown, or pink. Check out the following types of available shrimp:

- ✔ **White shrimp:** Coming from the Carolinas and the Gulf of Mexico, white shrimp grow to 8 inches long. Their flesh is sweet and firm.

- ✔ **Brown shrimp:** These shrimp come from the Texas-Louisiana coast. They're usually firmer than white shrimp, so they're ideal for being battered and fried, and they have a stronger flavor, too. The boys reach around 7 inches, the girls around 9.

- ✔ **Pink shrimp:** The color of these shrimp isn't always pink, and it's the color that often tells you where they hail from: Those from the Atlantic coast are usually brown; those from the northern Gulf coast are lemon-yellow; and those in the Florida Keys are pink. Pink shrimp are tender and sweet. They're also huge, reaching 11 inches long, which is great when the shrimp itself is the highlight of the presentation. (Think shrimp cocktail.)

You'll hear shrimp referred to as *green,* as in "How many green shrimp do you want?" or "We just got some green shrimp in today." This doesn't mean that the shrimp is actually the color green. Green shrimp is simply raw shrimp — pink, brown, or white — that's still in its shell.

Regardless of its original color, the shells of all shrimp turn red when cooked, and the meat turns white with reddish tinges.

Buying shrimp

Shrimp comes in different sizes, from very small to very large: *tiny, small, large, extra large, jumbo, colossal,* and *super-duper jumbo colossal* are just a few of the adjectives indicating size. These terms are descriptive, sure, but they don't really tell you how big that *big* really is, and what one fishmonger may call *extra large* may be another's *medium.*

Most grocery stores sell shrimp by the pound. You often see the count (how many shrimp you get per pound) accompanying the price. So, for example, shrimp with a 12 to 15 count means that a pound of that particular shrimp gives you between 12 and 15 pieces. The larger the shrimp, the fewer you get in a pound and the higher the cost (usually). Conversely, the smaller the shrimp, the more you get per pound and the lower the cost.

Storing shrimp

Ideally, you should buy shrimp fresh and use it the day that you purchase it. If you're going to eat it within the next day or two, you can store fresh shrimp in the refrigerator. Simply wrap the shrimp in ice and place it in a covered container. Then put the container in the coldest part of your refrigerator. As the ice melts, replace it and drain off the water.

If you have to store the shrimp longer than two days, place it in the freezer as soon as you bring it home. When you freeze fresh shrimp, leave the shell on, place the shrimp in a container that can hold water, such as a heavy-duty freezer bag, for example, or a covered Tupperware dish, fill it with water, and put it in the freezer. Freezing the shrimp in water maintains its freshness and flavor and keeps it from drying out. You can keep shrimp frozen this way in the freezer for up to seven months. If you're freezing shrimp in water, be sure that you divide your shrimp into useable portions.

Don't freeze thawed, shelled shrimp. The ice that surrounds it will destroy the shrimp's flesh, leaving it burned and shriveled.

When you're ready to thaw your shrimp, place it in the refrigerator or hold it under cold running water. Never thaw shrimp at room temperature. Thawing at room temperature is a health hazard. During the time it takes the food to thaw, bacteria can grow and multiply in the warm environment. Never thaw shrimp in hot water either, because the hot water temperature cooks the shrimp and makes it rubbery.

Deveining the shrimp

Most shrimp come with the head already removed, leaving just the legs, shell, and mud-vein for you to contend with. To devein and shell a shrimp at the same time, follow these instructions:

1. **Using a sharp knife, make a shallow slit along the shrimp's back from the head to the tail.**

    Buy easy-to-peel shrimp, which has already been slit.

2. **Pull the shell apart at the slit to loosen it; then pull off the shell by the legs.**

3. **Using your fingers or the tip of a knife and holding the shrimp under cold running water, pull the vein out.**

   The vein runs the length of the shrimp and is usually a mud-brown color, although sometimes it can be clear.

Scallops: Sea or Bay, sweet anyway

When you go shopping for scallops, you'll find two main types:

- ✔ **Sea scallops:** The larger of the two types of scallops, sea scallops are harvested in offshore ocean waters. They aren't as tender as bay scallops, but their meat is still sweet and moist. You get between 20 and 40 scallops in one pound.

- ✔ **Bay scallops:** Coming from the bays and estuaries along the East coast and into the Gulf of Mexico, bay scallops are the smaller of the two types of scallops; you usually get between 50 and 90 in a pound. The meat of bay scallops is sweeter and more succulent than the meat of sea scallops.

Buying and storing scallops

Scallops are usually sold *shucked* (removed from their shell). You can buy scallops fresh or frozen. When you buy fresh scallops, look for the following:

- ✔ **Color** that ranges from pale beige to creamy pink. Perfectly good scallops also have a slightly orange or pink hue due to the algae that the scallops ate.

  Stark white scallops have been soaked in water to increase their weight. This doesn't hurt anything and won't ruin the taste of the scallop, and it's not done to hide any particular flaws, but it's not entirely honest. Fresh scallops are juicy enough. The increased weight from the water soak simply means that you're getting fewer scallops for your money.

- ✔ **A sweet odor** is characteristic of fresh scallops.

- ✔ **Fresh, moist sheens** also indicate freshness. Avoid scallops that look shriveled or dry.

When you buy scallops, refrigerate them immediately and use them within a day or two. If you're not planning to cook them within a day or two, store them in the freezer in their original container or in an airtight container. When you're ready to use them, place them in the refrigerator to thaw.

Scallops freeze well. If you run across a sale or if you buy too many, freeze the extra. Use frozen scallops within 3 months.

Removing tendons from scallops

Most scallops that you buy at grocery stores are ready to be cooked. You don't need to do anything but pop them into the fryer, skewer them on the kebob, or do whatever else your recipe calls for. Occasionally, however, the muscle that held the scallop to the shell may still be attached. This crescent-shaped muscle has a rough texture, and it toughens when cooked. To remove it, simply peel it away from the scallop.

Cooking tips

Cooked properly, all scallops are sweet and tender yet firm. Scallops are key ingredients in soups, stews, and salads. And you can cook scallops using just about any technique you can think of: from sautéed to broiled to grilled to baked (the technique used in the Seafood Skillet recipe in this chapter). Ruining scallops is actually pretty difficult as long as you keep these tips in mind:

- ✔ Scallops benefit from brief cooking. If you overcook them, they turn tough. Be especially careful when you cook bay scallops, which are smaller than sea scallops and, therefore, easier to overcook.

- ✔ Scallops are done as soon as they lose their translucence and turn opaque.

- ✔ If you plan to put scallops in a sauce, cook the scallops and the sauce separately and combine them near the end of the cooking process. Cooking them separately ensures that your scallops won't be over-cooked and that the sauce doesn't get runny when the water cooks out from the scallops.

Seafood Skillet

You can cook this dish in a single skillet, as this recipe explains, or, if you have single-serving skillets (6 to 8 inches), you can cook each serving separately. Doing so requires a little more work and slightly more clean up, but you can take the hot skillets straight to the table for each diner. Tartar sauce and cocktail sauce work well with this dish.

Preparation time: *15 minutes*

Cooking time: *35 minutes*

Yield: *4 servings*

1 egg, beaten	*½ cup finely chopped celery*
½ cup dry breadcrumbs	*4 flounder fillets (or other thin, flaky white fish)*
Dash Louisiana-style hot sauce	*8 large shrimp, peeled and deveined*
1 teaspoon lemon juice	*8 sea scallops*
½ cup heavy cream	*½ cup cracker crumbs*
1 tablespoon vegetable oil, or butter	*2 teaspoons butter*
½ cup finely chopped onions	*Lemon wedges*

1 Preheat your oven to 350 degrees.

2 In a medium bowl, mix together the egg, breadcrumbs, hot sauce, lemon juice, and cream and set aside.

3 Heat the oil in a 12-inch cast-iron skillet and sauté the onions and celery until tender, about 5 minutes.

4 For each serving, layer one fish fillet, two shrimp, and two scallops on top of the onions and celery and repeat until all the seafood has been used.

5 Pour the breadcrumb mix evenly over each seafood serving. Top each serving with cracker crumbs and ½ teaspoon of the butter.

6 Bake for 30 minutes; then brown under the broiler for about 3 to 4 minutes. Serve with lemon wedges.

Per serving: Calories 466 (From Fat 197); Fat 22g (Saturated 10g); Cholesterol 225mg; Sodium 519mg; Carbohydrate 19g (Dietary Fiber 1g); Protein 45g.

Oysters aren't only for Rockefeller

Jonathan Swift's sentiment about oysters — "He was a bold man that first eat an oyster" — may be fitting, if your impression of oysters is formed by how they look and not by how they taste. Oysters, in fact, are one of the few dishes that are enjoyable both raw and cooked.

Three main types of oysters are sold in the United States:

- ✔ **Atlantic oysters:** Also called Eastern oysters, these come from the eastern seaboard (places like Cape Cod and Chesapeake Bay). They range in size from two to five inches. Bluepoint oysters, considered best for eating and often served on the half shell, are Atlantic oysters.

- ✔ **Pacific oysters:** Also called *Japanese oysters,* these come from the Pacific seaboard and can be up to a foot long. Because they're so big, Pacific oysters are generally cut to go in stews and soups.

- ✔ **Olympia oysters:** These are small (usually no larger than 1½ inches) and come from Puget Sound, Washington. They're a favorite eaten on the half shell.

Buying oysters

You can buy oysters canned, packed (already *shucked,* or out of their shells), or live (still in their shells, which you can shuck yourself or have the grocer/fishmonger do for you). How you buy oysters depends on how you plan to prepare them.

If you're serving raw oysters, for example, buy them live and shuck them yourself. Live oysters are also better for presentation purposes: Raw oysters and some cooked oyster dishes (Oysters Rockefeller, for example) are usually presented on the half shell — served with only the top shell removed — on a bed of crushed ice (raw) or a bed of rock salt.

When you buy live oysters, look for those whose shells are tightly closed. If the shell is open, the oyster has lost his grip, a sign that he's old, dying, or already dead.

For other recipes, however — like the ones in this chapter — you can buy already shucked oysters. You can ask your fishmonger to shuck the live oysters to order (the best way to gauge freshness), or you can buy canned or packed.

✔ **Canned:** Let's face it. Canned oysters aren't fresh. If you're making a recipe that includes the oysters primarily for flavor (oyster dressing, for example, or oyster stew), canned is okay — not great, mind you, but okay. Canned oysters have a stronger taste, and their texture can be rubbery or mushy. Freshly shucked oysters are preferable.

✔ **Packed:** Packed oysters are shucked oysters that come in a plastic container. These are perishable, so you need to use them within a day or two of buying them. When you buy packed oysters, follow these guidelines:

- Make sure that the lid on the container is tightly sealed and that the package shows no signs of being bloated, which is an indication that the oysters are old. Oysters release gas as they age.

- Look for plump oysters that are uniform in size, have a good color (light beige or pale tan), a fresh smell, and a clear, not cloudy, *liquor* (the oyster juice).

- Buy the pack with the sell-by date that's the farthest into the future.

Storing oysters

Fresh oysters, packed or live, are best if you use them the day that you purchase them. If you're planning to use them within a day or two, store fresh, shucked oysters in their original container with their juice in the coldest part of your refrigerator. Cover live oysters, larger shell down, with a damp towel and refrigerate them for up to three days.

If you aren't going to cook your shucked oysters within a day or two, freeze them. You can freeze packed oysters in an airtight container, or you can leave them in their original container; just be sure to pour out a little of the juice so that the juice doesn't' expand and cause the lid to pop. Oysters can remain in the freezer for up to 4 months. Thaw frozen oysters in the refrigerator hold or put the container under cold running water. Never refreeze thawed seafood.

Only freeze oysters that you're planning to cook. If you plan on eating raw oysters, you can forget about freezing them first.

Shucking oysters

To remove the shell of an oyster, hold the oyster cupped side down in a kitchen towel in the palm of your hand. Then follow these steps:

1. **Using the blade of a paring knife, find where the two halves separate.**

2. **Push the blade between the shells and wiggle it back and forth until you've pried the shell open wide enough to fit the top of your thumb inside.**

3. **Holding the oyster open with your thumb, cut the meat loose from the top shell (after you cut the muscle that holds the shell together, the shell pops open) and discard the top shell.**

4. **Detach the meat from the bottom shell.**

   If you're going to serve the oyster on the half-shell, save the bottom shell; otherwise, toss it.

The oyster liquor is full of flavor. Work over a bowl so that you can catch any that spills.

Soft-shell crabs

Next to shrimp, crabs are one of the most popular shellfish in the world. *Soft-shell crabs* are blue crabs that have been plucked from the ocean immediately after they shed their shell and before their new shell has a chance to harden. Unlike hard-shell crabs, whose meat must be removed, almost every single part of a soft-shell crab is edible. Crabs in general are noted for sweet, succulent meat, and soft-shell crabs are no exception.

Soft-shell crabs are always sold whole. They're in season from April to mid-September. When you buy soft-shell crabs, you buy them live. You can take them home and prepare them yourself for cooking, or you can ask your fishmonger to clean them for you. You may also be able to find them frozen.

When you buy fresh soft-shell crabs, look for crabs that have soft, gray skin and whose odor is fresh but not overpowering. (A crab that has begun to spoil has a horrible smell.)

Most parts of a soft-shell crab are edible. You simply need to remove the few parts that aren't: the mouth, the gills, and the triangular flap (called an *apron flap*) from the crab's belly. To remove these pieces, simply cut them off with a pair of kitchen shears. ***Note:*** You can remove the eyes if you want to, but you don't have to. The eyes are edible.

Be aware, though, that cleaning soft-shell crabs yourself can be a horrible task. The crabs are alive when you start; they die during cleaning, specifically when you cut off the mouth (or face, if you're snipping the eyes off, too). And they may twitch a little as they die. If this tasks sounds like a bit too much for you, ask your fishmonger to clean the crab for you.

Pan-Fried Soft-Shell Crabs

Soft-shell crabs are blue crabs that have been taken from the ocean as soon as they shed their shell, and they're delicious fried. Frying them, however, requires extra caution, because they splatter so much. After a crab sheds its shell, it swells with water to fill out its new, unhardened shell. Toss this creature, with its extra water, into a pan of hot butter, and you have to be extra careful. Using a splatter screen when frying soft shell crabs is *highly* recommended. Cocktail sauce and tartar sauce both make great dipping sauces for these crabs.

Preparation time: *10 minutes*

Cooking time: *6 minutes, each crab*

Yield: *4 servings*

Salt and pepper	½ cup cornmeal
8 medium soft-shell crabs, cleaned	4 tablespoons butter
½ cup all-purpose flour	Lemon wedges

1 Salt and pepper the crabs. In a medium bowl, combine the flour and cornmeal. Dredge the crabs in the flour mixture; shake off the excess.

2 Heat your 12-inch cast-iron skillet over medium-high heat until hot.

3 Drop the butter into the hot pan and swirl to keep the butter from burning as it melts.

4 Place the crabs, shell side down, into the pan. Cover with a splatter screen and cook until the crab turns reddish brown, about 3 minutes.

5 Turn the crabs over and cook until the other side is brown, about 3 minutes more. The crabs should be crispy and golden brown.

6 Drain crabs on paper towels and serve immediately with lemon wedges, or place in a warm oven.

Vary It! *Add some Cajun seasoning to the mix for a more heat.*

Per serving: *Calories 517 (From Fat 290); Fat 32g (Saturated 16g); Cholesterol 195mg; Sodium 600mg; Carbohydrate 26g (Dietary Fiber 2g); Protein 30g.*

Soft-shell clams

Soft-shell clams, also called *soft clams* or *long necks* (their entire body doesn't fit within the shell; the *snout,* or neck, hangs out), are a type of clam with thin shells that you can break with your fingers. You can buy soft-shell clams live in the shell or shucked.

When you buy soft-shell clams in the shell, make sure it's alive by lightly touching its neck. If it moves, it's alive. When you buy shucked clams, look for plumpness and clear liquid.

Store all live clams in the shell in the refrigerator for up to two days; shucked clams can be stored in the fridge for up to four days.

You can cook clams in a number of ways (steaming, baking, frying, and so on), but however you cook them, be sure not to overcook them. Like other types of shellfish, they get tough when they're overcooked.

You shuck clams in much the same way that you shuck oysters, with a variation or two:

1. **Steam the clams until they're open enough to allow you to insert the blade of a paring knife.**

2. **Pry the clam open with a paring knife and discard the top shell.**

   Be sure to hold the clam over a bowl to catch any juice that drips.

3. **Cut through the muscle that holds the meat to the bottom shell.**

   Unless you need the bottom shell, toss it, too.

The most popular East Coast soft-shell clam is the *steamer clam,* which as you can probably guess from its name, is great steamed; it's also good fried. The most famous West Coast soft-shell is the razor clam (it resembles an old-fashioned straight razor), which is also tasty steamed.

Fried Soft-Shell Clams

Soft-shell clams have thin, brittle shells that don't close entirely, so they tend to have a lot of sand inside. To get rid of most of the sand, soak your soft-shell clams in several batches of cold water. The water soak causes the clams to bloat up, pushing the sand out.

Preparation time: *10 minutes*

Cooking time: *About 5 minutes*

Yield: *4 servings*

8 cups soft-shell clams (about 32 clams), shucked and cleaned

1 cup all-purpose flour

1 cup cornmeal

1 teaspoon salt

1 teaspoon pepper

1 quart vegetable oil

1 Strain the clams. Combine the flour, cornmeal, salt, and pepper in a large bowl.

2 In a 12-inch cast-iron skillet, heat the oil over medium-high heat.

3 Dredge the clams, 8 at a time, into the flour mixture, until the clams are completely coated. Drop the clams into the hot oil (about 370 degrees) and fry until golden brown, about 1 minute.

4 Remove the clams and drain on paper towels. Bring the oil back up to temperature, and continue until all the clams are fried. Serve with tartar sauce.

Per serving: Calories 700 (From Fat 286); Fat 32g (Saturated 4g); Cholesterol 96mg; Sodium 907mg; Carbohydrate 58g (Dietary Fiber 4g); Protein 42g.

Hosting a Fish (and Shellfish) Fry — Cast-Iron Style

When you deep-fry fish and shellfish, you can't use the same guides to test doneness that you do when you steam or grill it. (These guidelines are explained in the "Basic cooking and handling techniques" section, earlier in the chapter.) How do you know, for example, whether your fish is flaky, your scallops opaque, or your shrimp white when they're covered in breading or batter? Use the guide in Table 8-2.

Table 8-2	Timetable for Deep-Fried Fish and Shellfish at 375 Degrees
Breaded Fish and Shellfish	*Cooking Time*
Fish, 3 to 4 ounce piece	4–6 minutes
Clams	2–3 minutes
Oysters	2–3 minutes
Scallops	2–4 minutes
Shrimp	2–3 minutes
Battered Fish and Shellfish	*Cooking Time*
Fish, 3 to 4 ounce piece	5-7 minutes
Scallops	3–4 minutes
Shrimp	4–5 minutes

To deep-fry fish or shellfish, you need a deep cast-iron pan. A Dutch oven or a fry kit is fine. (Head to Chapter 2 for descriptions of these items.) The key is the deep sides. You also want to have a thermometer, so you can keep tabs on the temperature of your oil. Other items you may find helpful are a splatter screen and a wire basket.

When you deep-fry, keep these tips in mind:

✔ You want the oil to be hot (between 350 and 375 degrees) so that the fish cooks quickly. The higher temperature also stops the batter or fish from absorbing too much oil.

✔ To keep the temperature steady, don't overcrowd your pan. Also be sure to check the oil temperature between batches.

✔ When deep-frying, choose lean fish (cod, snapper, and catfish, for example). The hot oil seals the batter almost instantly, keeping the moisture and flavor inside. Don't use fatty fish (like salmon, tuna, or mackerel). The same process that keeps lean fish moist and flavorful makes fatty fish taste oily and fishy.

✔ If you don't have a deep-fry basket, use a slotted spoon or spatula to remove the fish from the oil.

✔ To keep your food warm between batches, drain the seafood on paper towels, and then place it in on a warmed wire baking rack in a 200-degree oven.

Deep-Fried Shrimp and Oysters

This recipe is a fried favorite but don't let that stop you from experimenting. The cooking temperature for seafood and fish is always the same. Use Table 8-2 as a guide to cooking times and mix and match the fish and seafood that you use with this recipe.

Preparation time: *10 minutes*

Cooking time: *3 minutes per batch*

Yield: *6 servings*

Oil for deep-frying	*2 tablespoons Creole or spicy mustard*
2 dozen large shrimp	*1 tablespoon yellow mustard*
1 dozen shucked oysters	*Salt and pepper*
1 egg, beaten	*3 cups self-rising cornmeal*
1 cup milk	*2 tablespoons garlic powder*

1 Using a deep-sided cast-iron pan or deep-fryer, heat the oil to 375 degrees, about 10 minutes.

2 In a mixing bowl, combine the egg, milk, 1 cup of water, and mustards and season with salt and pepper.

3 In a separate mixing bowl, combine the cornmeal and garlic and season with salt and pepper. Set aside.

4 Dip the seafood in the egg mixture and then into the cornmeal mixture. Place into the basket and carefully lower into the hot oil.

5 Cook until the seafood floats, approximately 3 minutes. Remove, drain, and keep warm. Continue until all the seafood is cooked. Serve hot.

Per serving: Calories 461 (From Fat 165); Fat 18g (Saturated 3g); Cholesterol 103mg; Sodium 1,242mg; Carbohydrate 58g (Dietary Fiber 5g); Protein 15g.

Nice Legs, Baby

Frogs certainly aren't new to the dinner table. The Medieval European courts served young frogs, eaten whole, as a delicacy. Nowadays, the legs are the only part of a frog that's eaten (by humans, that is), and people compare their taste, as you may expect, with the white meat of a chicken.

You can find fresh frog's legs in the fish section in gourmet food markets, where they're usually sold in connected pairs. Look for legs that are plump and slightly pink. Fresh frog's legs are available from spring through summer. You can buy frozen frog's legs year-round. To store fresh frog's legs, wrap them loosely and place them the refrigerator for up to two days. You can also freeze frog's legs. Thaw them in the refrigerator overnight.

Fried Frog Legs

Be sure not to overcook your frog's legs. Doing so makes them tough.

Preparation time: *2 hours*

Cooking time: *5 minutes*

Yield: *3 servings*

12 small frog legs	*½ to 1 teaspoon Cajun seasoning*
1 egg	*Vegetable oil for deep-frying*
1 cup buttermilk	*½ cup self-rising flour*
1 teaspoon salt	*½ cup self-rising cornmeal mix*
1 teaspoon pepper	

1 Rinse the frog legs and pat dry.

2 In a large bowl, beat the egg, buttermilk, salt, pepper, and Cajun seasoning together. Add the frog legs and soak for up to 2 hours.

3 Heat 5 inches of the oil in a deep-fryer to 375 degrees.

4 In a medium bowl, combine flour and cornmeal. Dredge the frog legs in the flour mixture. Drop into the hot oil without crowding. Fry until golden brown, 4 to 5 minutes. Serve with tartar sauce.

Per serving: Calories 552 (From Fat 161); Fat 18g (Saturated 2g); Cholesterol 219mg; Sodium 1,652mg; Carbohydrate 38g (Dietary Fiber 2g); Protein 57g.

Chapter 9

One-Dish Meals

In This Chapter

▶ Making soups and stews

▶ Partaking of regional favorites: Chowders, gumbos, and jambalayas

▶ Rice dishes your whole family will love

▶ Cornbread as a main dish: Who'd a thunk?

*F*ew things are simpler than one-dish meals — especially for busy cooks. Toss all your ingredients into one pan, cook it for the required amount of time, and dinner's ready. Soup, rice-based dishes, and casseroles are all on the menu in this chapter.

All the recipes in this chapter can be served solo. They're hearty enough to satisfy the biggest appetites and delicious enough to please the pickiest eater. Of course, feel free to add accompaniments, such as bread or salad, if you like. You can find cornbread and biscuit recipes in Chapter 11. Hop on over to Chapter 13 for desserts, if you have any room left over, that is.

Several of the recipes in this chapter, particularly the ones featured in the "Soupy Sensations" and "Rallying around Rice" sections, include seafood. Chapter 8 tells you everything that you need to know about the fish and shellfish included in the recipes in this book. Hop on over to that chapter if you need information on how to select, prepare, and cook seafood.

Soupy Sensations

In a nutshell, soup is a liquid food. It can be creamy or chunky, hot or cold, the main dish or its beginning course. You can make soup from any combination of meat, vegetables, fish, shellfish, and pasta; the common factor is that all soups are cooked in liquid.

Keep reading for recipes and info on different varieties of soups, from the thick (gumbo) to the chunky (chowder), and a stew recipe for good measure. Cast iron is made for soups and stews. Chilis, chowders, and plenty of other soup dishes taste great and look especially appetizing when made and served in cast iron.

But keep in mind that liquid-based dishes (water- and tomato-based stocks and broths, in particular) can interact with the seasoning in your cast iron. Reserve these dishes for well-seasoned cast iron, which can tolerate the long cooking times that most soups, stews, and chilis require. If you're using a newly seasoned piece of cast iron, limit your soup repertoire to water- and milk-based soups (save the tomatoes for later) and be prepared to reseason the pan when you're done. In Chapter 3, I cover the signs that your pan requires reseasoning.

Many of the recipes in this chapter call for stock; others indicate broth. Here's the technical difference: *Broth* is the liquid that results when you cook vegetables, meat, or fish in water. *Stock* is the *strained* liquid you get when you cook vegetables, meat, or fish in water. As you can see, there's not much difference between the two, and for the recipes in this chapter, you can use them interchangeably. To find out how to make your own stock, check out the sidebar "Stocking up." Don't have the time — or the desire — to whip up your own stock? Then use canned broth instead. You can find it in the soup aisle of any grocery store.

Warming up to stew

I don't know about you, but I can't think of a better meal for a crisp and overcast fall afternoon than a hearty helping of stew. Meat and vegetables are the key players in stew, just as they are for other soups, but thick stew broth doesn't come solely from stock or broth; it comes from the cooking method as well. It's a product of the stewing liquid — usually a combination of wine or stock and water — and the juices from the meat as it cooks. Most stews require that the meat be lightly dredged in flour, which enhances the broth's thickness.

When you cook stew, let it simmer slowly for a long period of time. This tenderizes the meat and lets the various flavors blend. (Stew meat generally comes from the tougher flank portion of the cow, so it needs tenderizing; head to Chapter 6 for details on that.)

Brunswick Stew

Brunswick Stew gets its name from the region in Virginia from which it hails. Originally made with squirrel meat, most modern-day versions use chicken. This hearty version of the recipe calls for both chicken and pork.

Preparation time: *10 minutes*

Cooking time: *About 4 hours*

Yield: *8 servings*

3 pounds chicken pieces (or whole chicken)	1 teaspoon thyme
1 pound cubed pork (or ham)	1 teaspoon sugar
1 teaspoon plus 1 tablespoon salt	½ teaspoon pepper
2 medium onions, chopped	2 tablespoons Worcestershire sauce
1 quart or more of chicken stock (or bouillon)	1½ cups fresh or frozen baby lima beans
2 pounds fresh tomatoes, peeled, and seeded	4 medium potatoes, peeled and cubed
2 jalapeño peppers, seeded and diced	3 cups fresh corn
1 bay leaf	2 tablespoons butter

1 In 9-quart cast-iron Dutch oven, put the chicken and pork in enough water to cover. Add 1 teaspoon of salt and the onions. Bring to a boil, then lower the heat and simmer until meat falls off the bone, 1½ to 2 hours.

2 Remove chicken and bones from the Dutch oven. Cool chicken enough to remove skin and bones. Shred the chicken and return it to the pan.

3 Add the remaining tablespoon of salt, the chicken stock, tomatoes, jalapeños, bay leaf, thyme, sugar, pepper, and Worcestershire sauce, and simmer for 1 to 1½ hours, stirring occasionally.

4 Add lima beans, return to slight boil, and simmer for 30 minutes. If necessary, add more chicken stock to keep the desired, thick consistency of stew.

5 Add the potatoes and corn, return to slight boil, and simmer slowly another 45 minutes to 1 hour, or until potatoes are tender. Adjust seasoning if necessary. Remove the bay leaf and swirl in butter when ready to serve.

Per serving: *Calories 508 (From Fat 193); Fat 21g (Saturated 7g); Cholesterol 126mg; Sodium 1,905mg; Carbohydrate 43g (Dietary Fiber 6g); Protein 38g.*

Firing up great gumbos

Gumbos are a Creole specialty. Thick like stew, gumbos traditionally include okra (of African origin, the word *gumbo* means *okra),* as well as other vegetables, such as tomato and onion, and meat, chicken, seafood, sausage, ham — or any combination of these ingredients.

Many people think of Creole cooking and Cajun cooking as essentially the same style: Both rely on green peppers, onions, and celery and use prodigious amounts of filé powder. Despite the similarities, however, they represent two different cooking styles.

- ✔ **Creole:** French, Spanish, and African cuisines combined and more sophisticated than its Cajun counterpart, Creole cooking relies on butter and cream.

- ✔ **Cajun:** This combination of French and southern cuisine is more down-home. Cajun cooking relies on dark roux and plenty of animal fat — usually from pork.

You can thank the Creole cooks for gumbo; it was their creation. Cajun cooks get to take credit for jambalaya. (See the jambalaya recipe in the "Rallying around Rice" section, later in this chapter.) But nowadays, you're just as likely to find a Creole jambalaya recipe as you are a Cajun gumbo. In fact, one of the gumbo recipes in this chapter has a Cajun bent.

Most gumbos begin with a dark *roux* — a flour-fat mixture used in both Creole and Cajun cooking to thicken soups and sauces. Different types of roux are distinguished by color:

- ✔ **White roux:** This version is made with flour and butter and cooked just until it begins to turn beige. Folks use white roux to thicken white sauces and some soups.

- ✔ **Blond roux:** Like white roux, blond roux is also made with butter, but it is cooked a little longer, until it begins to turn golden. Also, like white roux, it's used in white sauces and soups.

- ✔ **Brown roux:** Also called *dark roux,* it can be made with butter, pork drippings, or beef fat. It's richer tasting and is cooked longer than white and blond roux; brown roux isn't ready until it turns a deep, rich brown. Brown roux is used in gumbo, as well as dark soups and sauces.

Many gumbo (and jambalaya) recipes, including the ones in this chapter, call for *andouille,* a heavily spiced smoked sausage. If you can't find andouille, you can substitute *kielbasa* (Polish sausage).

Louisiana Seafood Gumbo

To make *brown roux,* you cook a mixture of flour and fat (in this recipe, vegetable oil) over low heat, watching it carefully as it darkens. It's ready when the mixture is a deep mahogany color. But be careful, if you scorch the roux, you have to start all over again. Black specks are a clue that the roux has gone too far and needs to be thrown out.

Preparation time: *30 minutes*

Cooking time: *1 hour*

Yield: *12 servings*

1 cup vegetable oil	*2 cups sliced green onions*
1 cup all-purpose flour	*½ cup chopped parsley*
2 cups chopped onions	*Salt and pepper*
1 cup chopped celery	*Hot pepper sauce*
1 cup chopped bell pepper	*1 pound large shrimp, peeled, and deveined*
¼ cup diced garlic	*1 pound jumbo lump crabmeat*
½ pound sliced andouille	*2 dozen shucked oysters, reserve liquid*
1 pound claw crabmeat	*12 cups hot, cooked rice*
3 quarts warm shellfish stock, chicken broth, or vegetable broth	

1 In a 7-quart cast-iron Dutch oven, heat the oil over medium heat. After the oil is hot, add the flour, and using a wire whisk, stir constantly until you have brown roux, about 7 minutes.

2 After the roux is brown, add the onions, celery, bell pepper, and garlic. Sauté until the vegetables are wilted, approximately 3 to 5 minutes.

3 Add the andouille, blending well into the vegetable mixture. Sauté 2 to 3 minutes.

4 Add the claw crabmeat and stir into the roux. This will begin to add seafood flavor to the mixture. Then slowly add hot shellfish stock, one ladle at a time, stirring constantly until all is incorporated.

5 Bring to a low boil, reduce the heat to a simmer and cook approximately 30 minutes. Add additional stock if necessary to retain the volume.

6 Add the green onions and the parsley. Season to taste using the salt, pepper, and hot pepper sauce. Fold the shrimp, lump crabmeat, oysters, and reserved oyster liquid into the soup. Return to a low boil and cook approximately 10 minutes. Adjust seasonings and serve over the cooked rice.

Per serving: *Calories 709 (From Fat 273); Fat 30g (Saturated 5g); Cholesterol 183mg; Sodium 1,003mg; Carbohydrate 62g (Dietary Fiber 2g); Protein 43g.*

Cajun Shrimp and Okra Gumbo

If you don't have stock on hand, you can substitute broth or bouillon.

Preparation time: *20 minutes*

Cooking time: *1½ hours*

Yield: *6 servings*

⅓ cup bacon drippings

3 pounds okra, cut into ½-inch round slices

2½ tablespoons Cajun seasoning

2 cups finely chopped onions

6 cups chicken stock

4 cups vegetable stock

2 cups peeled and chopped tomatoes

1 teaspoon minced garlic

1 stick unsalted butter

1 pound andouille, cut into ¼-inch slices

1 pound medium shrimp, peeled

¼ cup finely chopped green onion

6 cups hot, cooked rice

1 Heat the bacon drippings in a cast-iron 7-quart cast-iron Dutch oven over high heat until smoking. Reduce the heat to medium-high, add ¾ of the okra, and cook about 3 minutes, stirring occasionally.

2 Stir in 1 tablespoon of the Cajun seasoning and continue cooking for about 10 minutes, stirring often.

3 Stir in the onions and cook until soft, about 5 minutes, stirring and scraping the bottom of the pan often to keep it from scorching.

4 Stir in 1 cup of either stock and cook 5 minutes, keeping the bottom of the pot scraped.

5 Add the tomatoes and cook for 8 minutes. Stir and scrape often.

6 Stir in another 2 cups of the stock, cooking for another 5 minutes. Continue to stir occasionally to avoid burning.

7 Turn heat to high and stir in the remaining 1½ tablespoons of Cajun seasoning and the garlic. Add the butter; cook and stir until butter is melted, scraping the bottom of the pot well. Add the remaining stock and bring it to a boil, stirring occasionally.

8 Add the sausage and, after the pot returns to a boil, reduce the heat and simmer for 45 minutes.

9 Add the remaining quarter of the okra and simmer for 10 minutes more.

10 Add the shrimp and return to a boil. Remove from the heat. Stir in the green onions. Mound the hot rice in the center of a bowl and ladle about 1½ cups of the gumbo from out of the Dutch oven around the rice.

Per serving: *Calories 892 (From Fat 460); Fat 51g (Saturated 22g); Cholesterol 219mg; Sodium 2,970mg; Carbohydrate 76g (Dietary Fiber 9g); Protein 35g.*

Stocking up

Stock is the liquid you get when you cook vegetables, meat, chicken, or seafood, in addition to other seasoning ingredients in water. Basically, stock is broth. It makes a nice base for soups. Whether you make beef, chicken, vegetable, or seafood stock, the steps are the same:

1. Add your ingredients to a *stockpot*. Cover with water. The ingredients include the following:

   ✔ **Meat, seafood, or vegetables:** These ingredients provide the main flavor. Many cooks make beef or chicken stock from leftover bones. Roast a chicken, for example, and instead of tossing the bones, use them to make chicken stock. For vegetable or seafood stock, use fresh, whole veggies or fresh seafood — or the parts that you're not cooking. For example, when you clean fish for dinner, save the heads and bones for the stock.

   ✔ **Other flavor-enhancing ingredients:** These ingredients often include celery, onion, carrots, and bay leaves.

2. Bring the stock to a boil; then reduce the heat to a slow simmer.

3. Let the stock simmer for several hours. During this time, skim off the foam and impurities that rise to the water's surface.

4. Strain the stock and toss out all solids (chicken, bones, vegetables, bay leaf, and any other ingredients, for example). You should have a clear liquid. Remove the fat from the stock. (You won't have to do this with vegetable stock.) Use or store the stock.

Making stock is becoming less common, because it takes time. Plus chicken and beef broth are readily available canned. Still, if you're inclined to make your own stock, keep these tips in mind:

✔ Don't let the water boil. You want the liquid to be clear, and boiling gets everything stirred up; it also breaks the fat down into droplets that are too small to be caught by a strainer. The result? Greasy stock.

✔ Don't use vegetables with strong individual flavors: Put broccoli in a vegetable stock, for example, and it pretty much obliterates all the other flavors.

✔ Store stock in the freezer in portion-size containers. You can use ice-cube trays (one cube equals about 2 tablespoons) or 1- and 2-cup containers. Divided this way, you can take out just as much stock as you need.

Talkin' chowdah

Chowders are thick, chunky soups. Traditionally, all chowders included seafood — the most famous being clam chowders — but now the term refers to any rich soup that has chunks of the main ingredient, such as corn chowder. The Seafood Chowder recipe in this section holds true to the original chowders: Seafood is its main ingredient. In addition to clams, it includes mussels, oysters, and salmon. For instructions on how to prepare these ingredients, head to Chapter 8.

Seafood Chowder

When you buy mussels, keep these tips in mind: Make sure the shell is tightly closed or snaps shut when you tap on it, indicating that the mussel is alive and kicking! Don't buy mussels with broken shells, mussels that feel heavy with sand, or that rattle when you shake them, because the mussel is dead. When you cook fresh mussels, they'll open, giving your chowder a fresh-from-the-sea appearance.

Preparation time: *20 minutes*

Cooking time: *45 minutes*

Yield: *6 to 8 servings*

¼ cup unsalted butter

2 medium onions, diced

½ cup diced celery

1 cup diced carrots

1 cup diced potatoes

1 cup sliced mushrooms

1 cup white wine

4 cups clam juice

Juice reserved from oysters

1 sprig fresh thyme

2 tablespoons chopped fresh parsley

1 can (6½ ounces) chopped clams

8 ounces shucked oysters, or 1 jar (8 ounces) shucked oysters

8 ounces mussels in shell

8 ounces salmon fillets, de-boned and cut into 1-inch cubes

Salt and pepper

1 cup heavy cream

1 In 7- to 9-quart cast-iron Dutch oven, melt the butter over medium-high heat. When the butter is bubbling, add the onions, celery, carrots, potatoes, and mushrooms. Sauté for 10 minutes.

2 Add the wine, clam juice, oyster juice (however much you have), thyme, and parsley. Bring the mixture to a rolling boil and reduce the heat and simmer for 15 minutes.

3 Add the clams, oysters, mussels, and salmon, stirring well. Cook for an additional 15 minutes or until the salmon begins to flake and the mussels open and rise to the surface. Season to taste using salt and pepper. Discard any muscles that don't open.

4 Add the heavy cream and continue to simmer for 5 minutes. Ladle the chowder into the soup bowls and serve hot.

Per serving: Calories 319 (From Fat 182); Fat 20g (Saturated 11g); Cholesterol 138mg; Sodium 549mg; Carbohydrate 13g (Dietary Fiber 2g); Protein 21g.

Rallying around Rice

In the race to see who's the leading food source for humankind, rice and wheat are neck and neck. Rice is a food staple for nearly half of the world's population. It's been grown for thousands of years and comes in over 7,000 varieties.

Before any rice can be eaten, the husk (hull and chaff) has to be removed. What remains is brown rice. Mill brown rice to remove the bran and germ, and you have white rice. Brown rice has a slightly nutty flavor, is chewy, takes a little longer to cook (because you have to get through the bran and germ), and offers more nutritional value that white rice.

When you go to buy rice, you'll notice that it's classified by its size; each size has different characteristics that are important for a cook to know:

✔ **Long-grain:** The longest rice, long grain can be white or brown. When cooked, it separates easily. You can buy various varieties of long-grain rice. One of the more exotic varieties is Basmati rice, which is grown in the foothills of the Himalaya Mountains and has a nutty flavor.

✔ **Medium-grain:** Medium-grain rice is, as its name implies, not as long as long-grain rice, nor is it as short as short-grain rice. It falls between the other two in its characteristics as well. It isn't as dry as long-grain rice, and it isn't as moist as short-grain rice. So whereas long-grain rice separates easily and short-grain rice clumps together nicely, medium-grain rice is fluffy and separates nicely right after its been cooked, but it gets clumpy as it cools.

✔ **Short-grain:** Short-grain rice, also called pearl rice because it's short and fat (almost round), has more starch that the other two grains. It's moist, and the grains stick together easily. Because it holds together so easily, it's the most popular rice in countries where chopsticks are used.

Gumbo, okra, and filé powder

Okra not only adds flavor to gumbo, but it also thickens the mixture. Another thickening agent, filé powder, is also used in traditional gumbo recipes. Made from the dried leaves of sassafras trees, filé powder is added to dishes right before serving because it turns stringy and tough if cooked too long. If you want to try filé powder, look for it in the spice sections of large supermarkets or gourmet shops.

Gullah Rice

Standard long-grain rice is ideal for this recipe, but you can use brown or white rice too. If you use brown, just add 5 minutes cooking time to Step 4. Don't use instant rice; it cooks too quickly and will break down before the rest of the ingredients are done.

The origins of this dish rest with the men, women, and children brought as slaves from West Africa to work the rice plantations on the coastal islands off of South Carolina and Georgia. Isolated from the mainland and eventually outnumbering their often-absent owners, these people preserved the language, religious practices, music, and social customs of their homeland. The result is a uniquely and literally African-American culture. These people and their descendents are known as the Gullah (in South Carolina) and Geechee (in Georgia) people. *Gullah* is also the name of their language, which is made up of English and over 4,000 words from many different African languages.

Preparation time: *20 minutes*

Cooking time: *50 to 60 minutes*

Yield: *6 servings*

2 pounds smoked sausage, sliced ½-inch thick	*2 cups uncooked rice*
2 tablespoons vegetable oil, if necessary	*1 teaspoon brown sugar*
1 cup chopped onion	*1 teaspoon salt*
1 cup chopped red bell pepper	*1 cup chopped tomatoes*
1 or 2 chopped jalapeño peppers, seeded	*2½ to 3 cups chicken stock*
	1 cup cooked black beans

1 In a 10-quart cast-iron Dutch oven, brown the sausage over medium-high heat. Remove the sausage and set aside; reserve the fat. Add enough of the vegetable oil so that the pan contains approximately 4 tablespoons of fat/oil.

2 Add the onion, bell pepper, and hot peppers. Cook over medium heat until the vegetables are wilted, approximately 10 minutes.

3 Add the rice and stir to coat the grains with the vegetable mixture. Stir in the sausage, sugar, salt, and tomatoes. Pour in 2½ cups of the chicken stock, one ladle at a time, blending well.

4 Bring the mixture to a rolling boil, reduce the heat to a simmer and cover. Cook for about 20 minutes, or until the rice is tender and the stock is absorbed. Check occasionally and, if necessary, add up to ½ cup additional stock as the rice cooks.

5 Remove the Dutch oven from the heat. Stir in the black beans, cover, and let it stand for 10 minutes. Serve warm.

Per serving: Calories 838 (From Fat 435); Fat 48g (Saturated 16g); Cholesterol 103mg; Sodium 2,437mg; Carbohydrate 70g (Dietary Fiber 5g); Protein 29g.

Pork and Sausage Jambalaya

Jambalaya combines rice, tomatoes, onion, green pepper, and just about any combination of meat, poultry, and shellfish that you can think of. Although ham was the original main ingredient in jambalaya (*jambon* is the French word for ham), ham has given way to smoked sausage or other heavily spiced meat, such as andouille.

Preparation time: *20 minutes*

Cooking time: *2 hours*

Yield: *8 servings*

¼ cup shortening or bacon drippings	8 cups beef or chicken stock
3 pounds cubed pork	2 cups sliced mushrooms
2 pounds sliced andouille	1 cup sliced green onions
2 cups chopped onions	½ cup chopped parsley
2 cups chopped celery	Salt and pepper
1 cup chopped bell pepper	Hot pepper sauce
½ cup diced garlic	3 cups long-grain rice

1 In a 7-quart cast-iron Dutch oven, heat the shortening or bacon drippings over medium-high heat.

2 Sauté the cubed pork until it's dark brown on all sides — approximately 30 minutes. This is important as the brown color of the jambalaya is derived from the color of the meat.

3 Add the andouille and sauté an additional 10 to 15 minutes. Remove the pork and andouille from the pan and set aside. Tilt the pan to one side and ladle out all the oil, except for one large cooking spoon.

4 Add the onions, celery, bell pepper, and garlic. Sauté until all the vegetables are dark golden brown, about 30 minutes. Be careful, as vegetables will tend to scorch because the pot is so hot.

5 Add the stock, bring to a rolling boil and reduce the heat to a simmer. Cook 15 minutes for flavors to develop.

6 Return the pork and andouille to the pan. Add the mushrooms, green onions, and parsley. Season to taste using salt, pepper, and hot pepper sauce. You may want to slightly over-season, because the rice tends to require a little extra seasoning.

7 Add the rice, reducing the heat to a simmer and cover. Cook the rice 25 minutes, stirring once.

Per serving: *Calories 1,006 (From Fat 476); Fat 53g (Saturated 18g); Cholesterol 175mg; Sodium 2,412mg; Carbohydrate 73g (Dietary Fiber 3g); Protein 55g.*

Making Cornbread the Main Dish

Cornbread is a southern staple, and many people think of it simply as an accompaniment to dinner rather than part of the main course. In the first three recipes in this section, the cornbread *is* the main dish. The last recipe — a cornbread salad — calls for freshly made cornbread.

Shrimp Cornbread Supreme

In this recipe, the cornbread binds the rest of the ingredients together. Make sure that you drain the broccoli well. Too much moisture makes the cornbread mixture soggy. Serve this with a small side salad, and you have a whole dinner.

Preparation time: *20 minutes*

Cooking time: *30 to 35 minutes*

Yield: *8 servings*

6 slices bacon	1 package (8¾ ounces) cornbread mix	1 pound cooked shrimp, shelled and deveined
4 eggs	6 dashes hot pepper sauce	2 cups finely shredded cheddar cheese
¼ cup milk	1 medium onion, chopped	
½ cup butter, melted and cooled	1 package (10 ounces) frozen chopped broccoli, thawed and drained	Chopped fresh parsley (optional)

1 Preheat oven to 375 degrees.

2 Fry the bacon until crisp in a 10-inch cast-iron skillet. Drain on a paper towel. Cool, crumble, and set aside.

3 Reserve 1 tablespoon of the bacon drippings. Drain off the remaining bacon drippings and wipe the skillet clean with a paper towel. Return the reserved bacon drippings to the skillet and place in the oven to heat.

4 Beat the eggs in a large bowl. Add the milk, butter, cornbread mix, and hot pepper sauce. Stir with a spoon until well blended. Stir in the onion, broccoli, shrimp, and 1½ cups of the cheese. Remove the skillet from the oven and carefully pour the batter into hot skillet.

5 Sprinkle the remaining ½ cup of cheese evenly over the top. Bake for 30 to 35 minutes, until golden brown. Remove from the oven and garnish with the bacon crumbles and parsley, if desired.

Per serving: Calories 494 (From Fat 287); Fat 32g (Saturated 17g); Cholesterol 285mg; Sodium 784mg; Carbohydrate 25g (Dietary Fiber 3g); Protein 27g.

Hamburger Cornbread Surprise

The cornbread in this recipe tops the meat mixture. When it's done, you serve this with a spoon to get at all the yummy good stuff hiding underneath the cornbread crust.

Preparation time: 10 minutes

Cooking time: 45 to 50 minutes

Yield: 6 to 8 servings

1 pound ground beef	*1 can (15 ounces) kidney beans, rinsed and drained*
⅓ cup chopped onion	*1 egg*
5 tablespoons vegetable oil	*1¼ cups milk*
1 can (14 ounces) stewed tomatoes, chopped	*2 cups white self-rising cornmeal mix*
1 teaspoon Worcestershire sauce	*2 cups finely grated sharp cheddar cheese*
¾ teaspoon salt	

1 Preheat oven to 425 degrees.

2 In a 10-inch cast-iron skillet, heat 1 tablespoon of vegetable oil and sauté the ground beef and the onion over medium-high heat. Drain the fat.

3 Add the tomatoes, Worcestershire sauce, and salt. Simmer for 15 minutes.

4 Stir in the beans. Simmer for another 5 minutes and remove from the heat.

5 In a medium bowl, mix together the egg, milk, and the remaining 4 tablespoons of vegetable oil with spoon. Add the cornmeal mix and mix well.

6 Spread cornmeal batter over the ground beef mixture in the skillet. Top with the grated cheese. Bake for 20 to 25 minutes, or until the center is set and the cornbread is golden brown.

Vary It! *For a Mexican, add a tablespoon of chili powder to ground beef mixture in Step 3 and eliminate the Worcestershire sauce.*

Per serving: Calories 510 (From Fat 248); Fat 28g (Saturated 10g); Cholesterol 107mg; Sodium 1,108mg; Carbohydrate 38g (Dietary Fiber 6g); Protein 27g.

Buffalo Chicken Cornbread with Blue Cheese Mayo

Buffalo wings, which hail from the Anchor Bar in Buffalo, New York, have become a favorite the nation over. The taste sensation of deep-fried chicken coated in hot sauce combined with cool bleu cheese dressing has inspired many a cook to give this new favorite a novel twist. In this recipe, the Yankee dish is paired with a Southern favorite.

Preparation time: *20 minutes*

Cooking time: *30 minutes*

Yield: *6 servings*

1 pound chicken breast tender strips	*⅔ cup chopped celery*
¼ cup Louisiana style hot sauce	*1 package (6 ounces) white cornbread mix*
Blue Cheese Mayonnaise (recipe follows)	*½ cup milk*
3 tablespoons butter	*1 egg*
½ cup chopped red onion	

1 Preheat oven to 425 degrees. In a medium bowl, combine the chicken and hot pepper sauce. Toss to coat. Marinate at room temperature for 20 minutes. Prepare the Blue Cheese Mayonnaise (recipe follows). Set aside until ready to use.

2 Melt 1 tablespoon of the butter in a 10-inch cast-iron skillet over medium heat. Cook and stir onion and celery in the butter until soft. Remove vegetable mixture from the skillet into a medium bowl.

3 In the same skillet, melt the remaining 2 tablespoons of butter over medium heat. Add the chicken mixture. Cook, stirring frequently, for 5 minutes. Reduce heat to low.

4 In a medium bowl, combine the vegetable mixture, the cornbread mix, milk, and egg. Mix well. Spoon evenly over the chicken mixture.

5 Bake at 425 degrees for about 20 minutes until topping is golden brown and set.

6 Cut into wedges and top each serving with the Blue Cheese Mayonnaise.

Blue Cheese Mayonnaise

½ cup mayonnaise	*½ teaspoon salt*
¼ cup plain yogurt	*2 teaspoons lemon juice*
2 ounces blue cheese, crumbled	

In a small bowl combine all ingredients. Cover and refrigerate until ready to use.

Per serving: Calories 446 (From Fat 263); Fat 29g (Saturated 9g); Cholesterol 115mg; Sodium 1,212mg; Carbohydrate 23g (Dietary Fiber 1g); Protein 22g.

Ham and Cheese Main Dish Cornbread Salad

Although this recipe calls for southern cornbread, you can vary the flavor simply by varying the cornbread. (You can find the Real Southern Cornbread recipe in Chapter 11.)

Preparation time: *10 minutes*

Chilling time: *4 hours*

Yield: *6 to 8 servings*

1 cup mayonnaise	*2 cups grated sharp cheddar cheese*
2 tablespoons olive juice	*3 hard boiled eggs, chopped*
1 tablespoon prepared mustard	*½ cup stuffed green olives, drained and sliced*
2 cups cubed baked ham	*1 skillet of southern cornbread, cooled and crumbled*
1 cup chopped celery	

1 In a medium bowl, combine the mayonnaise, olive juice, and the mustard.

2 In a very large bowl, mix together the ham, celery, grated cheese, chopped eggs, and the olives.

3 Blend the mayonnaise mixture into the ham mixture. Mix in the crumbled cornbread. Cover and refrigerate for four hours or overnight.

Per serving: *Calories 554 (From Fat 376); Fat 42g (Saturated 12g); Cholesterol 167mg; Sodium 1,299mg; Carbohydrate 24g (Dietary Fiber 2g); Protein 21g.*

Two a-peeling tomato options

Just as there's more than one way to skin a cat, there's more than one way to peel a tomato:

✔ **Method 1:** Rub the back edge of a knife over the entire tomato. Then make a slit in the skin and use the knife blade and your thumb to pull the skin from the meat of the tomato.

✔ **Method 2:** Cut a small X into the bottom of the tomato and then blanch it: Plunge it briefly into boiling water and then plunge it into cold water to stop the cooking process. This tightens the meat and loosens the skin. Then use a knife to pull the loosened skin away.

Part III
Cast-Iron Sides and Sweet Endings

The 5th Wave   By Rich Tennant

"I could be convinced not to store my cast-iron cookware on an overhead pot holder."

In this part . . .

Some of the best cast-iron recipes are side dishes, breads, and desserts, and this part contains the best of the best. Traditional cast-iron favorites (cornbread, muffins, and fried green tomatoes), modern delights (stir-fried vegetables), as well as delectable desserts and sweets (pineapple upside-down cakes and pralines) are all in this part. With these recipes, your side dishes will no longer be the thrown-together afterthoughts that rarely get the attention or notice they deserve.

Chapter 10

Vegetables Even Your Kids Will Love

*V*egetables offer plenty of variety. They can be prepared as side dishes, main dishes, appetizers, and sweetened enough to pass for desserts. Pairing such an adaptable foodstuff with the versatility of cast iron gives you all sorts of options. The best way to exploit these options is to experiment. Pair your favorite vegetables with your favorite herbs. You can try different cooking techniques — pan-fry, stir-fry, bake, braise, and caramelize — with all sorts of vegetables in any cast-iron skillet.

In this chapter, I introduce you to basic cast-iron vegetable recipes, using simple cooking techniques and easy-to-find vegetables. But don't misinterpret *basic* as *plain*. These dishes are simple, that's true. But they're also delicious, easily paired with just about any main dish and sure to be a hit around your kitchen table.

Cast-Iron Favorites: Potatoes and Beans

When you think cast iron and vegetables, two standards stand out: fried potatoes and home-style green beans. Because no cast-iron cookbook would be complete without these two favorites, I include both dishes, along with a bunch of other delicious potato and bean dishes.

This spud's for you

Potatoes can be mashed, fried, boiled, baked, scalloped, creamed — you name it, you can probably do it to a potato. Of all that you can do a potato, one of the nicest is to cook it in cast iron. Potato dishes, in short, are easy to make and hard to mess up.

Skillet-Fried Potatoes

The secrets to perfect fried potatoes are a heavy skillet (cast iron is perfect), even heat, and self-control. You have to let the potatoes cook long enough to brown and become crispy before you turn them. Also use a spatula, not a spoon, to turn the potatoes so that the potato slices retain their shape and don't get all mushed together.

Preparation time: *15 minutes*

Cooking time: *30 to 35 minutes*

Yield: *4 to 6 servings*

6 small Yukon gold potatoes, or 3 russets (about 2 pounds)	*2 tablespoons vegetable shortening*
1 medium onion	*2 tablespoons butter*
	Salt and pepper

1 Wash, peel, and slice the potatoes. Chop the onion.

2 Heat the shortening in a 10-inch cast-iron skillet until a drop of water skips and sizzles in the pan.

3 Arrange ⅓ of the potatoes in a layer in the bottom of the pan, sprinkle ⅓ of the onion over the potatoes, and then sprinkle with the salt and pepper. Dot with ⅓ of the butter. Repeat this step two more times, forming three potato layers.

4 Cover and cook for 20 minutes over medium heat. Don't lift the lid and don't turn the potatoes.

5 Remove the lid and continue to cook, turning the potatoes one or two more times, until crispy and done, about 10 to 15 minutes.

Vary It! *For a complete meal, include smoked sausage or cubed ham in the layers and reduce the amount of salt that you use.*

Per serving: Calories 204 (From Fat 73); Fat 8g (Saturated 3g); Cholesterol 10mg; Sodium 106mg; Carbohydrate 30g (Dietary Fiber 3g); Protein 3g.

Easy Dutch Oven Potatoes and Onions

This recipe uses many of the same ingredients as the Skillet-Fried Potatoes recipe earlier in this chapter, except the cooking method produces fork-tender potatoes instead of crispy ones. Baked in the oven, this dish is a great accompaniment to roast chicken or beef. And the cheese topping entices even the pickiest of little ones.

Preparation time: *10 minutes*

Cooking time: *1 hour, 15 minutes*

Yield: *8 to 10 servings*

4 to 5 pounds potatoes, sliced into ¼-inch rounds	½ cup (1 stick) butter, sliced into 10 pieces
2 pounds onions, sliced	8 to 12 ounces grated cheese of choice (optional)
Salt and pepper	

1 Preheat oven to 350 degrees. Coat a 5-quart cast-iron Dutch oven with cooking spray.

2 Place a layer of the potato slices and then a layer of the onion slices in the Dutch oven. Salt and pepper each layer.

3 Repeat layers until all the potato and onion slices are used up. Place the butter pieces onto the top. Cover and bake for about 1 hour. Check for doneness with a fork. Return to the oven and bake uncovered; cook until the potatoes are fork tender, about 15 minutes.

4 If desired, sprinkle the cheese on top during the last 15 minutes of baking.

Per serving: Calories 262 (From Fat 83); Fat 9g (Saturated 6g); Cholesterol 25mg; Sodium 68mg; Carbohydrate 41g (Dietary Fiber 4g); Protein 5g.

Oven-Roasted New Potatoes

Look for *new potatoes* (the small, rounded potatoes with the reddish skin) that have thin, papery skin and are free of blemishes or any tint of green (a sign that the potato isn't ripe). For this recipe, don't worry about size; small or large work equally well. But select potatoes of roughly the same size, so they all get done about the same time.

Preparation time: *10 minutes*

Cooking time: *40 minutes*

Yield: *4 servings*

6 tablespoons butter	½ teaspoon salt	¼ teaspoon cayenne pepper
10 or 12 medium new potatoes, skin on (about 3 pounds)	¼ teaspoon pepper	Kosher salt (optional)
	½ teaspoon garlic salt	1 tablespoon chopped fresh parsley

1 Preheat oven to 425 degrees. Put butter in 12-inch cast-iron skillet and put it into oven to heat.

2 Cut potatoes in half. Sprinkle salt, pepper, garlic salt, and cayenne into hot butter. Place potatoes cut side down in hot butter. Bake for 25 minutes.

3 Turn potatoes and bake an additional 15 minutes or until fork tender. Remove from oven, sprinkle with kosher salt, if desired, and garnish with parsley.

Per serving: Calories 369 (From Fat 157); Fat 17g (Saturated 11g); Cholesterol 46mg; Sodium 424mg; Carbohydrate 44g (Dietary Fiber 7g); Protein 9g.

Skillet Yum-Yum Sweet Potatoes

This is a less sweet, less caramel-y version of candied sweet potatoes — a holiday favorite. The subtle sweetness and tender but not mushy consistency of this dish makes it a perfect accompaniment for pork and poultry at any time of the year.

Preparation time: *10 minutes*

Cooking time: *30 minutes*

Yield: *4 servings*

2 to 3 tablespoons butter	3 or 4 medium sweet potatoes, peeled and sliced
¼ cup brown sugar	
1 teaspoon cinnamon	1 cup water

1 Heat the butter in a large (12- to 13-inch) cast-iron skillet on medium high.

2 Stir the sugar and cinnamon into the butter. Add the sweet potatoes and water. Cover, bring to a boil, and reduce the heat to medium. Continue to cook until the potatoes are fork tender, about 25 minutes, turning only to keep from burning.

3 Remove the lid and cook until liquid thickens, about 5 minutes, watching carefully.

Per serving: Calories 192 (From Fat 52); Fat 6g (Saturated 4g); Cholesterol 15mg; Sodium 15mg; Carbohydrate 35g (Dietary Fiber 3g); Protein 2g.

Herb Roasted New Potatoes

Although the recipe instructs you to bake these potatoes in a hot oven (400 degrees), they're also great for outdoor cooking. Pack the bag containing the seasoned potatoes with the rest of your outdoor cooking gear, and about an hour before you want to eat, place the seasoned potatoes in a cast-iron skillet or on a griddle and cook over hot coals until they're golden brown and tender. (For more outdoor recipes, head to Chapter 14.)

Preparation time: *20 minutes*

Cooking time: *45 minutes to 1 hour*

Yield: *4 servings*

2 pounds new potatoes, quartered	*2 tablespoons garlic, minced*	*¼ cup melted butter*
½ cup onion, sliced very thick	*2 tablespoons fresh thyme, chopped*	*2 tablespoons red wine vinegar*
½ cup red bell pepper, sliced very thick	*2 tablespoons fresh rosemary, chopped*	*2 teaspoons Creole seasoning*
½ cup yellow bell pepper, sliced very thick	*¼ cup olive oil*	*Salt and pepper*

1 Preheat oven to 400 degrees. Place the potatoes in a large, resealable plastic bag. Add the onion, bell pepper, garlic, and herbs. Pour in the olive oil, butter, and vinegar. Season using the Creole seasoning, salt, and pepper. Seal the bag and shake vigorously to completely season the potatoes.

2 Place the contents of the bag on a 12-inch cast-iron skillet and bake in the oven for 45 minutes to 1 hour, stirring occasionally, until the potatoes are tender and golden brown.

Per serving: Calories 390 (From Fat 227); Fat 25g (Saturated 9g); Cholesterol 31mg; Sodium 194mg; Carbohydrate 35g (Dietary Fiber 5g); Protein 7g.

Beans, beans, a wonderful fruit

Preparing traditional cast-iron bean dishes is a snap when you keep these secrets in mind:

- ✔ **Cooking time:** The key words are *long* and *slow*. The best-tasting dishes often cook for an hour or more.

- ✔ **Cooking liquid:** The beans pick up much of their flavor from the liquid they cook in and the ingredients you add to that liquid.

- ✔ **Fresh or frozen beans:** Canned green beans won't hold up to the long cooking times and will be mushy by the time that they're done. If you can't find fresh green beans (or you don't like the quality you find), use frozen.

Southern Green Beans

Finding fresh or even dried October beans can be hard. You'll probably have more luck finding canned October beans. If you use canned beans, add them during the last 30 minutes of cooking time.

Preparation time: 10 minutes

Cooking time: 2½ hours

Yield: 8 servings

4 pounds pole green beans, such as Kentucky Wonders	1 teaspoon sugar
1 pound October beans	¾ teaspoon pepper
1 ham hock or ½ pound salt pork	Salt

1 Wash, string, and break the green beans into pieces 1 to 2 inches in length, discarding the ends. Shell and rinse the October beans.

2 Place the ham hock in a 5-quart Dutch oven and cover it with water; add the sugar and pepper. Set the burner to medium high and bring to a boil.

3 Add the October beans. Reduce the heat and simmer for 2 hours.

4 Add the green beans and continue to simmer for 30 minutes, or until the beans are tender. Salt to taste during these last 30 minutes.

Per serving: Calories 444 (From Fat 27); Fat 3g (Saturated 3g); Cholesterol 7mg; Sodium 85mg; Carbohydrate 78g (Dietary Fiber 29g); Protein 29g.

Slow-Simmered Black Beans

This recipe puts a little spin on the traditional soup bean. Instead of navy beans, it uses black beans. You can find bags of black beans in the same aisle where you find soup or beans.

Preparation time: 10 minutes

Cooking time: 2½ hours

Yield: 6 servings

1 pound black beans	2 cloves garlic, chopped
¼ pound salt pork, sliced, or 4 to 5 slices thick bacon, cut into bite-sized pieces	1 carrot, peeled and sliced
	2 chicken bouillon cubes
1 medium onion, chopped	Salt, if necessary

1 Sort and rinse the beans.

2 Fry the salt pork or the bacon in a 3-quart cast-iron deep skillet over medium to medium-high heat. Reduce heat to medium low and cook the onion, garlic, and carrot, until the onion is transparent.

3 Add the beans and enough water to just cover. Add the bouillon cubes.

4 Increase the heat to bring to a boil and then reduce the heat to low and simmer, covered for 1½ to 2 hours. Stir occasionally and add water to keep the beans just covered with liquid.

5 During last 15 minutes of cooking, taste for seasoning and add the salt if necessary.

Per serving: Calories 388 (From Fat 139); Fat 16g (Saturated 5g); Cholesterol 16mg; Sodium 635mg; Carbohydrate 46g (Dietary Fiber 16g); Protein 18g.

Preparing the beans that the recipes in this section call for is simple. Just follow these instructions:

- ✔ **Black beans:** Simply rinse and *sort,* that is, sift through the beans and discard out any bad beans or small stones. Yes, you may find small rocks in your beanbag.

- ✔ **Green beans:** Wash, *string* (remove the tough fiber that connects the halves of the bean pod), and break off the ends of the beans. Then cut or break them into the sizes called for in the recipes.

- ✔ **October beans:** Simply shell and rinse.

Squash Anyone?

Although they come in a variety of shapes, sizes, and colors, all squash fits into one of two categories. (The following categories *don't* have anything to do with *when* the squash is grown.)

✔ **Summer squash:** So called because these squash are eaten when the plant is still immature, before the seeds and rind harden. You need to use your summer squash shortly after you purchase or pick it. Examples of summer squash include

- Crookneck
- Cymling
- Pattypan
- Straightneck
- Zucchini

When you buy summer squash, pay attention to the skin and its weight. The skin should be shiny and smooth and the squash should feel heavy for its size.

✔ **Winter squash:** So called, because these varieties are generally used when the plant is fully mature and the rind and seeds have hardened. Winter squash can be stored for several months. Examples of winter squash include

- Acorn
- Banana
- Buttercup
- Butternut

When you buy winter squash, pay attention to

- **Color:** Should be a nice yellow-orange.
- **Rind:** Make sure it's thick and hard, with no soft spots.
- **Weight:** Go for heavy.
- **Size:** Be careful not to get one that's too small — a sign that it hasn't developed its full flavor. And avoid one that's too big, too. The flesh may be seedy and stringy.

Acorn Squash with Sugar and Cranberries

The rind of an acorn squash (one of the winter squashes) is thick and hard. To remove the rind and seeds, cut the squash into quarters. Using a spoon, scrape the seeds from the flesh. Then take a sharp knife and carefully slice the flesh from the rind. This recipe is a great complement to poultry, pork, and game.

Preparation time: *5 minutes*

Cooking time: *35 minutes*

Yield: *6 servings*

3 acorn squash	*¼ cup chopped fresh parsley*
¼ cup butter	*1 cup chicken broth*
1 cup diced onion	*½ teaspoon salt*
½ cup brown sugar	*½ teaspoon pepper*
½ cup fresh cranberries	

1 Peel, seed, and dice squash into ½-inch cubes (about 4½ cups).

2 In a 12-inch cast-iron skillet, melt the butter over medium-high heat. Add the onions and sauté until translucent, about 5 minutes. Add the squash and continue cooking for 5 minutes.

3 Add the sugar, cranberries, and parsley; cook for an additional 5 minutes.

4 Stir in the broth, scraping the sides to remove any browned bits. Add the salt and pepper, and simmer for 20 minutes.

Per serving: Calories 245 (From Fat 77); Fat 9g (Saturated 5g); Cholesterol 21mg; Sodium 377mg; Carbohydrate 44g (Dietary Fiber 4g); Protein 2g.

Removing really rigid rind

The rinds of some winter squash are so hard that they're nearly impossible to remove. If this is the case, don't despair. Bake the squash first to soften the rind: If you can, cut the squash in half, remove any seeds, place it in a medium oven (325 to 375 degrees), and bake it until the rind is tender to the touch, about an hour. If the rind is so tough that cutting it in half is impossible, stick the whole squash in the oven and bake it. When the rind is soft, you can easily remove it from the flesh. Then prepare your recipe as usual.

Squash steals the show

Offering as many flavors as colors and shapes and loaded with nutrients, squash is a cook's and a nutritionist's delight. As a group, squash stands out in terms of vitamins and minerals. Even cooked squash is hard to beat for sheer good-for-you-ness. It provides vitamins A and C, potassium, and dietary fiber. Recent studies also show that it contains compounds, such as flavonoids, that fight cancer.

Patty Pan Squash and Vidalia Onion

Grown in Georgia and available in early summer, Vidalia onions are famous for their sweet flavor. If you can't find Vidalia onions for this recipe, you can substitute any other sweet onion.

Preparation time: *10 minutes*

Cooking time: *30 to 45 minutes*

Yield: *8 servings*

3 tablespoons butter

1 large Vidalia onion, sliced

6 Patty Pan squash, sliced

1 teaspoon sugar

¼ teaspoon pepper

1 Place the butter in a 12-inch cast-iron skillet and set your burner to medium high.

2 When the butter is bubbling, add the onion and sauté until almost brown. Add the squash, sugar, and pepper and toss with a spatula to combine. Reduce the heat to medium and continue cooking for about 15 minutes uncovered, turning once with the spatula. Cover and steam until the squash is tender, about 15 to 20 minutes. Reduce the heat if necessary.

3 Adjust seasoning with the pepper and sugar to taste during the last 5 minutes of cooking.

Per serving: *Calories 177 (From Fat 42); Fat 5g (Saturated 3g); Cholesterol 12mg; Sodium 11mg; Carbohydrate 36g (Dietary Fiber 5g); Protein 3g.*

Skillet Squash Casserole

You start this squash recipe on the stovetop and then finish it in the oven to let the juices and flavors blend. Any yellow summer squash — straightneck or crookneck will do.

Preparation time: *10 minutes*

Cooking time: *50 to 60 minutes*

Yield: *8 servings*

3 pounds yellow squash and zucchini
(about 7 total)

1 large onion, chopped

3 tablespoons butter

1 tablespoon sugar

1 teaspoon sage

1 cup processed cheese food, cubed

2 eggs, slightly beaten

Crushed round buttery crackers for topping
(about 16 crackers)

1 Preheat the oven to 350 degrees.

2 Cut the squash and zucchini into ½-inch-thick slices, discarding the ends.

3 In a 12-inch cast-iron skillet on medium heat, sauté the onion in the butter until tender. Add the squash and zucchini, sugar, and sage. Stir to combine ingredients.

4 Cover and cook until the squash and zucchini are almost tender. Check frequently, carefully turning and stirring with a spatula or large spoon. Try to keep the squash slices intact throughout the process. Remove from the heat and stir in the cheese until completely melted and combined. When the mixture is cool enough, add the eggs, and stir. Top with the crushed crackers.

5 Bake uncovered for 35 to 40 minutes or until all sides are bubbling, and the top is golden brown.

Per serving: Calories 198 (From Fat 107); Fat 12g (Saturated 6g); Cholesterol 80mg; Sodium 321mg; Carbohydrate 16g (Dietary Fiber 4g); Protein 8g.

Enjoying Corn On and Off the Cob

Although you can buy ears of corn in the produce section of any grocery, going out of your way to a farmers market often yields the most flavorful ears. By mid to late summer, you can find all kinds of corn varieties at local produce stands. Most of what's available, though, are the sweet corns — the favorite of American consumers.

TIP

When you shop for fresh ears of corn, don't pull back the husk to examine the kernels, as tempting as that may be. The husk protects the kernels and keeps them from drying out. In fact, some farmers make you buy any ear you even partially husk. Fortunately, you don't need to see the kernels to tell whether the ear is a good one. Using just a little pressure, run your fingers along the husk, feeling for the kernels underneath. A nice ear has smooth, plump, rounded kernels.

Creamy Corn Pudding

Not all corn recipes call for corn straight from the ear. This one uses cans of creamed and kernel corns. You combine these canned corns with a basic white sauce, add eggs to firm the concoction up, and bake. Voila! A corn pudding that you can serve with a spoon or spatula alongside any entree.

Preparation time: *10 minutes*

Cooking time: *1 hour and 15 minutes*

Yield: *6 to 8 servings*

3 tablespoons butter	*¾ cup milk*
3 tablespoons all-purpose flour	*1 can (14 ounces) cream-style corn*
1 tablespoon sugar	*1 can (14 ounces) whole corn*
¾ teaspoon salt	*3 eggs, well beaten*

1 Preheat your oven to 350 degrees.

2 In a 2-quart cast-iron serving pot, melt the butter over low heat. Add the flour, sugar, and salt, and stir until smooth. Cook one minute. Gradually add the milk and cook over medium low heat until thick and bubbly.

3 Remove from the heat and stir in the cream-style and whole corn.

4 Gradually add ¼ of the hot mixture to the eggs. Then add the egg mixture back to the hot corn mixture, stirring constantly.

5 Bake for 1 hour or until set.

Per serving: *Calories 168 (From Fat 70); Fat 8g (Saturated 4g); Cholesterol 94mg; Sodium 539mg; Carbohydrate 20g (Dietary Fiber 2g); Protein 5g.*

Corn Maque Choux

This Corn Maque Choux recipe that follows is a combination of vegetables, shrimp, and spicy meat that's closer to a meal than a side dish.

Select tender, well-developed ears of corn and remove shucks and silk. Using a sharp knife, cut lengthwise through the kernels to remove them from the cob. This is important since the richness of the dish will depend on how much milk and pulp can be scraped from the cobs.

Preparation time: *20 minutes*

Cooking time: *45 to 55 minutes*

Yield: *8 servings*

8 ears fresh corn (about 4 cups)

2 to 4 tablespoons bacon drippings

1 cup chopped onions

½ cup chopped celery

½ cup chopped green bell pepper

½ cup chopped red bell pepper

¼ cup diced garlic

¼ cup finely diced andouille, or quality Polish sausage

2 cups coarsely chopped tomatoes

2 tablespoons tomato sauce

2 cups small shrimp, peeled and deveined

1 cup sliced green onions (about 10)

Salt and pepper

1 Cut the corn kernels from the cobs and scrape each cob using the blade of the knife to remove all milk and additional pulp from the corn.

2 In a 3-quart cast-iron chicken fryer or deep-sided pan, melt the bacon drippings over medium-high heat.

3 Sauté the corn, onions, celery, bell peppers, garlic, and andouille for approximately 15 to 20 minutes or until the vegetables are wilted and the corn begins to tenderize.

4 Add the tomatoes and tomato sauce. Continue cooking until the juices from the tomatoes and are rendered into the dish, approximately 15 to 20 minutes.

5 Add the shrimp, green onions, and salt and pepper. Continue to cook an additional 15 minutes or until the flavors of the corn and shrimp are fully developed.

Per serving: Calories 186 (From Fat 56); Fat 6g (Saturated 2g); Cholesterol 59mg; Sodium 237mg; Carbohydrate 26g (Dietary Fiber 5g); Protein 11g.

Fried Corn

Unless you're from the South, and you've grown up eating Fried Corn, the result may be different from your expectations. This dish isn't really "fried" in the truest sense — or creamed or boiled for that matter. You simply cook the corn with bacon grease, butter, milk, and flour. The end result, though, speaks for itself.

This recipe calls for bacon drippings — but no bacon — which makes it a great side dish on the day that you had bacon for breakfast. If you don't have bacon grease on hand, you can fry a few (three or four) pieces now (and crumble the bacon over the dish when it's done or use it for something else) or you can use additional butter if you have to.

Preparation time: *20 minutes*

Cooking time: *45 minutes*

Yield: *6 to 8 servings*

6 to 8 ears of fresh corn, yellow or white	*¾ cup milk, more if needed*
1 tablespoon bacon drippings	*½ cup water, more if needed*
4 tablespoons butter	*Salt and pepper*
2 tablespoons all-purpose flour	

1 Shuck the corn, remove the silks, and rinse the ears.

2 In a large bowl, slice the kernels from the ears of corn. With the blunt edge of a knife blade, scrape the ears to get the last bits of kernels and the juice, or "milk"— so called because it's white and resembles milk — from the cob.

3 Put the bacon drippings and butter in a 12-inch cast-iron skillet and set on medium heat. When melted, stir in the flour. Add the milk, water, and corn.

4 Cook, stirring occasionally and using a spatula to turn. If necessary, add water or milk to keep the corn from drying out. Continue cooking for 30 to 45 minutes.

5 Salt and pepper to taste about half way through cooking time.

Per serving: Calories 147 (From Fat 80); Fat 9g (Saturated 5g); Cholesterol 20mg; Sodium 94mg; Carbohydrate 16g (Dietary Fiber 2g); Protein 3g.

Loading Up on Southern Staples

Some foods are associated with the southern United States: greens, gumbos, and fried green tomatoes all spring to mind. The main ingredients in the first of these two dishes — turnip greens and okra — are grown in the South. The main ingredient of the last dish — the ever-present tomato — has taken on a decidedly southern twist: picked green before it's ripe, dipped in batter, and deep fried.

O-K-R-A-H-O-M-A, Okrahoma, Okay!

Okra is technically a fruit, but that doesn't stop people from preparing, cooking, and serving it as a vegetable. A main ingredient in *gumbo* (a thick soup or stew), okra can also be served alone as a vegetable. (Check out Chapter 9 for great gumbo recipes.)

When you purchase okra at the store, look for tender, bright green pods that are about 4 inches long. To prepare okra for cooking, simply wash it, remove the ends, and cut it into lengths specified in your recipe.

Pan-Fried Okra

Pan-fried okra is a favorite of many folks. If you're lucky, your assistants in the kitchen won't have snatched it all away, and you'll still have some left to take to the table.

Preparation time: *10 minutes*

Cooking time: *20 minutes*

Yield: *4 servings*

2 pounds okra	*¼ teaspoon pepper*
1 cup white cornmeal	*Canola oil, or other vegetable oil to fill skillet ½-inch deep*
½ teaspoon salt	
½ teaspoon onion salt	

1 Wash the okra and remove the ends. Slice it into ½-inch slices.

2 In large bowl, combine the cornmeal, salt, onion salt, and pepper. Toss the okra into the cornmeal mixture to coat.

3 Put the oil in a 12-inch cast-iron skillet on a stovetop burner that's set on medium-high heat. When a few drops of water dance, add the okra. Cook, turning with a spatula, until the okra is brown, about 20 minutes.

4 Drain on several layers of paper towels.

Per serving: Calories 331 (From Fat 135); Fat 15g (Saturated 1g); Cholesterol 0mg; Sodium 531mg; Carbohydrate 45g (Dietary Fiber 9g); Protein 8g.

Spicy Stir-Fried Okra

This recipe includes gingerroot. To get the best ginger flavor from your gingerroot, choose wisely: Select a root whose skin is smooth. Shriveled skin means that the root is dried out. Cut away the tough outer peel, being careful to leave the flesh just beneath: That's where the best flavor is. You can store unused gingerroot in the refrigerator for up to a week and in the freezer for up to two months.

Preparation time: *5 minutes*

Cooking time: *7 to 10 minutes*

Yield: *6 servings*

1½ pounds fresh okra	*1 onion, sliced*
1 to 2 tablespoons olive oil	*2 fresh tomatoes, chopped*
1 teaspoon yellow mustard seeds	*¼ teaspoon ground cumin*
2 garlic cloves, minced	*1 teaspoon turmeric*
1 teaspoon grated fresh gingerroot	*Salt*

1 Wash the okra and cut it into ¾-inch diagonal slices, discarding the ends.

2 Heat the oil in a 12-inch cast-iron skillet or a cast-iron wok on medium high. Add the mustard seeds, cooking and stirring until the mustard seeds pop, about 2 minutes. If necessary, briefly cover and remove from heat until mustard seeds stop popping. Return to heat.

3 Add the garlic, ginger, onion, and okra and sauté for 2 minutes. Stir in the tomatoes, cumin, and turmeric. Cook and stir until the okra becomes slightly tender, 3 to 5 minutes, turning the heat down if necessary. Salt to taste.

Per serving: Calories 85 (From Fat 26; Fat 3g (Saturated 0g); Cholesterol 0mg; Sodium 106mg; Carbohydrate 14g (Dietary Fiber 4g); Protein 3g.

Going for the gold . . . er . . . greens

Turnip greens are the leafy tops of the turnip root and, in many areas, have surpassed the turnip itself for popularity and usefulness. The leaves are light green, thin, and covered in hair. The most challenging part of cooking turnip greens is cleaning them. To clean turnip greens (or any other leafy green vegetables), follow these steps:

1. **Place the batches of greens in a sink of cold water and soak the greens for 20 minutes.**

   Don't pack the sink too full. Greens need room to float. As they rise to the top of the water, the dirt is left at the bottom of the sink.

2. **Remove the greens from the water, being careful not to stir the water, and repeat Step 1.**

3. **Rinse greens thoroughly in a colander under running water.**

4. **Remove thick veins and stems; break leaves into medium-size pieces.**

Don't want to go to the hassle of cleaning your own greens? Buy them pre-cleaned from your grocery store. Many grocery stores now carry ready-to-cook greens and collards.

Turnip Greens Southern Style

This recipe calls for 3 pounds of greens. That's plenty of greens, but when cooked, they shrink to about one-quarter of their original volume.

Preparation time: 45 minutes (10 minutes with precleaned greens)

Cooking time: 3 hours

Yield: 6 servings

½ pound sliced salt pork (or thickly sliced bacon), chopped into 1-inch pieces	*3 pounds turnip greens* *½ cup chicken broth* *½ teaspoon sugar*	*Salt and pepper* *4 turnips, peeled and diced (optional)*

1 Clean the greens and tear into medium-size pieces.

2 In a large cast-iron Dutch oven (7 quarts or bigger), fry the salt pork over medium-high heat until cooked but not crisp. Add the greens, turning them over several times to coat with the pork drippings.

3 Add the broth, sugar, and salt and pepper. (You can adjust the salt and pepper to taste by adding more during the last part of cooking, so don't go crazy at this point.) Reduce heat and cover the Dutch oven, simmering the greens very gently.

4 Greens release liquid as they cook, but check occasionally to make sure the pan hasn't gone dry. You may have to add just enough water to keep it from scorching, but never cover the greens with water. Cook the greens until tender, about 2½ to 3 hours. If desired, add diced turnips about half way through cooking time.

Per serving: Calories 310 (From Fat 266); Fat 30g (Saturated 10g); Cholesterol 32mg; Sodium 713mg; Carbohydrate 8g (Dietary Fiber 6g); Protein 5g.

Frying green tomatoes

Native to South America and spreading around the world with the discovery of the New World, the tomato is an American classic. The Italians thought that tomatoes were an aphrodisiac when they first appeared in Italy, and the early American colonists thought tomatoes were poisonous. But the tomato is neither a love potion nor a death knell. It's another fruit that masquerades as a vegetable and comes in a number of varieties:

- ✔ **Cherry tomatoes:** These bite-size red tomatoes are used in salads and as appetizers.

- ✔ **Plum tomatoes:** Also known as *Italian tomatoes* or *Roma tomatoes,* they're egg-shaped and good for cooked dishes, such as sauces, stews, and chilis.

- ✔ **Round tomatoes:** Also called *beefsteak* tomatoes, these are the workhorses of the tomato varieties. Good for slicing, dicing, quartering, or leaving whole, these tomatoes are in everything from sandwiches to salads to stews and sauces.

But a tomato doesn't have to be ripe to be delicious, as the Fried Green Tomatoes recipe proves.

Fried Green Tomatoes

Until the popular movie *Fried Green Tomatoes at the Whistle Stop Café* (based on the novel of the same name by Fannie Flagg) came out in 1992, many people beyond the South had never heard of or experienced this Southern side dish and snack. When done right, fried green tomatoes have just the right mix of tang and crunch. Any unripe tomato will do.

Preparation time: *20 to 35 minutes*

Cooking time: *About 6 minutes per batch*

Yield: *6 servings*

4 firm medium green tomatoes

½ teaspoon salt

½ teaspoon garlic salt

¼ teaspoon pepper

½ to 1 cup all-purpose flour

1 stick butter

Vegetable oil

1 Wash and core the tomatoes but don't peel. Slice into ½-inch slices.

2 Lay the slices on wax paper or parchment paper. Sprinkle the salt, garlic salt, and pepper on both sides of the tomato slices. Set aside for 15 to 30 minutes.

3 Dredge the tomato slices in flour and place the slices on a baking sheet.

4 Put the butter in a 12-inch cast-iron skillet, and place the skillet on a burner set to medium high. Melt butter and, if needed, add enough vegetable oil to fill the skillet to about ¼ inch deep.

5 When the butter is hot (a pinch of flour sizzles but doesn't burn), add a layer of the tomato slices. Don't crowd the skillet, as the slices shouldn't touch. Fry each side until light golden brown, about 2 to 3 minutes per side, turning carefully with a spatula or tongs.

6 Remove to the paper towels to drain. Use a slotted spoon and skim the oil to keep it clean between batches. Add more butter and oil if necessary and repeat the frying process for the remainder of the tomatoes.

Vary It! *Use cornmeal to coat the tomatoes instead of flour. Or use a coating of half corn-meal and half flour. If you add cornmeal to the recipe, forgo the butter and simply use vegetable oil for frying.*

Per serving: *Calories 192 (From Fat 139); Fat 15g (Saturated 10g); Cholesterol 41mg; Sodium 287mg; Carbohydrate 12g (Dietary Fiber 1g); Protein 2g.*

Basic Veggie Crowd-Pleasers

No matter what kind of mood you're in, you can find a recipe from this section to fit the bill. When you want something more traditional, try the Surprise Veggies for a Crowd. With this vegetable medley, you can combine any vegetables you have on hand or feel inclined to include. (Of course, I offer some suggestions.)

And when you want to try something different and a little unexpected, check out the Cornbread Salad, which puts a traditional hot dish in a cold salad, or the Skillet Cabbage, which puts a traditional salad ingredient on the stove-top. If you just want to try something fun, get out the fry pan for the fried vegetables.

Surprise Veggies for a Crowd

You can prepare the vegetables for this dish the day before; just store them in plastic storage bags in the refrigerator, being careful to put each vegetable in its own bag. If you're in a hurry or just aren't inclined to clean and prep the veggies for this recipe yourself, buy already prepared bags of broccoli and cauliflower florets. You can find them — along with the baby carrots — in your grocer's produce section. You may even be able to find the bell peppers pre-cut, too. With these items prepared beforehand, you're just left with the rutabaga and squash. Also note that you need 1 cup of vegetables for every person that you plan to serve.

Preparation time: *20 minutes*

Cooking time: *20 to 30 minutes*

Yield: *8 servings*

1 cup broccoli florets	*1 onion, peeled and sliced into rings*
1 cup cauliflower florets	*1 rutabaga, peeled and cubed*
1 cup red bell pepper rings	*Salt and pepper*
1 cup yellow bell pepper rings	*1 stick of butter, cut into 8 pieces*
1 cup baby carrots	*16 ounces Parmesan cheese*
1 cup peeled, seeded, and cubed butternut squash	

1 Put about ¼ inch of water in a 5- or 7-quart cast-iron Dutch oven. Set the burner on the stovetop to medium high.

2 Layer the vegetables into the pot. Salt and pepper the vegetables — more than seems enough. Slice up the butter and place the butter slices on top.

3 Reduce the heat to medium low when vegetables are steaming. When the carrots are tender, remove the pan from the heat and use the baster to remove the water. Spread the grated Parmesan over the veggies and cover them with the lid until the cheese is melted. Stand back and wait for folks to ask for seconds.

Vary It! *You can use any vegetables you want for this recipe. Same goes for the cheese. Use one cheese or a combination of cheeses. Be creative!*

Per serving: *Calories 408 (From Fat 258); Fat 29g (Saturated 18g); Cholesterol 76mg; Sodium 1,151mg; Carbohydrate 14g (Dietary Fiber 3g); Protein 25g.*

Cornbread Salad

Who knew that you could use cornbread in a salad? Make the cornbread several hours or even the day before you assemble the rest of the salad. And even though the finished salad sets in the refrigerator overnight, the cornbread retains its consistency, giving the salad a nice texture and absorbing the flavors of the other ingredients.

Preparation time: *30 minutes*

Cooking time: *About 35 minutes*

Chilling time: *Overnight*

Yield: *8 servings*

8 slices bacon	1 cup finely chopped bell pepper
2 eggs	1½ cups chopped fresh tomato
8 ounces sour cream	1 cup sweet pickle relish or cubes
1 cup self-rising cornmeal mix	1 cup mayonnaise
1 cup finely chopped onion	8 to 12 ounces finely grated sharp cheddar cheese

1 Make the cornbread: Preheat oven to 400 degrees. Fry the bacon in a 10-inch cast-iron skillet until crisp over medium to medium-high heat. Drain the bacon on paper towels; let it cool. Crumble the bacon and set it aside. Reserve two tablespoons of the bacon drippings in a small cup.

2 Drain off the remaining drippings and wipe the skillet clean with a paper towel. Return the reserved bacon drippings to the skillet and place it in the oven to heat.

3 In a bowl, beat the eggs. Stir in the sour cream and the cornmeal and blend well with a spoon. Carefully remove the hot skillet from the oven and pour the hot bacon drippings into the batter. Blend well. Pour the batter into the hot skillet and bake it for 20 minutes or until it's golden brown. Remove it from the oven, let it cool for about 5 minutes, and turn onto a plate to cool completely. When it's completely cool, crumble it into a large bowl and set it aside.

4 Make the salad: In a bowl, stir together the onion, bell pepper, tomato, pickle relish, and mayonnaise. Add it to the crumbled cornbread and mix it well.

5 Cover and refrigerate the mixture overnight. Top it with grated cheese and bacon right before serving.

Per serving: *Calories 556 (From Fat 382); Fat 43g (Saturated 15g); Cholesterol 117mg; Sodium 1,022mg; Carbohydrate 32g (Dietary Fiber 3g); Protein 14g.*

Deep-Fried Veggies

Deep-fried vegetables are great as an appetizer. Broccoli, cauliflower, eggplant, onion, mushrooms, and zucchini are ideal vegetables for this recipe. Of course, no vegetable is a bad one, so get creative. Just be sure to have a fry basket on hand.

Preparation time: *10 minutes*

Cooking time: *2 to 3 minutes*

Yield: *2 servings*

Seasoning Mix (see the following recipe)

1 cup zucchini, peeled and cut into 1-inch pieces

1 cup mushrooms

½ cup all-purpose flour

½ cup bread crumbs

½ cup milk

1 egg

Oil for frying

1 Sprinkle ½ teaspoon of the Seasoning Mix evenly over the moist zucchini and mushrooms. Place the flour in a bowl and the breadcrumbs in a second bowl. Add 1 teaspoon of the Seasoning Mix to the flour and 1 teaspoon of the Seasoning Mix to the breadcrumbs and then mix each well.

2 In a separate bowl, combine the milk and egg.

3 Preheat the oil in a deep skillet or fry pan to 350 degrees.

4 Dredge the zucchini and mushrooms in the seasoned flour, shaking off the excess. Next, dip the vegetables into the milk mixture and then dredge them through the breadcrumb mixture, shaking off the excess.

5 Place the zucchini and mushrooms into the basket and carefully lower it into the hot oil and cook approximately 2 to 3 minutes or until golden brown. Drain on paper towels and serve immediately.

Seasoning Mix

1⅛ teaspoon salt

¾ teaspoon paprika

½ teaspoon white pepper

¼ teaspoon onion powder

¼ teaspoon garlic powder

¼ teaspoon cayenne pepper

¼ teaspoon pepper

¼ teaspoon dried thyme

⅛ teaspoon dried basil

In a bowl, combine all the ingredients and blend thoroughly.

Per serving: Calories 438 (From Fat 185); Fat 21g (Saturated 4g); Cholesterol 115mg; Sodium 522mg; Carbohydrate 50g (Dietary Fiber 3g); Protein 14g.

Skillet Cabbage

Although you may be tempted to save time on this recipe by buying prechopped cabbage at the grocery store, try to resist the urge. Prepackaged cabbage is generally shredded rather than chopped and is best reserved for salads and slaws. In this recipe, the smaller shredded pieces will turn mushy during cooking.

Preparation time: *10 minutes*

Cooking time: *15 to 20 minutes*

Yield: *6 servings*

3 tablespoons canola oil

2 large onions, sliced

1 green pepper, seeded and chopped

4 cups red or green cabbage, chopped

2 tomatoes, peeled and chopped

2 teaspoons sugar

Salt and pepper

1 Heat the oil in your cast-iron deep skillet on medium-high heat.

2 Sauté the onion and green pepper until the onions are translucent, about 10 minutes. Reduce the heat to medium.

3 Add the cabbage, tomatoes, and sugar. Stir and toss to combine.

4 Cook over medium heat for about 10 to 15 minutes, until the cabbage is tender but not mushy.

5 Add the salt and pepper to taste during last 2 minutes.

Per serving: *Calories 121 (From Fat 67); Fat 7g (Saturated 1g); Cholesterol 0mg; Sodium 107mg; Carbohydrate 13g (Dietary Fiber 3g); Protein 2g.*

Fried Eggplant

When you buy eggplant, look for ones that are smooth and firm and have an even, dark-purple color. One medium eggplant (approximately 1½ pounds) is enough to feed four people.

Preparation time: *35 minutes*

Cooking time: *6 minutes per batch*

Yield: *6 servings*

2 eggplants	*½ cup milk*
Salt and pepper	*1 cup of all-purpose flour, or more*
1 egg, slightly beaten	*Vegetable oil to fill skillet ½-inch deep*

1 To prepare the eggplant, peel and slice it into ½-inch-thick rounds. Place the eggplant slices in a very large bowl with very cold salted water. Cover with a plate to keep the eggplant submerged in the water. Let it stand for about 30 minutes. Discard the water and drain the eggplant in a colander. Lay the eggplant slices on wax paper and sprinkle them with the salt and pepper.

2 In a shallow, wide-mouthed bowl, combine the egg and milk. Put the flour on another piece of wax paper.

3 Prepare a baking sheet covered with wax paper.

4 Dip the eggplant slices into the milk mixture; then dredge them in flour. Lay the eggplant slices on the baking sheet.

5 Pour the vegetable oil in your 12-inch skillet; set it on a burner to medium-high heat. If a pinch of flour sizzles but doesn't burn, the oil is hot.

6 Place the eggplant slices in the skillet so that they don't touch. Cook the eggplant slices until they're golden brown on both sides, about 3 minutes per side.

7 In between batches, clean the oil by skimming with a slotted spoon or skimmer. Adjust the heat if necessary to keep the oil from becoming too hot or cool.

Per serving: *Calories 264 (From Fat 144); Fat 16g (Saturated 2g); Cholesterol 38mg; Sodium 123mg; Carbohydrate 26g (Dietary Fiber 4g); Protein 5g.*

Chapter 11

Cornbread and Biscuits

In This Chapter

▶ Reviewing some corny tricks

▶ Trying some tried and true cornbread recipes

▶ Discovering the secret of fluffy biscuits

▶ Adding variety to basic and flavored biscuit recipes

Cornbread and biscuits are two foods that are ridiculously simple to make. They don't require you to assemble a long list of ingredients, spend much time preparing them, or master hard-to-learn cooking methods. In fact, from start to finish, you can get a version of either to the table in less than 30 minutes.

So why do cornbread and biscuits have a reputation for being hard to make? Because just as making good cornbread and biscuits is easy, making bad cornbread and biscuits is even easier — not inedible, mind you, but uninspired, flat, tough, gritty, dense, and dry. Making cornbread and biscuits isn't a mystery. In this chapter, I explain what you need to know about the ingredients and the mixing methods. (It matters, especially when you make biscuits.) And share a few other trade secrets. Before you know it, your biscuits and cornbread will be the highlight of the meal.

Anybody can make great cornbread and biscuits. All it takes is a little know-how and a cast-iron skillet.

You're Cookin' Cornbreads Now

Good cornbread is moist on the inside and has a nice golden crust — not gritty, not dry. And it doesn't crumble like 2,000-year-old plaster. Cornbread is also versatile. You can serve it with soups and stews or anything else that has gravy that you want to sop up. You can crumble it for salads. (Chapter 10 has a recipe.) You can use it in stuffing. You can even make a milkshake out of it. (No kidding! Check out the "Tennessee milkshake" sidebar in this chapter.)

The biggest factor affecting the taste and texture of your cornbread is the type of cornmeal you use. Cornmeal is divided by color and by the *milling* (grinding) method.

- **Color:** Although the recipes in this section specify a type of cornmeal, you can use whatever you have available. Just keep in mind that using a different meal than the one specified will influence the flavor of your bread.

  - **Yellow:** This cornmeal, the favorite in the northern states, has a more potent corn flavor.

  - **White:** Folks in the South favor white cornmeal, which has a milder corn flavor.

  - **Blue:** The recipes in this chapter don't call for the blue stuff. But if you're feeling creative, go for it.

- **Grinding method:** Most of the cornmeal you buy from supermarkets is milled in either of two ways. The milling method is usually specified on the package; if it isn't specified, assume that it's been milled in the first of the following two methods:

  - **Ground by steel rollers:** Many major supermarket brands are ground using steel rollers. The result is meal that's finer in texture. Cornmeal ground this way is almost always *degermed* — that is, it has had the *germ,* the outer coating of the kernel, removed. Its uniform color tells you that it's degermed cornmeal. You can store this cornmeal for up to a year in a cool, dry place, such as your kitchen cabinet or pantry.

  - **Stone ground:** In this milling method, which is sometimes called *water ground,* the corn is ground with millstones. The result is a meal that's slightly coarser in texture than cornmeal ground by steel rollers. Cornmeal that's stone ground isn't completely *degermed,* which means that you can see flecks of different colors in the meal. You need to store stone-ground meal in an airtight container in your refrigerator or freezer because of its higher oil and moisture content. Simply bring it to room temperature before you use it.

People, like cornmeal, fall into categories: Those who have a favorite type of cornmeal and those who don't care and will use whatever's available. If you know that you like sweet cornbread, for example, or cornbread that has a crisper rather than moister texture, you can buy the cornmeal that produces the kind of cornbread you like. If you're not a cornbread aficionado and have a container of Quaker cornmeal that you want to use up, use away. Remember, it's *all* good.

Basic cornbread recipes

Generally, southern folks prefer unsweetened cornbread with a crisp crust. They like white cornmeal. Northerners prefer sweeter cornbread with a more cake-like consistency. They go with yellow cornmeal. Whatever kind of cornmeal you go with, keep this tip in mind:

Always preheat your skillet or pan with shortening in it. The hot skillet and melted shortening gives your cornbread a crispier, tastier crust.

Real Southern Cornbread

Real southern cornbread isn't sweet. In fact, it uses little or no sugar. The tang in the buttermilk and the bacon grease give this cornbread its flavor.

Preparation time: *10 minutes*

Cooking time: *30 to 40 minutes*

Yield: *8 slices*

3 tablespoons bacon grease, or vegetable oil

2 cups white, self-rising cornmeal mix

½ teaspoon baking soda

2 eggs, beaten

2 cups buttermilk

1 Preheat your oven to 450 degrees.

2 Put the bacon grease into a 9-inch cast-iron skillet and place it in the oven to get really hot.

3 Blend the cornmeal mix, baking soda, eggs, and buttermilk in a bowl, using a spoon or fork.

4 When the skillet and bacon grease are really hot, carefully remove the skillet from the oven and pour the hot bacon grease into the batter. Quickly stir the bacon grease into the batter.

5 Pour the batter into the hot skillet. It should sizzle and may splatter. Bake for 30 to 40 minutes or until golden brown.

6 Remove from the oven and let it cool 5 to 10 minutes. Invert onto a plate, revealing crispy brown crust. Cut into wedges and serve hot (with plenty of butter).

Per serving: Calories 204 (From Fat 58); Fat 6g (Saturated 2g); Cholesterol 60mg; Sodium 692mg; Carbohydrate 29g (Dietary Fiber 2g); Protein 7g.

Yankee Cornbread

This recipe is for folks who like their cornbread yellow and sweet. You can influence how sweet your cornbread is by experimenting with the amount of sugar you add. If this recipe is just a touch too sweet, add less sugar — 2 tablespoons instead of the ¼ cup, for example.

Preparation time: 10 minutes

Cooking time: 20 to 25 minutes

Yield: 8 slices

2½ cups yellow self-rising cornmeal mix

¼ cup sugar

1 cup milk

¼ cup vegetable oil

2 eggs, slightly beaten

1 Preheat your oven to 425 degrees. Grease a 10-inch cast-iron skillet.

2 In a large bowl, combine the cornmeal mix, sugar, milk, oil, and eggs and blend well with a spoon; pour into skillet.

3 Bake for 20 to 25 minutes or until a toothpick inserted in the center comes out clean.

Vary It! *For corn muffins, grease muffin cups, fill with batter about ⅔ full and bake for 15 to 20 minutes.*

Per serving: Calories 290 (From Fat 94); Fat 10g (Saturated 2g); Cholesterol 57mg; Sodium 491mg; Carbohydrate 43g (Dietary Fiber 2g); Protein 6g.

The self-rising cornmeal story

With *self-rising cornmeal mix* the flour, salt, and leavening (the stuff that makes the bread rise) is already added. If a recipe calls for self-rising cornmeal mix, and you have only plain cornmeal, you can make your own: Combine 1 cup cornmeal, 1 cup flour, 1 tablespoon baking powder, 1 teaspoon salt; then cut in ¼ cup butter or shortening. In some regions of the country that are more cornbread crazy than others, *self-rising cornmeal* is available. Self-rising cornmeal (no *mix* on the end) contains cornmeal, salt, and the leavening agent but doesn't contain flour.

Spoon Bread

Spoon bread is a cross between cornbread and a soufflé, rising sky high when you cook it and falling when you remove it from the oven. So named because you serve it with a spoon and eat it with a fork, spoon bread is great as a side dish in place of potatoes or rice. ***Note:*** The key to good spoon bread is a lump-free mush. Pour the meal into the hot liquid quickly and to stir like crazy, using a wire whisk; then keep stirring until the mush begins to thicken.

Preparation time: *15 minutes*

Cooking time: *35 minutes*

Yield: *8 to 10 servings*

2 cups whole milk	*2 tablespoons melted butter*
½ cup cornmeal	*2 eggs, separated*
1 teaspoon salt	*½ teaspoon baking powder*

1 Preheat your oven to 400 degrees. Grease a 12-inch, deep, cast-iron skillet and place it in your hot oven.

2 In a 3-quart saucepan, heat the milk until simmering. Gradually add the cornmeal and salt to the hot milk, stirring constantly. Continue to blend until the cornmeal has absorbed the milk and becomes stiff. Add the butter, blend well, and remove from the heat.

3 Using an electric mixer, beat the egg yolks and baking powder in a separate bowl until well blended.

4 Pour the egg mixture into the cornmeal batter. Blend well and set aside.

5 In a separate mixing bowl, beat the egg whites until stiff. Using a large serving spoon, gently fold the egg whites into the batter.

6 Pour the batter into a preheated 12-inch skillet and bake for 35 minutes. The bread will be done when firm to the touch and golden brown.

Vary It! *Add shredded cheese when you add the butter in Step 2.*

Per serving: *Calories 90 (From Fat 45); Fat 5g (Saturated 3g); Cholesterol 55mg; Sodium 287mg; Carbohydrate 8g (Dietary Fiber 1g); Protein 4g.*

Hushpuppies

Legend has it that the Ursuline nuns developed the hushpuppy in the early 1700s. Native Americans gave the nuns some cornmeal, which the nuns converted into a delicious fritter called *croquettes de maise*. The name *hushpuppy* came about when an old Creole cook was frying a batch of catfish and croquettes. His hungry dogs began to howl in anticipation of a chance to savor some of the catfish. The innovative Creole instead tossed a few of the croquettes de maise to the dogs and yelled, "Hush, puppies!" The name has since been associated with this cornmeal delicacy.

Preparation time: 15 minutes

Cooking time: 3 minutes

Yield: 6 to 8 servings

1 cup self-rising flour	*1 egg, beaten*
1 cup self-rising cornmeal mix	*1 cup buttermilk*
½ teaspoon salt	*½ cup chopped green onion*
1 teaspoon sugar	

1 In a cast-iron deep fryer, preheat the oil to 375 degrees.

2 Combine the flour, cornmeal mix, salt, and sugar in a mixing bowl. Add the egg and ½ cup of the buttermilk to mix to a stiff batter. Stir in the onions.

3 Add more buttermilk a little at a time until the batter is well mixed and let it stand for 10 minutes.

4 Drop it by spoonfuls into the hot oil and fry until golden brown.

Per serving: Calories 266 (From Fat 139); Fat 15g (Saturated 1g); Cholesterol 28mg; Sodium 617mg; Carbohydrate 27g (Dietary Fiber 2g); Protein 5g.

Flavored cornbreads

Cornbread purists like their cornbread plain, with a little (or much) butter. Others like to experiment, tossing in a few herbs here or some cheese there, to create their own special breads. If you want the variety that flavored cornbread offers but aren't the kind to experiment yourself, try these recipes. They just may inspire you.

Broccoli Cornbread

Don't worry about the moisture from the thawed broccoli causing your cornbread to go soggy. This recipe uses the moisture of the broccoli and the melted butter as the liquid that binds the ingredients.

Preparation time: *10 minutes*

Cooking time: *35 to 45 minutes*

Yield: *8 to 10 slices*

2 sticks butter

4 eggs

10 ounces frozen chopped broccoli, thawed

1 medium onion, finely chopped

8 ounces cottage cheese

2 boxes corn muffin mix

½ cup self-rising cornmeal mix

1 Preheat your oven to 375 degrees. Put the butter in a 12-inch cast-iron skillet and place the skillet in the oven to melt the butter while preparing the batter.

2 In a large bowl, beat the eggs. Add the broccoli, onion, cottage cheese, muffin mix, and cornmeal mix and mix well.

3 Remove the skillet from the oven and pour the hot, melted butter into the cornbread mixture. Mix well.

4 Pour the mixture into the hot skillet and bake for 35 to 45 minutes or until golden brown. Serve warm.

Per serving: Calories 454 (From Fat 247); Fat 27g (Saturated 14g); Cholesterol 138mg; Sodium 785mg; Carbohydrate 42g (Dietary Fiber 5g); Protein 10g.

Quick breads

Cornbread is considered a quick bread, just as muffins and biscuits are, because you don't have to use yeast as a *leavener* (rising agent): The upshot? You can mix all the ingredients in the time it takes to preheat your oven. These breads, unlike yeast breads, don't take hours to rise. The leaveners that you use in quick breads are baking soda and baking powder. If you use self-rising cornmeal mix, you can do so without these leaveners entirely, because the cornmeal contains them already.

Sour Cream Cornbread

The combination of white cornmeal, sour cream, and cream-style corn make this cornbread especially moist.

Preparation time: *10 minutes*

Cooking time: *45 minutes*

Yield: *8 slices*

½ cup vegetable oil	*1 cup white, self-rising cornmeal mix*
1 can (8 ounces) cream-style corn	*3 eggs, beaten*
1 cup sour cream	*¾ teaspoon salt*

1 Preheat your oven to 400 degrees. Place ¼ cup of the oil in a 9-inch cast-iron skillet and place the skillet in the oven to heat.

2 Mix the rest of the oil with the corn, sour cream, cornmeal mix, eggs, and salt.

3 When the skillet and oil are really hot, remove the skillet from the oven and carefully pour the hot oil into the batter. Mix well.

4 Pour the batter into the hot skillet. Bake for about 45 minutes or until golden brown.

Per serving: *Calories 314 (From Fat 205); Fat 23g (Saturated 5g); Cholesterol 92mg; Sodium 339mg; Carbohydrate 22g (Dietary Fiber 2g); Protein 6g.*

Mexican Cornbread

You can make this cornbread as mild or as hot as you like by using more or fewer hot peppers.

Preparation time: *10 minutes*

Cooking time: *40 to 45 minutes*

Yield: *12 squares*

1¼ cup white, self-rising cornmeal mix	*⅓ cup cooking oil*	*¼ cup finely diced onion*
2 eggs, beaten	*1 can (8 ounces) cream-style corn*	*1 small jalapeno pepper, seeded and chopped*
¾ cup milk	*½ green bell pepper, seeded and diced*	*½ teaspoon salt*
¾ cup grated cheddar cheese		*½ teaspoon baking powder*

1 Preheat your oven to 400 degrees. Grease a 10-inch cast-iron skillet or spray it with cooking spray.

2 Mix all the ingredients together.

3 Bake for 40 to 45 minutes or until golden brown.

Per serving: Calories 180 (From Fat 94); Fat 11g (Saturated 3g); Cholesterol 45mg; Sodium 429mg; Carbohydrate 16g (Dietary Fiber 2g); Protein 5g.

Cheesy Green Pepper Corn Muffins

A cheesy cornbread with a twist: green pepper and onion. If you don't have a muffin pan, use a 10-inch skillet and bake for 30 to 40 minutes or until golden.

Preparation time: *10 minutes*

Cooking time: *15 to 18 minutes*

Yield: *18 muffins*

2 cups all-purpose flour	*½ cup finely shredded cheddar cheese*
1 cup yellow cornmeal	*2 tablespoons finely chopped green pepper*
⅓ cup sugar	*¼ cup chopped onion*
4½ teaspoons baking powder	*1½ cups milk*
1½ teaspoons salt	*2 eggs, beaten*
½ cup vegetable shortening	

1 Preheat your oven and well-greased cast-iron muffin pan to 400 degrees.

2 In a large bowl, combine the flour, cornmeal, sugar, baking powder, and salt; cut in the shortening until the mixture resembles coarse crumbs. Stir in the cheese, pepper, and onion.

3 In a small bowl, combine the milk and eggs; stir into the dry ingredients just until blended.

4 Fill the muffin molds almost full. Bake at 400 degrees for 15 to 18 minutes or until golden brown.

Per serving: Calories 178 (From Fat 74); Fat 8g (Saturated 3g); Cholesterol 30mg; Sodium 326mg; Carbohydrate 22g (Dietary Fiber 1g); Protein 4g.

Raspberry Dazzler Cornbread

More of a cake than a traditional cornbread, you can serve this in place of coffeecake for breakfast or after dinner as dessert.

Preparation time: *10 minutes*

Cooking time: *30 minutes*

Yield: *18 servings*

1 cup self-rising flour	*2 egg yolks*
1 cup self-rising cornmeal mix	*1½ sticks butter, melted and cooled*
¾ cup sugar	*¾ cup milk*
1½ tablespoons finely grated lemon zest	*1½ cups fresh raspberries*
1 egg	*2 to 3 tablespoons sugar*

1 Preheat your oven to 400 degrees. Grease a 9-inch cast-iron skillet with shortening.

2 In a large bowl, mix the flour, cornmeal mix, sugar, and lemon zest.

3 In another bowl, beat the egg and egg yolks, butter, and milk. Stir it into the flour mixture. Gently stir in the raspberries.

4 Pour the mixture into the skillet and bake in the middle of the oven for 25 minutes. Sprinkle the top with sugar and bake for an additional 5 minutes.

Per serving: *Calories 179 (From Fat 81); Fat 9g (Saturated 5g); Cholesterol 57mg; Sodium 202mg; Carbohydrate 22g (Dietary Fiber 2g); Protein 3g.*

Tennessee milkshake

Forget the ice cream. In Tennessee, you can make a milkshake with just cornbread and milk. Here's how:

1. Fill a glass a little over half full of milk.

2. Crumble plain, old cornbread into the milk until the glass is almost full.

3. Stir it around a little to get the bread saturated.

Pretty simple. In fact, this recipe has no science or precise measurement. If you like your shake thicker, use less milk and more cornbread. Want it thinner? More milk and less cornbread. You can even be daring and add a little sugar to the mix.

Cornsticks

Cornsticks are basically cornbread cooked in single-serving portions. The benefit of making cornsticks is that you end up with more crispy edges, my favorite part of cornbread, and I'm sure I'm not alone on this one.

A traditional favorite shape for cornstick molds is the ear of corn. But don't be bound by tradition. If you're whimsical, you can find cornstick molds with other shapes: stars, fish, cacti, and more. If you do use a specially molded pan, make sure that the batter fills the entire impression. After all, what good's a fish without its fin?

Simple Cornsticks

To help the cornstick release from the pan, grease and sprinkle a little cornmeal into each impression.

Preparation time: *10 minutes*

Cooking time: *15 to 20 minutes*

Yield: *14 cornsticks*

2 tablespoon bacon drippings

2 tablespoons vegetable oil

1 cup white, self-rising cornmeal mix

2 tablespoons all-purpose flour

1 tablespoon sugar

1 egg, beaten

1 cup buttermilk

1 Heat your oven to 450 degrees. Grease the impressions of cast-iron cornstick pans with bacon grease. Place the cornstick pan in the oven while preheating to get really hot. Heat the vegetable oil on the stovetop in a small saucepan.

2 In a large bowl, mix the cornmeal mix, flour, sugar, egg, and buttermilk together with spoon. Pour the hot oil into the batter and blend.

3 Remove the hot cornstick pan from the oven, lightly sprinkle some cornmeal into the bottom of the cornstick impressions, and fill the impressions about ⅔ full with batter. Bake for 15 to 20 minutes or until golden brown.

Per serving: *Calories 90 (From Fat 43); Fat 5g (Saturated 1g); Cholesterol 18mg; Sodium 169mg; Carbohydrate 10g (Dietary Fiber 1g); Protein 2g.*

Buttermilk Cornsticks

Another variation of a basic cornstick recipe, this one doesn't require bacon grease — an ingredient that many cooks don't keep as staples in their pantries.

Preparation time: *10 minutes*

Cooking time: *15 minutes*

Yield: *14 cornsticks*

1 cup yellow cornmeal	1 teaspoon salt
1 cup all-purpose flour	¼ cup margarine
2 teaspoons baking powder	1 cup buttermilk
¼ teaspoon baking soda	2 eggs

1 Preheat your oven and well-greased cast-iron cornstick pans to 475 degrees.

2 In a mixing bowl, combine the cornmeal, flour, baking powder, baking soda, and salt. Cut in the margarine. Add the buttermilk and eggs, blending well.

3 Pour the batter into hot pans. Bake at 475 degrees for 15 minutes.

Per serving: Calories 115 (From Fat 39); Fat 4g (Saturated 1g); Cholesterol 31mg; Sodium 309mg; Carbohydrate 15g (Dietary Fiber 1g); Protein 3g.

Dilly Cornsticks

Dill weed (the leaves of the dill plant) has a milder flavor than *dill seed* (the seeds of the plant). If you want a stronger dill flavor, don't substitute dill seed. Instead increase the amount of dill weed slightly.

Preparation time: *10 minutes*

Cooking time: *15 to 18 minutes*

Yield: *15 cornsticks*

1 cup all-purpose flour	1 teaspoon dill weed
1 cup yellow cornmeal	1 tablespoon minced onion
2 tablespoons sugar	2 eggs
1 tablespoon baking soda	1 cup plus 2 tablespoons milk
½ teaspoon salt	¼ cup oil

1 Preheat your oven to 425 degrees. Place a greased cast-iron cornstick pan in the oven while preheating.

2 In a large mixing bowl, combine the flour, cornmeal, sugar, baking soda, salt, dill weed, and onion.

3 In another bowl, beat the eggs, milk, and oil together.

4 Pour the liquid into the dry ingredients. Mix until just blended.

5 Fill the cornstick impressions a scant ¾ full.

6 Bake for 15 to 18 minutes or until golden brown. Serve hot and spread a little butter on it.

Per serving: Calories 125 (From Fat 47); Fat 5g (Saturated 1g); Cholesterol 31mg; Sodium 347mg; Carbohydrate 16g (Dietary Fiber 1g); Protein 3g.

Ain't Nothin' Better Than Biscuits

Biscuits are one of the simplest quick breads to make — if you know how. But many people don't know the tips and tricks, and that's probably why biscuits intimidate many cooks.

Making a good biscuit requires a little know-how. A basic biscuit requires only four ingredients — the flour, the fat (usually shortening), the leavener, and the liquid. So, as you can see, the ingredients aren't the key. When you make biscuits, the *process* — how you combine the ingredients — is more important than the ingredients themselves.

Keep reading to find out what it takes to make a light, fluffy biscuits. You'll find plenty of recipes that let you show off your new skill.

Cutting to the biscuit basics

You use a certain mixing technique when you make biscuits: First, cut the shortening or other fat into the dry ingredients, using a pastry cutter or two knives, and then stir in the liquid. This simple technique doesn't seem fraught with peril, but it is. Cutting in the shortening is the part that gives people the most trouble, whether they realize it or not.

When you cut *(rub)* in the shortening, you have to make sure that it's evenly distributed throughout the mixture *without* over-mixing it. The mixture should resemble coarse crumbs; if it has the consistency of paste, you've gone too far. (If you want to know why this is important, hop to the sidebar "High-rise biscuits need gas" in this chapter.) Keep these suggestions in mind:

- ✔ **Keep your shortening or butter cold.** Never make biscuits with butter that's warmed to room temperature. For that matter, refrigerate your shortening for a while to give it a nice chill before you begin. If your shortening or butter is too warm, you'll end up with a paste, which is bad for fluffy biscuits.

- ✔ **Cut the shortening in quickly** — as fast as you can without throwing dough all over your countertop. Use your fingertips (*not* your whole hand — it's too warm), two knives, a pastry blender, a food processor, or an electric blender on pulse.

When you make biscuits, you also want to keep the following in mind:

- ✔ **Don't overknead your dough.** Over kneading makes your biscuits tough.

- ✔ **Don't roll out the dough too thin.** You don't want it any thinner that ½ inch. Better yet, don't roll the dough out at all. Instead shape it by hand.

- ✔ **Don't leave out the salt,** which you may be tempted to do if you're watching your salt intake. The salt activates the leavening ingredients. Without it, your biscuits won't rise.

- ✔ **For crisper sides, place biscuits so they will not touch.** For softer sides, place biscuits so they're barely touching.

Whipping up traditional biscuits

Although you can use any type of flour when you make biscuits, the type does make a difference in the consistency of the biscuit.

- ✔ **Cake:** Also known as *soft flour,* cake flour gives your biscuits a tenderer, moister, more cake-like texture.

- ✔ **All-purpose:** Also known as *strong flour,* all-purpose flour makes the crust crisper and the crumb drier.

Baking Powder Biscuits

You can say plenty about plain biscuits. They're delicious. They go with anything. And you can't beat them when you have some butter and honey that you're anxious to get rid of. These biscuits are also great topped with sausage gravy.

Preparation time: *10 minutes*

Cooking time: *12 minutes*

Yield: *12 biscuits*

2 cups all-purpose flour	*Dash of sugar*
2 teaspoons baking powder	*3 tablespoons vegetable shortening*
¾ teaspoon salt	*⅔ cup milk*

1 Preheat your oven to 450 degrees.

2 In a large bowl, sift together the flour, baking powder, salt, and sugar. Work in the shortening with a pastry cutter or your fingers, until the mixture resembles coarse crumbs.

3 Gradually add the milk, mixing it in with a spoon. The dough should be as soft as can be handled without sticking.

4 Turn the dough onto a lightly floured board and knead for about 30 seconds. Roll out to ½ inch thickness. Cut with a floured biscuit cutter or a can with both ends cut away.

5 Bake in a cast-iron griddle or skillet coated with cooking spray for about 12 minutes.

Per serving: Calories 113 (From Fat 35); Fat 4g (Saturated 1g); Cholesterol 2mg; Sodium 216mg; Carbohydrate 17g (Dietary Fiber 1g); Protein 3g.

High-rise biscuits need gas

For biscuits to rise, the fat needs to be evenly distributed throughout the dough. When your biscuits cook, two actions take place at the same time. The leavener, as it warms, releases gas, and the shortening, as it warms, melts. If the shortening and leavener are evenly distributed, the melting shortening gives the released gas a place to go. This combination of events — the gas releasing into little bubbles that pop in the spaces the melting shortening has opened up — is what causes your biscuits to rise.

If the shortening isn't mixed in very well, the gas doesn't have anywhere to go and just dissipates. If you overmix the shortening (and end up with a paste instead of crumbs), the dough is too heavy and collapses around the gas pockets.

Buttermilk Biscuits

Buttermilk is a key ingredient in many biscuit recipes. It adds flavor and makes a lighter, airier biscuit than regular milk does.

Preparation time: *10 minutes*

Cooking time: *12 minutes*

Yield: *12 to 14 biscuits*

2 cups all-purpose flour	*½ teaspoon baking soda*	*4 tablespoons vegetable shortening*
½ teaspoon salt	*2 teaspoons baking powder*	*1 cup buttermilk*

1 Preheat oven to 450 degrees.

2 In a large bowl, sift together the flour, salt, baking soda, and baking powder. Work in the shortening with a pastry blender or your fingers, until the mixture resembles coarse meal. Slowly stir in the buttermilk until the dough pulls away from the bowl.

3 Turn the dough onto a lightly floured surface, knead for about 30 seconds, and roll to ½ inch thickness. Cut with a floured biscuit cutter, and place on a cast-iron griddle or skillet coated with cooking spray.

4 Bake for about 12 minutes until golden brown on top.

Per serving: Calories 104 (From Fat 36); Fat 4g (Saturated 1g); Cholesterol 1mg; Sodium 201mg; Carbohydrate 15g (Dietary Fiber 1g); Protein 2g.

Buttermilk Drop Biscuits

Drop biscuits are perhaps the easiest to make. Simply mix the ingredients and then drop the spoonfuls of dough into your pan. You can even find special cast-iron pans made especially for drop biscuits so that they'll come out nice and round.

Preparation time: *10 minutes*

Cooking time: *15 to 18 minutes*

Yield: *14 biscuits*

2 cups all-purpose flour	*½ teaspoon cream of tartar*	*1¼ cups buttermilk*
1 tablespoon baking powder	*¼ teaspoon salt*	*2 tablespoons chopped fresh parsley (optional)*
¼ teaspoon baking soda	*½ cup butter or vegetable shortening*	
2 teaspoons sugar		

1 Preheat your oven to 450 degrees.

2 In a bowl, stir together the flour and the baking powder, baking soda, sugar, cream of tartar, and salt. Cut in the butter with a fork or pastry blender, until the mixture resembles coarse crumbs.

3 Add the buttermilk (and parsley, if desired) and stir until just blended.

4 Using a spoon, drop the dough into a greased cast-iron drop biscuit pan (fill quite full) or onto a skillet or griddle.

5 Bake for 15 to 18 minutes or until golden brown. Serve while hot.

Per serving: Calories 134 (From Fat 62); Fat 7g (Saturated 4g); Cholesterol 18mg; Sodium 170mg; Carbohydrate 15g (Dietary Fiber 1g); Protein 3g.

Cornmeal Biscuits

This recipe combines all-purpose flour and cornmeal to create a light and airy biscuit that can stand up to any broth or gravy. These biscuits are perfect for soups and stews.

Preparation time: *10 minutes*

Cooking time: *12 to 15 minutes*

Yield: *8 biscuits*

1¼ cups all-purpose flour	*3 teaspoons baking powder*
¾ cup cornmeal	*4 tablespoons vegetable shortening*
1 teaspoon salt	*⅔ cup milk*
2 teaspoons sugar	

1 Preheat your oven to 375 degrees.

2 In a large bowl, sift together the flour, cornmeal, salt, sugar, and baking powder. Cut in shortening with a pastry blender or fork until the mixture resembles coarse crumbs.

3 Stir in the milk with a fork until the dough just pulls away from the bowl.

4 Turn onto lightly floured surface and roll out to ½ inch thickness. Cut out the biscuits with a floured biscuit cutter.

5 Place on a lightly greased cast-iron skillet or griddle. Bake for 12 to 15 minutes.

Per serving: Calories 145 (From Fat 66); Fat 7g (Saturated 2g); Cholesterol 3mg; Sodium 444mg; Carbohydrate 17g (Dietary Fiber 1g); Protein 3g.

Drop Biscuits

This is just about the simplest biscuit recipe: five basic ingredients sure to be found in any kitchen and no rolling and cutting required. It's perfect for the hurried cook.

Preparation time: *10 minutes*

Cooking time: *10 to 12 minutes*

Yield: *14 biscuits*

2 cups all-purpose flour	3 tablespoons vegetable shortening
3 teaspoons baking powder	2 tablespoons butter
1 teaspoon salt	1 cup milk

1 Heat your oven to 450 degrees.

2 Combine the flour, baking powder, and salt in a bowl.

3 Cut the shortening and butter into dry mixture with a fork or pastry blender until it resembles coarse meal. Add the milk and stir.

4 Drop by spoonfuls onto a greased cast-iron drop biscuit pan, griddle, or skillet.

5 Bake for 10 to 12 minutes.

Per serving: Calories 144 (From Fat 46); Fat 5g (Saturated 2g); Cholesterol 7mg; Sodium 257mg; Carbohydrate 14g (Dietary Fiber 1g); Protein 2g.

The birth of the biscuit

The soft-wheat flours of the South didn't (and still don't) bond well with yeast. To make yeast breads, southern cooks had to import good bread flour from the North. Folks couldn't afford to purchase it. Biscuits were born when commercially prepared baking powder and baking soda became readily available to the southern cook. These ingredients could be combined with the South's soft flour to make biscuits, a yummy substitute for the yeast breads that were common in the North.

When the leavening agents of baking soda and baking powder became available, biscuits became as much a part of southern meals as cornbread and hoe cakes had been before that time.

Flavored biscuits

Many people go no farther when flavoring biscuits than spreading butter and jam or honey on them. But flavored biscuits — that special breed of biscuit with special flavors cooked right in — are a treat not to be missed. In fact, flavored biscuits can stand on their own: No butter needed.

Bacon Biscuits

To enhance the bacon flavor of these biscuits, cook them in the skillet that you used to fry the bacon. Pour out the excess bacon grease (save it for other recipes if you want), wiping the sides of the pan with just enough grease to keep the biscuits from sticking.

Preparation time: *15 minutes*

Cooking time: *10 to 12 minutes*

Yield: *14 biscuits*

8 slices bacon	*2 teaspoons baking powder*
2 cups all-purpose flour	*4 tablespoons vegetable shortening*
½ teaspoon salt	*¾ cup milk*

1 Place a cast-iron skillet on a stovetop burner on medium heat. Fry the bacon until crisp and drain on paper towels. Crumble and set aside.

2 Preheat your oven to 450 degrees.

3 Sift the flour, salt, and baking powder together in a large bowl. Cut in shortening with a fork or pastry blender until the mixture resembles coarse crumbs. Stir in cooked bacon.

4 Stir in the milk with a fork just until dough pulls away from bowl.

5 Turn onto a lightly floured surface and knead it for about 30 seconds or just until smooth. Cut out the biscuits with a floured biscuit cutter.

6 Place on a lightly greased cast-iron skillet or griddle. Bake for 10 to 12 minutes or until golden brown.

Per serving: Calories 126 (From Fat 54); Fat 6g (Saturated 2g); Cholesterol 5mg; Sodium 210mg; Carbohydrate 14g (Dietary Fiber 1g); Protein 3g.

Cheese Biscuits

Pair these flavorful biscuits with a nice dinner salad or bowl of soup for a (relatively) light meal.

Preparation time: *10 minutes*

Cooking time: *12 minutes*

Yield: *12 to 14 biscuits*

2 cups all-purpose flour	1 cup finely shredded sharp cheddar cheese
3 teaspoons baking powder	½ teaspoon dry mustard
¾ teaspoon salt	Scant ¾ cup milk
4 tablespoons vegetable shortening	

1 Preheat your oven to 450 degrees.

2 Sift the flour, baking powder, and salt together in a bowl.

3 With a pastry blender or fork, cut in the shortening until mixture resembles coarse crumbs. Stir in cheese and dry mustard.

4 Stir in the milk with a fork until the dough pulls away from the sides of the bowl.

5 Turn onto lightly floured surface and knead about 10 times or just until the dough is smooth. Roll out the dough to a ½ inch thickness. Cut out the biscuits with a floured biscuit cutter.

6 Place on lightly greased cast-iron skillet or griddle. Bake for about 12 minutes or until golden brown.

Per serving: Calories 139 (From Fat 63); Fat 7g (Saturated 3g); Cholesterol 10mg; Sodium 263mg; Carbohydrate 14g (Dietary Fiber 1g); Protein 4g.

Chapter 12

Pancakes, Muffins, and More

● ●

In This Chapter

▶ Getting a rise out of yeast breads

▶ You want muffins? Oh, I've got muffins

▶ Cooking up breads from America's past

● ●

The reason that cast iron is such a great cookware for breads is because it makes the crusts so much better than anything else you can find. Whether you're making yeast breads, quick breads, or pancakes, the same holds true: The even heat and dark color of cast iron produces a nicer, more consistent crust: one that's uniformly golden and tender.

Even with a well-seasoned cast-iron pan, you may have a problem with the batter or dough sticking. The solution is to simply make sure that you grease your pan with oil or shortening. Well-seasoned cast iron requires only a little greasing; newer cast-iron needs a bit more. If you don't want to add calories and fat, you can use cooking spray. That's just one of many tips that awaits you as you make your way through the fabulous breads, muffins, and pancakes in this chapter. And what cast-iron cookbook would be complete without historical bread recipes? Not this one — I include a few at the end of this chapter.

Baking Easy Yeast Breads

Few things beat a warm, fresh loaf of bread or rolls hot from the oven. But many cooks nowadays leave the actual bread- and roll-making to the pros. If they decide to do it themselves, they rely on a bread machine. And, really, who can blame them? Producing yeast breads that rise the way that they're supposed to, have golden crusts, and are light and airy inside is a feat many cooks struggle with. But I'm here to tell you that it is possible, and this section proves it by including easy-to-make bread recipes.

When you make yeast breads, keep these pointers in mind:

- ✔ Use warm water to activate the yeast. Water that's too hot (warmer than 125 degrees) kills the yeast; water that's too cold (below 105 degrees) makes the yeast sluggish. A good temp is between 110 and 115 degrees.

- ✔ Most recipes expect that you'll add some flour while you knead the dough, but many people keep adding flour until the dough is no longer sticky. The result is bread that's tough and dry. To avoid this problem, just cover your hands in a thin film of oil or shortening and keep kneading. As you do, the flour in the dough begins to absorb more of the liquid in the dough, and the dough grows less sticky.

Savory Dill Bread

The sugar in the recipe isn't strictly for taste; it actually affects how your loaf rises. This little bit of added sugar gives the yeast more sugar to act on, creating more rise.

Preparation time: *2 to 3 hours, including rising time*

Cooking time*: 40 to 50 minutes*

Yield: *12 to 14 servings*

1 package yeast	*1 unbeaten egg*
1 cup creamed cottage cheese	*1 tablespoon dried dill weed*
2 tablespoons sugar	*¼ teaspoon soda*
1 tablespoon butter	*1 tablespoon instant onion*
1 teaspoon salt	*2½ cups bread flour*

1 Combine the yeast with ¼ cup warm water in a bowl large enough to hold all the ingredients and double in size. Let stand about 10 minutes until bubbly.

2 Mix the cottage cheese, sugar, butter, salt, egg, dill weed, soda, and instant onion into the yeast and water.

3 Gradually add the flour, beating well after each addition. The dough will be a little sticky at this point, but it's more manageable after the first rise.

4 Let the dough rise in a warm place until doubled in size, about 1 to 1½ hours. Stir down dough.

5 Preheat your oven to 350 degrees. Turn the dough into a well-greased 3-inch deep cast-iron skillet. Let rise until doubled in size again, about 1 hour.

6 Bake for 40 to 50 minutes. The finished loaf makes a hollow sound when you thump it. Brush with melted butter. Sprinkle with Kosher salt. Makes one round, 10-inch loaf.

Per serving: Calories 126 (From Fat 21); Fat 2g (Saturated 1g); Cholesterol 20mg; Sodium 257mg; Carbohydrate 21g (Dietary Fiber 1g); Protein 6g.

Sheepherders Bread

Sheepherders Bread calls for bread flour, which is processed to have more *gluten*, a type of flour protein that traps bubbles that form when the yeast feeds on the sugars in the dough. More gluten means higher rise and a better structure, which is ideal for any yeast bread.

Preparation time: *About 2½ hours, including rising time*

Cooking time: *About 1 hour*

Yield: *14 to 16 servings*

2½ teaspoons salt

1 stick butter, slightly melted

½ cup sugar

2 packages (¼ ounce, each) dry yeast

8 to 10 cups bread flour

1 Put 3 cups warm tap water (no hotter than 120 degrees), salt, butter, and sugar into a bowl and stir. Add yeast and let it stand for 15 minutes, until bubbly.

2 Using a wooden spoon, add 5 cups of the flour, beating it into batter a little at a time. Add 3 more cups of the flour and beat well with a wooden spoon.

3 Turn the dough onto a floured surface and knead, adding up to 1 more cup of flour, until the dough feels smooth and elastic. Turn into a large, greased bowl and let it rise in a warm place until it's doubled in size (about ½ hours).

4 Punch down and place into a 6- or 7-quart cast-iron Dutch oven lined with nonstick aluminum foil or aluminum foil that's greased with shortening or butter. Leave enough aluminum foil to make handles for removing the bread from the Dutch oven when the baking process is complete. Cover with a lid that's also been greased. Let it rise until doubled (about 1½ hours) in a warm place.

5 Bake, covered, in a 350-degree oven for 12 minutes. Remove the lid and continue to bake for 45 to 60 minutes longer. Bread should be brown on top and sound hollow when thumped.

6 Lift the bread from the Dutch oven with the aluminum foil and let it cool. Makes one large round loaf of bread, 12 inches in diameter.

Per serving: Calories 324 (From Fat 62); Fat 7g (Saturated 4g); Cholesterol 15mg; Sodium 366mg; Carbohydrate 56g (Dietary Fiber 2g); Protein 8g.

Spoon Rolls

This recipe gives you the distinctive taste of yeast rolls without all the prep work. No kneading, rising, rolling, or shaping required. Simply prepare your dough and drop it by spoonfuls into your muffin pan. Because the batter can be kept in the refrigerator for a week, make as many rolls as you want and save the rest of the batter for your next dinner.

Preparation time: *15 minutes*

Cooking time: *20 minutes*

Yield: *14 rolls*

1 package dry yeast	*¾ cup butter, melted*
¼ cup sugar	*4 cups self-rising flour*
1 egg, beaten	

1 Preheat oven to 400 degrees.

2 Using a bowl large enough to hold all the ingredients, dissolve the yeast in 2 cups warm water and let stand for about 20 minutes for yeast to swell.

3 With a wooden spoon, mix in the sugar, egg, butter, and flour.

4 Spoon the batter into a well-greased cast-iron drop biscuit pan or muffin pan until each well is slightly over ½ full. Bake for 20 minutes.

Per serving: Calories 233 (From Fat 94); Fat 11g (Saturated 6g); Cholesterol 42mg; Sodium 460mg; Carbohydrate 30g (Dietary Fiber 1g); Protein 4g.

Setting the Pace with Quick Breads and Muffins

Quick breads and muffins rely on chemical leaveners (baking soda and baking powder) rather than yeast for their rise. (See the section "Baking Easy Yeast Breads," earlier in this chapter; Chapter 11 has tips and recipes for making cornbread and biscuits, two other popular quick breads.) You can use several mixing methods when you make quick breads, but the two most common are

✔ **Method 1:** Mix the dry ingredients separately from the wet ingredients and then combine them.

✔ **Method 2:** Cream the sugar and eggs until they're light and fluffy, stir in the eggs and extracts, and then alternately add the wet and dry ingredients into the creamed sugar and eggs.

Regardless of the mixing method you use, when you combine the wet and dry ingredients, don't overmix your batter. Doing so results in tough muffins and breads. Simply stir gently — don't beat. Mix the ingredients just enough to incorporate all the flour. (You don't want flour streaks.) But don't mix so much that the batter is smooth.

Old-Time Banana Bread

Banana bread is a wonderful way to use up overripe bananas. To get a nice rise out of your banana bread, don't over-stir the batter. Good banana-bread batter should be thick and chunky.

Preparation time: 10 minutes

Cooking time: 55 to 60 minutes

Yield: 12 to 14 slices

½ teaspoon baking soda	⅔ cup bananas (2 medium) mashed
¼ cup buttermilk	2 cups all-purpose flour
¼ cup vegetable shortening	½ teaspoon baking powder
¾ cup sugar	¼ teaspoon salt
1 egg	½ cup chopped nuts

1 Preheat your oven and well-greased cast-iron loaf pan to 350 degrees.

2 Add the baking soda to the buttermilk in a measuring cup and let it stand.

3 In a large bowl, combine the shortening and sugar, beating it until fluffy. Add the egg and bananas. Beat until mixed.

4 In a small bowl, combine the flour, baking powder, and salt. Add the dry ingredients and buttermilk mixture alternately to the shortening, sugar, egg, and banana mixture. Stir in the nuts.

5 Carefully pour the batter into the preheated and greased loaf pan and bake at 350 degrees for 55 to 60 minutes or until bread tests done — a toothpick inserted into the center comes out clean.

6 Remove from the oven and place on wire rack until cooled.

Per serving: *Calories 190 (From Fat 63); Fat 7g (Saturated 1g); Cholesterol 15mg; Sodium 110mg; Carbohydrate 29g (Dietary Fiber 1g); Protein 3g.*

Breakfast Muffins

This standard muffin recipe lends itself to all sorts of variations. I've included a few traditional modifications at the end of the recipe, but don't let my suggestions limit your culinary creativity.

Preparation time: *10 minutes*

Cooking time: *15 minutes*

Yield: *18 muffins*

2 cups all-purpose flour	*2 eggs*
2 tablespoons sugar	*1 cup milk*
3 teaspoons baking powder	*2 tablespoons melted vegetable shortening*
½ teaspoon salt	

1 Preheat your oven and well-greased cast-iron muffin pans to 450 degrees.

2 In a bowl, combine the flour, sugar, baking soda, and salt.

3 In a separate bowl, beat the eggs; then add the milk and shortening. Blend with dry ingredients.

4 Spoon into muffin cups. Carefully fill each cup ⅔ full. Bake at 450 degrees for 15 minutes.

Vary It! *To make buttermilk muffins, use 2 teaspoons baking powder and ½ teaspoon baking soda. Substitute buttermilk for the milk.*

To make nut muffins, add ½ cup of chopped pecans or walnuts to the batter.

To make blueberry muffins, fold 1½ cups of dry berries into the batter.

To make banana muffins, add 1 cup mashed bananas to the batter.

To make bran muffins, mix 1 cup bran with milk before adding it to the mixture.

Per serving: *Calories 85 (From Fat 23); Fat 3g (Saturated 1g); Cholesterol 26mg; Sodium 142mg; Carbohydrate 13g (Dietary Fiber 0g); Protein 3g.*

Chocolate Muffin Cakes

You can call this a breakfast muffin if you want to, but the richness of the sour cream and the melted chocolate make this muffin suitable for an after-dinner dessert — if you can keep the children away from it that long.

Preparation time: *10 minutes*

Cooking time: *30 minutes*

Yield: *16 muffins*

½ cup butter	*½ teaspoon salt*
½ cup vegetable shortening	*¼ teaspoon soda*
2 cups sugar	*1 cup sour cream*
3 eggs	*1 package (12 ounces) chocolate chips*
1 teaspoon vanilla	*3 ounces German chocolate, melted*
3 cups all-purpose flour	

1 Preheat your oven and well-greased, cast-iron muffin pan to 325 degrees.

2 Blend the butter, shortening, and sugar until fluffy. Add the eggs, one at a time, and the vanilla.

3 In a separate bowl, stir together the flour, salt, and soda until blended. Add to the butter mixture alternately with sour cream. Stir in both chocolates.

4 Spoon the batter into the greased muffin pan and bake for 30 minutes. Be careful with the hot muffin pan.

Per serving: Calories 461 (From Fat 217); Fat 24g (Saturated 12g); Cholesterol 62mg; Sodium 116mg; Carbohydrate 60g (Dietary Fiber 2g); Protein 5g.

Paper liners or not?

Breads baked in cast iron have a nicer crust. Papering a cast-iron muffin pan defeats the purpose of using cast iron. If getting the muffin out the pan is your main concern, just make sure that each compartment of your cast-iron pan is well greased. Also, make sure to grease around the top rim so that the muffin crown releases, too.

Mini-Muffins

The touch of cinnamon-sugar, added after baking, gives these muffins a little additional sweetness. If you want more pronounced sweetness, add a dollop of jam or jelly — any flavor — to the top of each uncooked muffin and then let it bake right in. You can find more variations at the end of this recipe.

Preparation time: *10 minutes*

Cooking time: *16 to 18 minutes*

Yield: *18 muffins*

1¾ cups all-purpose flour	¾ cup milk
⅓ cup sugar	¼ cup oil
2 teaspoons baking powder	¼ cup sugar
¼ teaspoon salt	1 teaspoon cinnamon
1 beaten egg	3 tablespoons melted butter

1 Preheat your oven and well-greased cast-iron muffin pan to 400 degrees.

2 Combine the flour, sugar, baking powder, and salt. Make a well in the center.

3 Combine the egg, milk, and oil. Pour it into the well of the flour mixture all at once. Mix until blended. Batter will be lumpy.

4 Fill the preheated and greased muffin pan ⅔ full. Bake at 400 degrees 16 to 18 minutes (until golden brown). Let the muffins sit for 10 minutes and then remove from the pan.

5 In a small bowl, combine the sugar and cinnamon. Brush the tops with butter. Sprinkle a mixture of sugar and cinnamon on the tops. Serve warm.

Vary It! *Add ¾ cups fresh or frozen blueberries to the batter.*

Add 1 cup coarsely chopped cranberries and 2 tablespoons sugar.

Add ⅔ cups chopped dates and ⅓ cup chopped nuts.

Add ½ cup shredded cheese.

Add 1 medium, finely chopped apple.

Reduce milk to ½ cup and add ¾ cup mashed banana and ½ cup chopped nuts.

Per serving: *Calories 124 (From Fat 52); Fat 6g (Saturated 2g); Cholesterol 18mg; Sodium 84mg; Carbohydrate 16g (Dietary Fiber 0g); Protein 2g.*

Pumpkin Muffins

Fresh pumpkin imparts a milder flavor than its canned cousin. To prepare fresh pumpkin, cut a small pumpkin in half and remove the seed and fiber — the stringy stuff. Place the pumpkin, cut side up, in a baking dish filled with a ¼-inch of water. Cover and bake for one hour at 400 degrees. Scoop the tender pumpkin from the shell and mash. Store the unused portion in the refrigerator.

Preparation time: *10 minutes*

Cooking time: *20 minutes*

Yield: *12 muffins*

⅔ cup sugar	*2 teaspoons baking powder*
1 egg	*¼ teaspoon salt*
¼ cup vegetable shortening	*1 teaspoon ground cinnamon*
½ cup cooked fresh or canned pumpkin	*⅛ teaspoon ground cloves*
2 tablespoons milk	*Lemon Glaze (see the following recipe)*
1 cup all-purpose flour	

1 Preheat your oven and well-greased cast-iron muffin pan to 350 degrees.

2 In a large bowl, cream together the sugar, egg, and shortening. Add the pumpkin and milk.

3 In another bowl, blend the flour, baking powder, salt, cinnamon, and cloves. Mix the dry ingredients into the wet.

4 Carefully spoon the batter into the cast-iron muffin pan, ½ to ⅔ full. Bake at 350 degrees for 20 minutes until a toothpick inserted into the center comes out clean.

5 Drizzle with the Lemon Glaze.

Lemon Glaze

1½ tablespoons melted butter	*1 tablespoon lemon juice*
½ cup powdered sugar	*⅛ teaspoon grated lemon rind*

In a small bowl, combine the butter, powdered sugar, lemon juice, and lemon rind.

Per serving: Calories 163 (From Fat 57); Fat 6g (Saturated 2g); Cholesterol 22mg; Sodium 119mg; Carbohydrate 25g (Dietary Fiber 1g); Protein 2g.

Sugar Muffins

Sugar Muffins, whose tops are given a brush of melted butter and then rolled in sugar, are the next best thing to a streusel topping — without the work. The key is to perform this final step while the muffin is still hot enough that the sugar partially melts, leaving you with a sweet, crusty crown.

Preparation time: 10 minutes

Cooking time: 20 to 25 minutes

Yield: 9 muffins

⅓ cup vegetable shortening	1½ teaspoon baking powder	½ cup milk
½ cup sugar	½ teaspoon salt	½ cup melted butter
1 egg	¼ teaspoon cinnamon	½ cup sugar
1½ cups cake flour		

1 Preheat your oven and the well-greased cast-iron muffin pan to 325 degrees.

2 Cream the shortening and sugar. Add the egg.

3 Combine the flour, baking powder, salt, and cinnamon. Add to the creamed sugar mixture alternately with the milk.

4 Carefully fill the preheated and greased muffin pan ⅔ full. Bake at 325 degrees for 20 to 25 minutes or until golden.

5 Cool 3 to 4 minutes. Brush the top with the melted butter and roll in the sugar. Serve warm.

Vary It! *For a different flavor, roll the muffin top in cinnamon sugar.*

Per serving: Calories 324 (From Fat 169); Fat 19g (Saturated 9g); Cholesterol 53mg; Sodium 208mg; Carbohydrate 37g (Dietary Fiber 0g); Protein 3g.

How yeast works

Yeast, the leavening agent in many breads, is a living organism that feeds on sugar and starch in the flour, converting these substances into carbon dioxide and alcohol. The carbon dioxide gas gives yeast bread its rise, and the alcohol gives it its characteristic flavor. Kneading is important, because it distributes the yeast evenly throughout the bread dough.

So, when you bite into a dinner roll, are you eating tiny little live organisms? No. You're eating tiny little dead organisms. The heat of the oven kills the yeast.

What to do if the syrup runs dry

If you discover that you don't have any syrup, don't panic. Don't make any sudden movements or rash decisions — such as throwing out those golden griddle cakes. Put the bottle down and slowly back away from the refrigerator. After you regain your composure, try one of these suggestions instead:

✔ Spread butter and jam or marmalade on top.

✔ Serve your pancakes with cut fresh fruit and whipped cream to please the kids.

✔ Serve them with a dollop of ricotta or small curd cottage cheese.

✔ Use the pancakes as bread and wrap sausage or bacon in them or make a scrambled egg taco.

✔ Make your own syrup: Heat up 1 cup corn syrup and 1 tablespoon butter until the butter melts. Then add ¼ teaspoon maple flavoring and just a touch of vanilla extract.

Flipping Over Pancakes and Popovers

The heat is what turns out perfect pancakes and popovers. A hot griddle and a hot muffin pan are musts when you make these two dishes. The heat helps with the rise and keeps the pancakes tender, but overcooking makes them tough and rubbery. Turning up the heat is especially important for popovers, which lack leavening ingredients in the mix and rely on the combination of heat and eggs to make them rise.

When you're making pancakes for a crowd and want to keep the pancakes warm until all are done, line the bottom of the baking sheet with a clean dish towel preheat it in a 200-degree oven. As you remove pancakes from the griddle, put them on the lined baking sheet. (The dishtowel keeps the bottom pancakes from cooking on the baking sheet and getting hard.) If you have a convection setting on your oven, *don't* use it when you're keeping pancakes warm. The circulating air will just dry them out. And no one likes dry pancakes.

When you make pancakes, don't turn them until they're ready — the top will be full of bubbles — and turn them only once. Also be sure to keep the griddle hot and well greased through the entire cooking process.

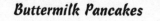

Buttermilk Pancakes

Hot off the griddle, these moist and delicious pancakes will stir up memories of days gone by.

Preparation time: 5 minutes

Cooking time: 1 to 2 minutes per side

Yield: 8 pancakes

1 egg	*1 scant cup all-purpose flour*	*½ teaspoon baking soda*
1 cup buttermilk	*½ tablespoon sugar*	*½ teaspoon salt*
2 tablespoons vegetable oil	*1 teaspoon baking powder*	

1 Heat a cast-iron griddle to medium-high heat.

2 In a bowl, beat the egg. Stir in the buttermilk and oil. Add the flour, sugar, baking powder, baking soda, and salt and stir. Some small lumps will remain.

3 Grease your hot griddle. Sprinkle a few drops of water on the griddle. If the drops dance in beads, the griddle is at the correct temperature.

4 Pour ¼ cup of the batter onto the hot griddle. Turn the pancake when to top is full of bubbles. Cook until golden brown. Continue until all batter is used. Be sure that the griddle is still greased and hot between batches.

Vary It! *For fruit pancakes, gently stir ½ cup cut up fruit or berries into your batter.*

Per serving: *Calories 112 (From Fat 41); Fat 5g (Saturated 1g); Cholesterol 28mg; Sodium 312mg; Carbohydrate 14g (Dietary Fiber 0g); Protein 3g.*

Kosher salt versus table salt

Many cooks prefer kosher salt to table salt, and some recipes specifically call for kosher salt. Some important differences between the two types of salt are that table salt is a finer grained salt with additives to make it pour freely. Kosher salt is usually additive-free and has a courser grain. In addition, kosher salt has a milder salt flavor than table salt.

When you cook with kosher salt, remember that kosher salt has less salt per volume (due to the coarser grains) than table salt does. For that reason, you need to use more kosher salt on it to attain the same level of saltiness that table salt yields. Similarly, if you're substituting table salt in a recipe that specifically calls for kosher salt, you use less. The difference in saltiness depends on the brands that you're comparing; sometimes kosher salt is half as salty as table salt. If you're substituting salts and the recipe doesn't include the alternative quantity, season to taste.

Corncakes

Sturdier than traditional pancakes and flavored with bacon grease, these corncakes have much in common with a quick bread. Although you can eat them with syrup, they're just as good — some say even better — with just a dollop of butter. When you make corncakes, be sure to keep your griddle hot and grease it with each batch.

Preparation time: *5 minutes*

Cooking time: *5 minutes*

Yield: *16 corncakes*

1 cup white cornmeal	*2 eggs*
1 cup white cornmeal mix	*2 cups buttermilk*
1 teaspoon baking soda	*2 tablespoons bacon grease, melted*
2 teaspoons baking powder	*2 tablespoons vegetable shortening, melted*
1 teaspoon salt	

1 In a large bowl, combine the cornmeal, cornmeal mix, baking soda, baking powder, and salt. Set aside.

2 In a smaller bowl, beat the eggs, the buttermilk, bacon grease, and shortening. Pour the liquid into the dry ingredients and beat together hard.

3 Heat a cast-iron griddle to medium-high on your stovetop. Grease the hot griddle. Pour about ¼ cup of the batter onto the hot griddle and turn when bubbles appear, about 3 minutes. Cook until the other side is golden brown, about 2 minutes. Continue until all the batter is used. Be sure that the griddle is still greased and hot between batches.

Per serving: *Calories 83 (From Fat 39); Fat 4g (Saturated 2g); Cholesterol 30mg; Sodium 321mg; Carbohydrate 8g (Dietary Fiber 1g); Protein 3g.*

German Pancakes

German pancakes, also called *Dutch pancakes, puff pancakes, apple pancakes,* and quite a few other names, are the giants of the pancake world that you cook in a skillet in the oven rather than in a griddle on the stovetop. Like popovers, these pancakes don't use leaveners (baking powder or soda). Instead the combination of the eggs and high oven temperature causes them to rise.

Preparation time: *10 minutes*

Cooking time: *30 to 35 minutes*

Yield: *4 servings*

6 tablespoons butter	½ lemon
1 cup all-purpose flour	Powdered sugar
1 teaspoon salt	Cinnamon
6 eggs	1½ cups applesauce or fried apples
1 cup milk	

1 Preheat your oven to 400 degrees. Spread the bottom and sides of a 12-inch cold cast-iron skillet with the butter.

2 Sift the flour and salt together and set aside. Beat the eggs until very light. Add the milk to the eggs. Add the dry ingredients to the eggs and milk.

3 Pour the batter into a skillet and bake for 30 to 35 minutes, or until cooked through and golden brown. Remove from the oven.

4 Squeeze the juice of a ½ lemon over the top. Top with a sprinkle of powdered sugar and cinnamon. Serve with applesauce or fried apples.

Per serving: Calories 495 (From Fat 244); Fat 27g (Saturated 14g); Cholesterol 373mg; Sodium 712mg; Carbohydrate 49g (Dietary Fiber 2g); Protein 15g.

Basic Popovers

Popovers are best served piping hot, straight from the oven. If you let them sit long enough to cool, they lose the texture that makes them so delectable.

Preparation time: *5 minutes*

Cooking time: *20 minutes*

Yield: *6 popovers*

1 cup all-purpose flour	*1 cup milk*
¼ teaspoon salt	*1 tablespoon vegetable shortening*
2 eggs	

1 Preheat your oven and well-greased cast-iron muffin pan to 450 degrees.

2 In a mixing bowl, sift together the flour and salt.

3 Make a well in the center of the flour and break the eggs into it. Add your milk and shortening to the well and stir with a wooden spoon until smooth.

4 Pour the batter into a hot muffin pan ⅔ full. Bake at 450 degrees for 20 minutes.

5 Split the popovers when baked and fill with butter or jam or serve with roast beef and gravy.

Vary It! *Change a regular popover into Yorkshire pudding: Put about ¼ to ½ cup drippings from any roasted beef into a 10-inch skillet or casserole dish and heat in a hot oven until very hot but not smoking. Pour your popover batter into the hot skillet and bake in a 425-degree oven for 25 to 30 minutes. Serve immediately.*

Per serving: *Calories 145 (From Fat 48); Fat 5g (Saturated 2g); Cholesterol 76mg; Sodium 138mg; Carbohydrate 18g (Dietary Fiber 1g); Protein 6g.*

Breads at Home on the Range and in the History Books

Bread is, I believe someone once said, the staff of life. Well, staff of life or not, bread certainly has had a popular run over the years. It's been at the top of the charts since our prehistoric ancestors first realized that grain mixed with liquid wasn't just a mess but an edible concoction.

Early breads were simple breads with a simple purpose: to feed hungry people. Bread owes its historical popularity to other factors as well:

✔ Bread is transportable and an ideal food for travelers. Think about it. You can't eat a salad while you're driving, but you can eat a bagel. Hardtack, for example — a dried, unleavened and unsalted bread — has been a staple of sailors' diets since the 1800s.

The recipes in this section are great for outdoor cooking. They require only a few ingredients and very little prep. They're recipes that American colonials, pioneers, and adventurers relied on to supplement — or comprise — their diets. If you want a real authentic cooking experience (or as close to authentic as you can come with a minivan parked around the bend), cook these breads outdoors. Chapter 14 tells you what you need to know to convert recipes for outdoor cooking.

✔ Bread is easy to make. Believe it or not, you don't need a bread machine to turn out a nice loaf, and people 100 years ago made loaves daily, often on the open range or prairie.

✔ Nothing beats bread for sopping up juices and gravy — absolutely mandatory for an era when the axiom "Waste not, want not" wasn't just a hen-pecking catchphrase but a guide for survival.

So enjoy the recipes in this section. What they may lack in "style" they more than make up for as culinary Americana.

Skillet Bread

Originally from Mexico, and called *pan de campo,* this bread was made in heavy skillet over the campfire. But this bread has also played a prominent role in U.S. history. Most likely, Lewis and Clark used a version during their Corps of Discovery. And it's definitely fed many hungry cowboys during cattle drives. A simple-tasting bread, cowboy cooks would have served it with chili, beans, stew, or gravy to make up for the relative lack of flavor.

This historical recipe uses less liquid than most modern-day breads, so don't work the dough very much, or it will become tough.

Preparation time: *5 minutes*

Cooking time: *8 to 10 minutes*

Yield: *8 servings*

4 cups all-purpose flour	*2 teaspoons baking powder*
2 tablespoons sugar	*6 tablespoons solid vegetable shortening*
2 teaspoons salt	

1 In a large mixing bowl, combine the flour, sugar, salt, and baking powder. Cut the shortening into the flour mixture. Add 2 cups water and mix briefly with a spoon. Don't overwork the dough.

2 Place the dough onto a floured surface and roll or pat to ¼-inch thickness. Cut a round of dough to fit a 10-inch cast-iron skillet.

3 Preheat a 10-inch cast-iron skillet over medium-low heat. Add enough shortening to coat the bottom.

4 Carefully place the dough in the skillet and cook until brown on one side, about 7 minutes. Carefully flip the dough (it'll want to fold in half) and cook on other side until brown, about 5 minutes.

5 Slice into pie-shaped wedges and serve while piping hot.

Vary It! *Contemporary versions of skillet bread often use milk instead of water and oil instead of shortening.*

Per serving: *Calories 325 (From Fat 92); Fat 10g (Saturated 3g); Cholesterol 0mg; Sodium 678mg; Carbohydrate 51g (Dietary Fiber 2g); Protein 7g.*

Hoecakes (Johnnycakes)

The precursor to pancakes, hoecakes, which are sometimes called *Johnnycakes,* go back to colonial times. According to legend, the name *Johnnycake* may have come from *journey cakes,* which people would pack to snack on during long journeys on horseback. And the name *hoecake* could have come from a preferred cooking method — on a hoe over the fire — but that history is difficult to confirm. Johnnycakes were a favorite of President William McKinley's — along with bacon and eggs — all fried in cast iron.

These tasty cakes resemble thin-ish cornmeal pancakes. Not as common as they were, in the past, hoecakes are still a hit with outdoor enthusiasts, because they don't require an oven. Indoors, you can serve them as a bread for dinner just like you would cornbread. And you can serve them for breakfast with honey or jam in place of pancakes, toast, or biscuits.

Preparation time: *5 minutes*

Cooking time: *3 minutes*

Yield: *24 cakes*

1 cup white cornmeal

½ cup all-purpose flour

1¼ teaspoon baking powder

¼ teaspoon baking soda

1 teaspoon salt

1 tablespoon sugar

About 1⅓ cup buttermilk

1 Heat your cast-iron griddle to medium-high heat on your stovetop.

2 In a medium bowl, combine cornmeal, flour, baking powder, baking soda, salt, and sugar. Add buttermilk to the desired consistency — think of a thin, cornmeal pancake batter.

3 Grease a hot griddle with solid vegetable shortening. Test the griddle for correct temperature by splashing a few drops of water onto the surface. If the water dances in beads, the griddle is hot enough.

4 Pour ¼ cup of the batter onto the hot griddle. Turn when the surface is full of bubbles. Fry until the second side is golden brown as well. Keep griddle well greased and hot with each batch. Serve hot with butter.

Per serving: *Calories 43 (From Fat 7); Fat 1g (Saturated 0g); Cholesterol 1mg; Sodium 144mg; Carbohydrate 8g (Dietary Fiber 1g); Protein 1g.*

Scalded Hoecakes

This cattle-trail recipe became bread for dinner with a pot of beans any time fresh milk was out of reach. If you were close to water, you may have served it with freshly-caught fried fish. Though seldom used today (most folks prefer hoecakes made with milk or buttermilk), they can be a staple on back woods hiking or hunting trips or any wilderness situation. If you're outdoors, you won't be able to refrigerate the batter, as the recipe instructs, so just let it rest at room temperature for 30 minutes.

In this recipe, boiling water is used as the liquid (hence the *scalded* in the recipe's name). This is important, because it softens the cornmeal grain to the desired consistency. Use cold water or water at room temperature, and your hoecakes will be gritty.

Preparation time: *25 minutes*

Cooking time: *5 minutes*

Yield: *20 cakes*

Bacon drippings or oil for frying	*1 teaspoon salt*
1¾ cup white cornmeal	*2 cups boiling water*

1 Heat a 10-inch cast-iron skillet to medium-high with enough bacon drippings and/or oil to fill the skillet — about ½-inch deep.

2 Combine the cornmeal and salt in a bowl. Slowly but steadily, pour boiling water into the dry mixture, stirring constantly. Beat until the batter is smooth. Refrigerate for 20 minutes.

3 Shape into balls and make thin patties about 2-inches in diameter. Fry about 5 minutes, turning once, until both sides are browned.

Per serving: Calories 81 (From Fat 51); Fat 6g (Saturated 3g); Cholesterol 6mg; Sodium 147mg; Carbohydrate 7g (Dietary Fiber 1g); Protein 1g.

Chapter 13

Delectable Desserts

*T*he favorite part of most meals is dessert. The promise of dessert inspires kids to eat whatever mom or dad places in front of them. If you're accustomed to making main dishes and sides in cast iron and have never tried any baking beyond cornbread, biscuits, or a cobbler or two, you may be in for a surprise.

Cast iron is a great cookware for cakes, pies, and other sweet fare. This chapter includes all types of cast-iron sweets, as well as general cooking tips and suggestions for making moist cakes, flaky pie crusts, and great candy.

Having Your Cake and Eating It, Too

Most cakes include relatively few ingredients. You have your four basic ingredients — fat, flour, sugar, and eggs. Leavener, liquid, and flavoring are also commonly found in cake recipes. The basic procedure is pretty simple, too: Whip the ingredients into a batter, pour the batter into a pan, and bake.

Amazingly, these few ingredients, combined in different amounts and mixed in slightly different ways, create a bounty of different cakes. But you have to get the proportions right.

Following are some tips to ensure that your cakes come out right:

✔ **Use the type of flour specified in the recipe.** Different flours have different protein levels, and this level directly affects how your cake rises. For general cake baking, use all-purpose flour.

✔ **Use the finest grain sugar that you can find.** If a recipe calls for sugar and the granule is too large, it won't hold enough air when it's creamed or beaten into eggs. The sugar also may not dissolve completely as the cake cooks, leaving you with dark spots of crystallized sugar.

✔ **Bring the eggs to room temperature.** Because cold eggs hold less air, your cake will be lighter when you use eggs at room temperature. Beating your eggs also incorporates more air, enhancing your cake's rise.

Don't let eggs stand at room temperature for longer than an hour. Researchers indicate that after that time, they become a health risk.

✔ **Let your butter warm to room temperature before you add it.** Butter that's too cold doesn't cream well; butter that's too warm breaks down during the creaming process, so don't let it get soft. Also, unless otherwise specified, use unsalted butter for a better tasting cake.

✔ **Use pure vanilla extract.** For the sake of taste, don't use imitation.

✔ **Roast nuts before you use them.** They're more flavorful that way.

Chemical reactions take the cake

When you bake a cake, a variety of chemical reactions occur:

✔ **Flour,** which gives the cake its substance, contains *gluten,* a protein that, when activated, makes the flour bind together and retain gas. This protein, combined with the protein from the egg, creates an elastic pocket that traps the gas released from the leaveners.

✔ **Leaveners** produce gas when they come in contact with liquid and when the heat from the oven activates them. Baking powder and baking soda are the most common ones used in cakes.

✔ **Sugar** adds sweetness, volume, and color.

✔ **Eggs** bind the other ingredients and add color, flavor, and moistness. Eggs act as a leavener too: When you beat eggs, you create millions of tiny air pockets that, when heated, expand and make the cake rise.

✔ **Butter** adds richness and moistness.

✔ **Milk** adds moistness, flavor, and color to your cake. It also changes the protein in the flour to gluten and jump-starts the chemical reaction in the leaveners.

Together, all these ingredients give your cake its color, flavor, texture, moistness, and rise.

Almond Star Cakes

This recipe calls for an All Star pan, which is really a cast-iron muffin pan with star-shaped molds. You can use a regular muffin pan instead or any fun-shaped muffin pan you have.

Preparation time: *10 minutes*

Cooking time: *40 minutes*

Yield: *8 to 10 cakes*

½ cup butter or margarine	2 eggs, beaten
1 cup all-purpose flour	1 teaspoon almond extract
1 cup sugar	Almond Cake Glaze (recipe follows)
1 teaspoon salt	¼ cup chopped nuts (optional)
1 teaspoon baking soda	5 maraschino cherries, halved (optional)
¼ cup sour cream	

1 Preheat the oven and your well-greased cast-iron muffin pan to 375 degrees.

2 Bring ½ cup water and the butter to a boil in a large saucepan. Remove from the heat. Stir in the flour, sugar, salt, baking powder, sour cream, eggs, and almond extract until smooth. Pour into a preheated and greased muffin pan. Carefully fill the molds ¾ full.

3 Bake at 375 degrees for 20 minutes. Cool for 20 minutes. Remove the muffins from the pan.

4 Spread the Almond Cake Glaze on top of the cakes. If desired, sprinkle each with the nuts or top with maraschino cherry halves.

Almond Cake Glaze

2 cups confectioners' sugar	¼ to ½ teaspoon almond extract

Mix the confectioners' sugar, 2 to 3 tablespoons of water, and the almond extract to make a glaze.

Per serving: *Calories 327 (From Fat 103); Fat 11g (Saturated 7g); Cholesterol 70mg; Sodium 376mg; Carbohydrate 54g (Dietary Fiber 0g); Protein 3g.*

Double Cherry Tea Cake

Be sure to drain the crushed pineapple well for this recipe. Too much moisture produces a soggy cake.

Preparation time: *15 minutes*

Cooking time: *25 to 30 minutes*

Yield: *10 to 12 cup cakes*

1¼ cup all-purpose flour

2 cups candied red and green cherries, chopped

1 cup walnuts, chopped

½ cup butter

½ cup sugar

½ teaspoon baking powder

½ teaspoon salt

3 eggs

¼ cup drained crushed pineapple

Orange Glaze (recipe follows)

1 Preheat the oven and the well-greased cast-iron muffin pan to 350 degrees.

2 Combine the flour with the cherries and nuts. Set aside.

3 Cream the butter. Add the sugar, baking powder, and salt. Cream thoroughly for about 5 minutes. Add the eggs, one at a time. Stir in flour mixture and pineapple.

4 Carefully spoon into a greased muffin pan, ½ full. Bake at 350 degrees for 25 to 30 minutes or until golden brown.

5 Cool and frost with Orange Glaze.

Orange Glaze

2 cups confectioners' sugar

1 teaspoon orange rind

2 to 3 tablespoons orange juice

Mix confectioners' sugar and orange rind. Blend in orange juice until the mixture has a glaze consistency.

Per serving: Calories 373 (From Fat 140); Fat 16g (Saturated 6g); Cholesterol 74mg; Sodium 145mg; Carbohydrate 56g (Dietary Fiber 1g); Protein 5g.

Nutty Funnel Cakes

A summertime fairground favorite, funnel cakes can be topped with cinnamon-sugar, as this recipe specifies, or powdered sugar, fruit, and just about anything else you feel like putting on top. They're even delicious served plain.

Preparation time: *10 minutes*

Cooking time: *2 minutes per cake*

Yield: *8 to 10 cakes*

¾ cup powdered sugar, sifted	*1⅔ cup milk*
1 teaspoon cinnamon	*2 eggs*
⅔ cup pecans	*½ teaspoon vanilla*
2½ cups self-rising flour	*Vegetable oil for frying*
¼ cup sugar	

1 Combine the powdered sugar and cinnamon in a small bowl and set aside.

2 With the knife blade in a food processor bowl, add pecans, and chop until fine. Add the flour, sugar, milk, eggs, and vanilla. Process for 30 seconds or until smooth.

3 In your cast-iron deep skillet or Dutch oven, heat the vegetable oil to 375 degrees.

4 Using a measuring cup or a funnel to make a thin stream of batter, pour ¼ cup batter in a circle to form spiral in oil. Fry 1 minute until edges are golden brown. Turn and fry until golden, about 1 minute. Drain on paper towels.

5 Sprinkle with sugar-cinnamon mixture. Serve immediately. Continue making funnel cakes in batches. If the remaining batter gets thick while standing, stir in 1 to 2 tablespoons of additional milk about halfway through the process.

Per serving: *Calories 401 (From Fat 22); Fat 22g (Saturated 3g); Cholesterol 48mg; Sodium 430mg; Carbohydrate 41g (Dietary Fiber 2g); Protein 6g.*

Pineapple Upside-Down Cake

The key to a great pineapple upside-down cake is caramelized fruit and brown-sugar topping. Started on the stovetop in a cast-iron skillet and finished in the oven, this cake is a contrast in delicious things: the rich, buttery topping and the moist, sweet cake. When you use cast iron, you can determine how caramel-y your topping is. Leave it on the stovetop just long enough to melt the butter; or leave it a couple minutes longer so that the brown sugar begins to melt, too. Either way, you're creating a classic cast-iron dessert.

Preparation time: *15 minutes*

Cooking time: *45 minutes*

Yield: *8 servings*

3 tablespoons butter	*3 eggs*
1 cup light brown sugar	*1½ cups white sugar*
7 slices canned pineapple	*1 teaspoon vanilla*
½ cup pineapple juice reserved	*1½ cups all-purpose flour*
7 candied cherries	*1½ teaspoons baking powder*
10 to 12 pecan halves (optional)	*¼ teaspoon salt*
¼ cup raisins (optional but makes a prettier and tastier cake)	

1 Preheat oven to 350 degrees.

2 Melt butter in 10-inch cast-iron skillet over low heat. Sprinkle the brown sugar over the butter. Remove from heat.

3 Arrange the pineapple rings in the skillet, cutting a few in half, if necessary, to fit all the rings in the pan. Place candied cherries in the center of each pineapple ring. Place the pecan halves and raisins, if desired, between pineapple rings.

4 In a mixing bowl, beat the eggs. Stir in the sugar. Add the vanilla and reserved pineapple juice and blend well.

5 In a separate bowl or on parchment paper, combine the flour, baking powder, and salt. Add the dry ingredients to the egg mixture and blend.

6 Pour batter over brown sugar and pineapple rings in a skillet. Bake for 45 minutes or until nicely brown. Invert onto a platter while warm.

Per serving: Calories 445 (From Fat 58); Fat 6g (Saturated 3g); Cholesterol 91mg; Sodium 184mg; Carbohydrate 94g (Dietary Fiber 1g); Protein 5g.

January 1900 Jam Cake

A precious recipe, handed down from generation to generation, as so many cast-iron recipes are. For this recipe, you need three 10-inch skillets.

Preparation time: *15 minutes*

Cooking time*: 30 minutes*

Yield: *8 to 10 servings*

½ cup butter	*3 cups all-purpose flour*	*3 tablespoons cocoa*
2 cups sugar	*2 teaspoons cinnamon*	*2 cups jam, usually blackberry*
6 egg yolks	*2 teaspoons ground cloves*	*1 cup raisins*
2 cups buttermilk	*2 teaspoons nutmeg*	*Old-Time Icing (recipe follows)*
2 teaspoons baking soda	*2 teaspoons allspice*	

1 Preheat your oven to 325 degrees. Line two 10-inch cast-iron skillets with wax paper because the jam can make the cake stick. In a large bowl, cream the butter and sugar and then add the egg yolks, one at a time. Set aside.

2 In another small bowl, mix the buttermilk and the baking soda and let stand for 3 minutes.

3 To the creamed butter, sugar, and egg yolks mixture, add the flour alternately with the buttermilk mixture. Add the cinnamon, cloves, nutmeg, allspice, cocoa, jam, and raisins.

4 Divide the batter evenly into two skillets and bake at 325 degrees for 30 minutes.

5 Remove the skillets from the oven and place the Old-Time Icing between the two layers and on top of the cake.

Old-Time Icing

2 cups milk	*1 cup butter*
4 cups sugar	*⅛ teaspoon baking soda*

Combine the milk, sugar, butter, and baking soda in deep cast-iron skillet. Cook for about 20 minutes until mixture reaches the hardball stage on a candy thermometer (250 to 265 degrees). At this point the mixture will form thick threads from the spoon and form a hard ball when dropped into cold water.

Per serving: Calories 1,167 (From Fat 300); Fat 33g (Saturated 20g); Cholesterol 210mg; Sodium 379mg; Carbohydrate 212g (Dietary Fiber 4g); Protein 10g.

Skillet Caramel Frosting

Skillet Caramel Frosting makes an "old-time" golden, hard caramel frosting that's great on cupcakes and pound cakes. As with all frosting, be sure to measure the ingredients carefully. Even a tad too much or too little liquid can make the frosting too hard or impossible to spread. With this kind of hard frosting, altitude and humidity can also factor into the end result. For example, in the South, making this frosting is difficult on rainy days.

Preparation time: *15 minutes*

Cooking time: *5 minutes*

Yield: *Frosts about 12 cupcakes or an 8-inch layer cake*

½ cup butter

1 cup firmly packed light brown sugar

¼ cup dark corn syrup

2 teaspoons cream of tartar

3 cups powdered sugar, sifted

3 tablespoons whipping cream

2 teaspoons vanilla

1 Melt the butter in a 3-inch deep cast-iron skillet over medium-high heat. Make sure you use a deep skillet because the frosting will bubble up and can boil over the sides of a regular skillet.

2 Stir in the brown sugar, corn syrup, and cream of tartar. Bring to a boil and boil for 5 minutes without stirring. When the mixture is thick and brown, remove from the heat.

3 Stir in the powdered sugar, whipping cream, and vanilla. Be careful when adding the cream to the hot mixture — it can splatter. Beat at medium speed in the pan with an electric mixer for 2 minutes. Spread immediately on cupcakes or a cake.

Per serving: Calories 288 (From Fat 81); Fat 9g (Saturated 6g); Cholesterol 26mg; Sodium 21mg; Carbohydrate 53g (Dietary Fiber 0g); Protein 0g.

Perfectly Easy Pastries and Other Super Sweets

You can make traditional one-crust and two-crust pies in a cast-iron skillet. Just follow the directions for any pie recipe you have, but instead of using a pie plate, use a skillet — a 9- or 10-inch skillet is a good substitute.

Don't worry about your pie crust sticking to your cast-iron skillet. The high-fat content of pastry combined with a seasoned cast-iron pan makes for a stick-free crust.

The trickiest part of making a good pie is making a good crust. Good pie crusts are flaky, tender, and golden. They literally melt in your mouth.

Following are a few guidelines for nailing your pie crust every time:

- ✔ Cut the shortening or butter into the flour until the mixture resembles course, pea-size crumbs.

- ✔ Add only the amount of liquid that the recipe specifies. Too much water or milk, as the case may be, makes the dough tough. If the dough is dry, add a little more shortening or butter instead.

- ✔ Make sure that your water or liquid is ice cold. As the shortening or butter in the dough warms through handling, the dough becomes pasty — a bad thing for a tender crust. The cold liquid helps you avoid this problem.

- ✔ Don't over flour your pastry board or countertop. If your dough is too soft to roll out easily, stick it in the refrigerator to firm it up a bit and then try again.

- ✔ Don't overwork the dough. Mix the ingredients and roll the dough as expediently as you can. Too much handling makes the crust tough.

And don't limit yourself to pies (and cakes) when you want to make sweet temptations in cast iron. Cobblers and candies also fit the bill. This section includes a couple of recipes to get you started.

Skillet Chocolate Pie

Pretty hard to resist a title like that, huh? The filling for this recipe is essentially a chocolate pudding. But don't substitute boxed pudding for the chocolate mixture. What you save in time can't make up for what you lose in flavor.

Preparation time: *20 minutes*

Cooking time: *25 to 35 minutes*

Yield: *8 servings*

1 cup sugar

1 rounded tablespoon flour

3 tablespoons cocoa

3 egg yolks (reserve the whites for The Best Meringue, recipe follows)

1 cup milk

1 heaping tablespoon butter

1 tablespoon pure vanilla extract

1 deep 8-inch pie shell, baked

The Best Meringue (recipe follows)

1 Mix together the sugar, flour, and cocoa and set aside.

2 In another bowl, beat the egg yolks and add the milk.

3 Preheat your oven to 350 degrees.

4 In a 3-inch deep cast-iron skillet, melt the butter over medium heat. Stir in the sugar, flour, and cocoa mixture. Remove from the heat and stir in the milk and egg yolk mixture. Place it back on the burner and cook on medium heat until very thick. This should take about 15 to 20 minutes.

5 Remove from the heat and stir in the vanilla. Pour into a baked pie crust.

6 Top with The Best Meringue and bake at 350 degrees until the meringue peaks are slightly brown. Don't leave the kitchen, because it only takes 10 to 15 minutes.

The Best Meringue

Would you like your meringue to be the envy of every cook? Want it to turn out light and fluffy every time? Then be sure to separate your eggs carefully; even a tiny bit of yolk can blunt the peaks. Use whites that are at room temperature and beat them in a cold and dry glass or metal bowl. And add your sugar slowly and continue beating until it's completely dissolved. You can use this meringue to top almost any 8- or 9-inch pie and make it that much better.

3 egg whites

¼ teaspoon cream of tartar

¼ teaspoon vanilla extract

¼ teaspoon almond extract

⅛ teaspoon salt

½ cup sugar

1 In a bowl, beat the egg whites at high speed with an electric mixer until the egg whites are foamy.

2 Sprinkle the cream of tartar, vanilla extract, almond extract, and salt over the egg whites. Continue beating until soft peaks form.

3 Gradually add the sugar, 1 tablespoon at a time, beating until stiff peaks form. Spread over hot pie filling or, using a pastry bag, pipe the meringue onto a pie in desired shapes, being sure to spread or pipe it all the way to the pie crust.

Per serving: Calories 368 (From Fat 132); Fat 15g (Saturated 4g); Cholesterol 88mg; Sodium 216mg; Carbohydrate 55g (Dietary Fiber 1g); Protein 5g.

The Tatin sisters and their tart

Here's one of the stories behind the origins of Tart Tatin: Stephanie and Caroline Tatin, French sisters who ran their father's hotel after his death in the late 19th century, were in a hurry to prepare an apple tart for their hungry guests returning from a hunt. Behind schedule and rushed, Stephanie threw together the apple mixture for the tart and then tossed the mixture into the pan and the pan into the oven. To her horror, about half way through the baking time, Stephanie realized that she had forgotten the crust. The two sisters pulled the half-cooked concoction from the oven and, desperate, added the crust on top. Hoping to hide their mistake, they inverted the upside-down apple tart onto a plate and served it to their guests. Although perhaps not the traditional *tarte aux pommes* they'd been expecting, the guests nonetheless devoured the hot, golden, caramel-y tart: A dessert was born.

Less exciting versions of the dessert's origins? The sisters got the recipe from their father or they got it from the chef who worked for some French count.

Apple Maple Tart Tatin

This recipe is essentially an upside-down pie. The filling is on the bottom, and the crust is on top. To get it right-side up again, carefully invert it onto a large serving platter.

Preparation time: *15 minutes*

Cooking time: *30 minutes*

Yield: *8 servings*

6 Cortland or Fuji apples	*¼ cup all-purpose flour*
2 tablespoons lemon juice	*½ teaspoon cinnamon*
¼ cup butter	*Dough for Apple Maple Tart Tatin*
½ cup sugar	*(recipe follows)*
¾ cup maple syrup	

1 Preheat your oven to 400 degrees. Peel and core the apples. Cut the apples into quarters and sprinkle with lemon juice. Set aside.

2 In a 12-inch cast-iron skillet, melt the butter over medium-high heat. Dust the bottom of the skillet with ½ cup sugar until completely covered. Remove from the heat and set aside.

3 In a large mixing bowl, place the apples, syrup, flour, and cinnamon. Toss the apples, coating completely with syrup mixture. Line the bottom of the skillet with the apples in a decorative fashion.

4 Top with the Dough for Apple Maple Tart Tatin and trim away the excess dough. Place the skillet over medium heat. When the edges of the pan begin to bubble, about 3½ to 4 minutes, remove skillet.

5 Place the tart in the oven and bake for 15 minutes or until the crust is brown. Carefully turn hot tart over onto a large serving platter. Allow tart to cool slightly before serving.

Dough for Apple Maple Tart Tatin

2 cups all-purpose flour	*pinch of sugar*
½ cup butter	*½ teaspoon salt*
1 egg	*3 teaspoons milk*

Place the flour on a flat surface. Cut in the butter. Add the egg, sugar, and salt. Knead the dough until it forms a ball. Add the milk and knead several times until smooth. Roll the dough into a ¼-inch thick circle, large enough to cover the skillet.

Per serving: Calories 472 (From Fat 166); Fat 18g (Saturated 11g); Cholesterol 73mg; Sodium 160mg; Carbohydrate 74g (Dietary Fiber 3g); Protein 5g.

Blueberry French Toast Cobbler

French bread has the perfect texture and weight for French toast, but it isn't the only bread you can use. If you don't have French bread, substitute any bread with solid texture. The solid texture is key. Fresh, brand-name white sandwich breads are too soft; they fall apart in the egg mixture. *Note:* This recipe is an old outdoor favorite and was particularly popular with drovers on cattle drives. Head to Chapter 14 for instructions on outdoor cooking.

Preparation time: *1 hour 10 minutes*

Cooking time: *25 minutes*

Yield: *8 servings*

1 loaf French bread, sliced ¾-inch thick	*4½ cup blueberries*
5 eggs	*½ cup sugar*
¼ cup sugar	*1 teaspoon cinnamon*
¼ teaspoon baking powder	*1 teaspoon cornstarch*
1 teaspoon vanilla	*Powdered sugar*
¾ cup milk	*¼ cup blueberries for garnish*
3 tablespoon butter	

1 Place the bread slices in a single layer in a large dish.

2 In a large mixing bowl, combine the eggs, ¼ cup sugar, baking powder and vanilla. Using a wire whisk, blend all the ingredients thoroughly. Slowly add the milk until all is incorporated.

3 Pour the egg mixture over the bread, turning once to coat evenly. Cover and allow to set for 1 hour at room temperature.

4 Preheat your oven to 450 degrees. In 14-inch cast-iron skillet, melt butter over medium-high heat.

5 In another large mixing bowl, combine the blueberries, sugar, cinnamon, and cornstarch. Pour blueberry mixture into the skillet. Using a spatula, place bread, wettest side up, on top of blueberries.

6 Bake for 25 minutes or until the blueberries are bubbling around the bread, and the bread is golden brown.

7 Remove from the oven and sprinkle with the powdered sugar. Top with additional fresh blueberries.

Per serving: Calories 353 (From Fat 89); Fat 10g (Saturated 4g); Cholesterol 147mg; Sodium 350mg; Carbohydrate 58g (Dietary Fiber 4g); Protein 9g.

North Carolina Hillbilly Apple Sonker

Sonker is an Appalachian term for a deep-dish fruit pie. In areas outside Appalachia, it's better known as a cobbler. Spooned on individual serving plates and topped with whipped cream, this dessert is called delicious in any part of the country.

Preparation time: *15 minutes*

Cooking time: *1 hour to 1 hour and 15 minutes*

Yield: *8 servings*

6 large or 12 small apples, peeled, cored, and sliced

2 tablespoons butter

2½ cups sugar

½ cup all-purpose flour

½ teaspoon cinnamon

Dough for North Carolina Hillbilly Apple Sonker (recipe follows)

1 cup whipping cream

1 teaspoon vanilla

1 Preheat your oven to 350 degrees. Grease a 10-inch cast-iron skillet with butter.

2 Place the apples, 2 cups of the sugar, flour, and cinnamon in a large mixing bowl. Toss lightly to coat the apples with the sugar mixture.

3 Place the apples into the preheated skillet and top with the Dough for North Carolina Hillbilly Apple Sonker. (The recipe follows.) Using a paring knife, cut 1-inch steam holes in the top of the pastry for ventilation.

4 Bake the sonker for 1 hour to 1 hour and 15 minutes, or until crust is golden brown and flaky. Remove from your oven and cool slightly.

5 Place the whipping cream, ½ cup sugar, and vanilla in the bowl of an electric mixer. Beat on high speed until soft peaks form. Using a serving spoon, place a generous portion of the sonker in the center of an 8-inch plate and top with fresh whipped cream.

Dough for North Carolina Hillbilly Apple Sonker

This recipe yields a total of three crusts. You can freeze two of the three crusts for later use by wrapping them in wax paper and placing them in a resealable plastic bag.

1 egg

2 teaspoons vinegar

3 cups all-purpose flour

1 teaspoon salt

¾ cup vegetable shortening, or butter

1 Beat the egg, 10 tablespoons tap water, and vinegar together in the bowl of an electric mixer.

2 Sift together the flour and salt in a large mixing bowl.

3 Using your hands, crumble the shortening or butter into the flour mixture, blending thoroughly until mixture resembles the texture of cornmeal. Pour in the water mixture and blend until the dough forms.

4 Turn the dough out onto a lightly floured surface and knead until smooth.

5 Divide into 3 equal portions and roll each crust into a circle until ¼ inch thick.

Per serving: Calories 831 (From Fat 312); Fat 35g (Saturated 14g); Cholesterol 75mg; Sodium 312mg; Carbohydrate 127g (Dietary Fiber 4g); Protein 7g.

New Orleans Pralines

Many candy and custard recipes do very well in cast iron because of cast iron's weight and heating properties. Cast iron is great for caramelizing sugar. When you make candy, temperature is key. Use a good candy thermometer: They're cheap, easy to find, and essential for candy making.

Preparation time: *5 minutes*

Cooking time: *About 20 minutes*

Yield: *2½ dozen pralines*

1½ cups sugar	¼ cup butter
1½ cups brown sugar	2 cups pecan halves, toasted
1 cup evaporated milk	1 teaspoon pure vanilla extract

1 Bring the sugar, brown sugar, and milk to a boil in a deep cast-iron skillet or Dutch oven. Cook over medium heat, stirring often for 10 minutes, or until candy thermometer registers 228 degrees.

2 Stir in the butter and pecans. Continue cooking, stirring constantly, until candy thermometer registers 236 degrees. (At this stage, called the *softball stage,* a small amount of the candy, when dropped into cold water, will form a soft ball.)

3 Remove from the heat and stir in vanilla. Beat with a wooden spoon for 2 minutes to thicken.

4 Quickly drop by heaping tablespoons onto buttered wax paper or a slab of marble. Let the candy stand until firm.

Per serving: Calories 154 (From Fat 65); Fat 7g (Saturated 2g); Cholesterol 23mg; Sodium 13mg; Carbohydrate 23g (Dietary Fiber 1g); Protein 1g.

Part IV

Cast-Iron Cooking for the Great Outdoors — and Beyond

The 5th Wave   By Rich Tennant

"I'm just saying, you see someone cooking with cast iron you think cornbread and chili, not osso buco and an artichoke soufflé."

In this part . . .

Cast-iron cooking has been an outdoor affair for as
many years as people have been cooking in cast iron.
It's the cookware of the colonists and the settlers who
moved westward. Today, it's the cookware of campers,
Scouts, and outdoor enthusiasts. In this part, you can find
all the information that you need to know to use your cast
iron outdoors and to find others who share this pastime.

You can also find game recipes (what better meal to cook
outdoors?) and cast-iron recipes based on global favorites.
After all, while you're on the road, so to speak, why not
travel farther afield and sample cuisine that originated
elsewhere?

Chapter 14

Cooking Around the Campfire

In This Chapter

▶ Gathering gear: From pokers to cauldrons

▶ Digging out a pit for your cast-iron coals

▶ Getting in touch with other camp-oven enthusiasts

▶ Going ape for campfire desserts

Cast iron is a nearly perfect outdoor cookware. It travels well, cooks evenly, and cleans up easily — just what you need when you're sometimes miles from home and without the luxuries that you take for granted, such as electric or gas ranges and running water. Anyone can cook in the great outdoors, preparing everything from simple one-dish entrees and desserts to complete multicourse meals. Doing so successfully isn't rocket science. It just takes a few hot coals, the right tools, and a few tricks up your sleeve. This chapter tells you what you need to know and includes easy recipes for the beginning camp cook.

If you're just beginning as an outdoor cook, or you haven't had much success in the past and want to try again, this chapter is for you. It tells you about the tools you need (including pan types) and how to control your cooking temperatures. I also offer advice on outdoor-cooking techniques.

Outdoor cast-iron cooking is a big-time hobby for many people. Because you may become its next enthusiast, you can also find information in this chapter about how to locate others who share this interest.

Roundin' Up the Outdoor Hardware

Anyone can cook outdoors, using any kind of cast-iron cookware they have, but most people rely on one or two pieces: Dutch ovens (called *camp ovens*, when they're designed for outdoor use) and skillets with lids. With either of these pieces, you can cook any dish. (**Note:** All the recipes in this chapter use a skillet or a Dutch oven.) But many outdoor cooks consider other items necessary, too.

Cookware: Anything you want

Although you can use any Dutch oven outside, cookware that has legs and a flanged lid, called a *camp oven,* makes outdoor cooking a little easier. The legs let you keep the Dutch oven itself off the coals (and thus avoid getting the cookware too hot), and the flanged lid lets you put coals on top without worrying about them rolling off onto the ground or, when you lift the lid, into your food. The recipes in this book are intended for outdoor cooking, so many of them recommend that you use a camp oven. (See Chapter 2 for more on Dutch ovens and camp ovens.)

If you're shopping for a camp oven, look for one that has a reversible lid. These lids function as both a lid and, when flipped over, a griddle. The griddle side is usually slightly concave, which keeps anything you cook in it — pancakes, eggs, bacon, and so on — from spilling or dripping over into the coals.

Like Dutch ovens, you can also find skillets with flanged lids and legs that keep the bottoms of the pans off of the hot coals.

If you don't want to spring for skillets and ovens designed specifically for outdoor use, you can use a *spyder* (essentially a cast-iron trivet) to turn any stovetop cast-iron skillet or Dutch oven into an outdoor cooking machine. See the "Going for convenience and comfort" section, that's coming up next, for more info on spyders.

Going for convenience and comfort

Although the following items aren't absolutely necessary when you cook outside, they can make your task a little easier and safer:

- **Brush:** You use a brush to remove ashes and coals from on top of lids and around your pan. Any plain old ash brush will do.

- **Oven gloves:** These gloves are essentially extra long, extra thick fire-resistant oven mitts that are sometimes made of leather.

- **Long utensils:** You want utensils that are as long as possible and that you can still comfortably and safely wield. The longer the utensil, the further from the fire you are. You need the standards — spoon, spatula, meat fork, and anything else you need to stir, turn, or prod your food. But you may also want to invest in a pair of tongs or a poker that let you move charcoal coals around safely.

✔ **Heavy-duty aluminum foil or metal trash can lid:** Although not a necessity, using aluminum foil or an upside-down aluminum trash can lid (placed in such a way that it doesn't wobble) can help you control the temperature of the coals, especially if the ground is damp or cool. See the "Making adjustments for weather conditions" section, later in this chapter, for more information.

✔ **Lid hook:** Also called a *lid lifter,* this tool shown in Figure 14-1 lets you remove the lid from your camp oven or skillet without spilling coals and ashes into your dish. Because they're generally long (around 18 inches), they also keep you away from the heat and all the hair on your arms intact. Lid hooks come in a variety of lengths. Choose the longest one you can that still lets you comfortably lift the lid.

✔ **Spyder:** Shown in Figure 14-2, a spyder (also known as a *trivet* or *lid stand*) is a three- or four-legged stand that can hold your pans over the fire as the food cooks, functioning as the "legs" for any flat-bottomed cast iron that you have, essentially turning it into outdoor cookware. Just place the spyder over the coals and your pan on top of the spyder. Instant legs! It can also serve as a place to set a hot lid when you're checking on the food. These come in varying heights.

If you use a spyder, you may want to have two or three of different heights so that you can adjust how close your pan is to the coals.

✔ **Charcoal chimney starter:** A charcoal chimney starter is beneficial for starting hot coals. See Figure 14-3. You're also going to need to replenish the hot coals that you use, especially for dishes that cook for a long time. This tool lets you keep extra coals ready and nearby as you cook.

Figure 14-1:
Give that
lid a lift.

Photograph courtesy of Lodge Manufacturing Co.

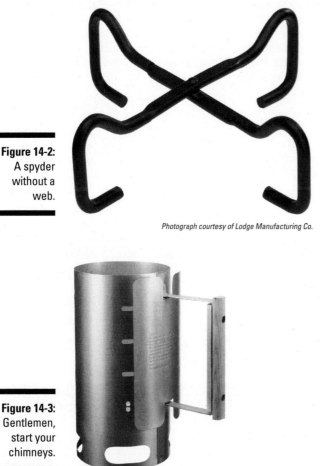

Figure 14-2: A spyder without a web.

Photograph courtesy of Lodge Manufacturing Co.

Figure 14-3: Gentlemen, start your chimneys.

Photograph courtesy of Lodge Manufacturing Co.

Temperature Control

In principal, outdoor cooking is just like indoor cooking: Using the right cookware and the right temperature, you can make any dish your heart — or your hungry brood — desires. The main difference between the two is *how* you control the temperature. Your stove has control dials; the rocks or grassy hill that you build your campfire on — even the fire pit in your own backyard — probably won't.

When you're cooking outside, your heat source is either wood or charcoal briquettes. Although some people prefer wood embers, most prefer charcoal, because it lasts longer and gives you more even heat. For that reason, the recipes in this chapter refer only to charcoal.

Charcoal coals generally give you between 45 minutes and an hour's worth of cooking time, provided that the day isn't windy, which can make the coals burn faster. Avoid charcoal that comes presoaked in lighter fluid: It burns faster.

When you cook outside, you generally don't put your cookware over an open flame. With an open flame, the only way that you can control the cooking temperature is to lift and lower the pan, a task that, although possible, isn't easy either. (To make raising and lowering the vessel manageable, you need a tripod or cooking rig.)

The heat source isn't the only added variable when you move from the cozy confines of your kitchen to great outdoors (or the great backyard). You also have to contend with air temperature, wind, humidity, and the other climactic conditions that Mother Nature doles out. Temperature control in outdoor cooking is as much an art as a science. You control cooking temps with the following:

- ✔ Number of coals and their placement on the lid and under the pan
- ✔ Location of the heat source
- ✔ Adjustments for weather conditions
- ✔ Your cooking techniques

I go into much greater detail about each of these variables in the following sections.

The best way to figure out how to control your cooking temperatures is simply to practice and experiment. Before you know it, you'll be cooking up a storm, maybe even in a storm.

Number and placement of coals

To control the temperature when you cook in a camp oven, the number of coals you use and where you put the coals are key factors. For some cooking techniques (boiling, frying, and sautéing, for example), you put all your coals under the pan. For these techniques, obviously, you don't need a lid. For other techniques (such as baking and simmering, for example), you arrange some coals on top (hence you need a lid) and some coals underneath, as shown in Figure 14-4. Simple enough.

Well, almost. Keep reading for explanations of the finer points.

Figure 14-4:
Pans designed for outdoor cooking have flanged lids and feet so that you can place coals on top and underneath.

Photograph courtesy of Lodge Manufacturing Co.

Counting coals

All the recipes in this chapter and many recipes in other outdoor cast-iron cooking books tell you how many coals to place on the lid and how many to place underneath your camp oven or skillet to get the appropriate temperature.

The trick is figuring out how many coals you need when the recipe doesn't specify. Fortunately, cooking temperatures are about the same for indoor conventional ovens as they are for outdoor cooking. So if you'd roast a chicken indoors in a 325-degree oven, you'd use the same temperature when you roast a chicken outdoors. Table 14-1 shows you how many coals you need to attain certain temperatures. The "Heat sources and cooking methods" section, later in this chapter, tells you where to put these coals for different cooking techniques. With this information, you can convert indoor oven recipes (baking, roasting, and so on) for use outdoors.

Table 14-1		Total Number of Coals to Reach Certain Temperatures				
Dutch Oven	**325 Degrees**	**350 Degrees**	**375 Degrees**	**400 Degrees**	**425 Degrees**	**450 Degrees**
8-inch	15	16	17	18	19	20
10-inch	19	21	23	25	27	29

Dutch Oven	325 Degrees	350 Degrees	375 Degrees	400 Degrees	425 Degrees	450 Degrees
12-inch	23	25	27	29	31	33
14-inch	30	32	34	36	38	40

To increase the temp, you simply add coals; to decrease the temp, you remove them. Although not precise, assume that every coal adds between 10 and 20 degrees of heat. When you just want to keep your food warm, remove all the coals except for a few under and over the dish.

These guidelines are just that — guidelines. If no other factor impacts the actual heat of the coals, the conversions in Table 14-1 are pretty accurate. But add in the factors that often affect cooking temperatures outdoors (wind, air temp, and so on), and you're going to have to make adjustments. See the section "Making adjustments for weather conditions" for information, later in this chapter.

Heat sources and cooking methods

After you know how many coals you need total (see the preceding "Counting coals" section), you need to figure out where they should go: on the lid, underneath, or both. How you divide the coals and where you place them depend on the cooking method.

In a cast-iron skillet or Dutch oven, you can braise, bake, boil, simmer, sauté, deep-fry and just about anything else. You can perform all these cooking techniques outside, too. You just need to know where most (or all) the heat should come from. If you're baking, for example, you need the heat to surround your pan; if you're frying, all the heat should come from underneath. Table 14-2 outlines where the heat source should be for the various cooking methods.

Converting old recipes

Many old recipes don't specify temperature settings. Instead, they offer vague descriptions — to the modern cook's thinking, anyway. If you find old recipes — a common occurrence when you go hunting specifically for cast-iron recipes — don't be surprised if the only temperature guide is "Cook (whatever) in a slow oven until done." Some equivalents are as follows:

Description	Temperature Equivalent
Slow	250 to 350 degrees
Moderate	350 to 400 degrees
Hot	400 to 450 degrees
Very hot	450 to 500 degrees

Table 14-2	Location of Heat Source	
Cooking Method	Where the Heat Should Come From	Coal Distribution
Baking	More from the top than bottom	For every coal under the bottom, you need three on the lid.
Boiling	Bottom	All coals under the bottom.
Frying	Bottom	All coals under the bottom.
Roasting	Top and bottom equally	Same number of coals on the lid and under the bottom.
Sautéing	Bottom	All coals under the bottom.
Simmering	More from the bottom than top	For every coal on the lid, you need four under the bottom.
Stewing	More from the bottom than top	For every coal on the lid, you need four under the bottom.

Spacing out: Oooh, pretty patterns!

When you know how many coals you need and where they should go (as explained in Tables 14-1 and 14-2 in this chapter), you need to arrange them properly. You can't just lump a bunch of coals under the pan and slap another bunch of coals on top. If you do, you create hot spots that can either burn your food or make it cook unevenly. Here's how to arrange the coals:

- ✔ **For coals under the pan:** Space the coals evenly in a circular pattern, starting at least ½-inch within the outer edge of the pan's bottom.
- ✔ **For coals on the lid:** Space the coals evenly in a checkerboard pattern.

Making adjustments for weather conditions

After you figure out how many coals to place where, you then have to take the weather into account. The air temperature, wind speed, humidity levels, ground temperature, and so on can affect the temperature of your coals. With this information, you can add or subtract coals as necessary to get the temperature that you want.

Your coals will burn hotter if

✔ You have warm breezes or wind.

✔ You're cooking in direct sunlight.

✔ The air temperature is high.

Your coals will be cooler if

✔ The humidity is high.

✔ You're cooking in the shade.

✔ You're cooking at high altitudes.

✔ The ground temperature is cool or the ground is damp.

To take ground temperature out of the mix, consider not putting your coals directly on the ground. Instead, use heavy-duty aluminum foil, an old charcoal grill pan, or an overturned aluminum trash can lid as a base for your fire. If you find that you cook outdoors a lot, you may want to use a metal table specifically designed for outdoor cooking. The table has a lip around the edge that keeps your coals from falling off of it and a metal wall on three sides that keeps the wind away. Such a table accomplishes what the other bases do plus, because you're cooking on a table, you don't bend over all the time.

What a hole in the ground! Outdoor cooking techniques

Cooking outdoors can be as authentic or as convenient as you want it to be. After all, technically speaking, you can place your cast-iron pot inside a covered barbecue grill, set the temperature to whatever you want and call yourself an outdoor cook. Most people, however, use one of the following techniques:

✔ **Cooking a single dish over hot embers or coals.** This technique is the one that the recipes in this chapter require. It's the easiest cooking technique for the beginning outdoor cook, because you only have to manage a single dish at a time.

✔ **Stacking pans over hot embers or coals to cook more than one dish at a time.** This technique lets you cook plenty of food without taking up any more ground space than single-dish cooking requires. (See Figure 14-5.) You actually stack cast-iron pans on top of each other over a heat source. The food that requires the most heat goes on the bottom of the stack, and the food that requires the least goes on top. As you gain more experience with outdoor cast-iron cooking and want to broaden your repertoire, you may find yourself stacking pans.

This technique works best for foods that require an even distribution of heat rather than foods that require that the heat source come primarily from the top or the bottom of the pan. (Refer to the section "Heat sources and cooking methods" earlier in this chapter for information.)

A challenge in stacked cooking is that, if you want to check or stir a dish that isn't on the top of the heap, you have to move all the pans above it. Of course, some would argue that this is part of the fun.

✔ **Cooking in a pit:** If you're so inclined, you can actually bury your Dutch oven in a pit of coals. In this method, you build a fire in a hole that you've dug and lined with aluminum foil or stone and, when the coals are ready, place your covered cast-iron dish inside, cover it with dirt and more coals, and let it cook. This cooking technique is slow. Most dishes cooked in this method take 4 to 6 hours. It's best reserved for dishes that don't need to be tended and that (for obvious reasons) are covered.

Figure 14-5:
Stacked
ovens let
you cook
more than
one item
at a time.

Photograph courtesy of Lodge Manufacturing Co.

More tips for the outdoor cook

Cooking outdoors isn't rocket science, but it does take a little special know-how. With the basic knowledge outlined in this chapter and the following tips, chances are, your outdoor cooking experience will be a positive one:

✔ When you figure outdoor cooking times, don't forget to figure in how long it takes to get your coals ready. For charcoal, start your coals 15 to 20 minutes before you need them.

✔ If a dish takes a long time to cook, have hot coals available to replenish the ones you use up. (A charcoal chimney starter is good for this. See the section "Going for convenience and comfort" earlier in the chapter.) Add new coals when the old coals start to break up. When you add new coals, increase the amount proportionally on both the top and bottom. Don't add only to the top, for example, or you'll end up with uneven cooking.

✔ To keep the cooking temperature even within the pan or Dutch oven, rotate the lid and the pan in opposite directions regularly. Every 10 to 15 minutes, give the lid a quarter turn in one direction and the pan or Dutch oven a quarter turn in the other direction.

✔ If you have to move coals around (and chances are you will, either to replenish the coals you've used up or to increase or decrease the temperature by adding and removing coals), use long-handled tongs and wear thick oven mitts. After all, you're playing with fire, and what fun is cooking outdoors if you spend all your time indoors rubbing salve on your burns?

✔ When you remove the lid to check on your dish or rotate the lid, be careful not to let ashes from the lid drop into your food. When the dish is done, go ahead and brush the ashes away entirely.

When you're first starting out, start simple. Although you can cook anything in a Dutch oven, try your hand at easy dishes (stew, chili, cobbler, and roasted chicken, for example) first. The recipes in this chapter are all great beginner recipes: easy to assemble, easy to make, and delicious.

Finding Other Folks Who Like to Cook Outdoors

If you discover that outdoor cooking is your thing, you have quite a bit of company. You can find several Dutch oven societies across the United States and in other places in the world. Here are a few:

✔ **International Dutch Oven Society:** Based in Utah, the IDOS has chapters in Texas, Southern California, New York, Pennsylvania, and Ontario, Canada. For information, call the IDOS at (801) 752-2631, or visit its Web site at www.idos.com.

✔ **Lone Star Dutch Oven Society:** Based in San Antonio, Texas, the LSDOS has local chapters throughout the state of Texas. For information about the LSDOS, call (972) 296-9157 or visit the Web site at www.lsdos.com.

✔ **Northwest Dutch Oven Society:** Based in Tacoma, the NWDOS has chapters throughout Washington. For society information, contact the society at www.nwdos.org.

✔ **Suncoast Dutch Oven Society:** Based in Tampa Bay, the Suncoast DOS has local chapters throughout Florida. For information, contact the society at www.geocities.com/suncoastidos/.

✔ **Japan Dutch Oven Society:** For information about the JDOS, visit its Web site at www.jdos.com. (To get very far on this site, however, you need to be fluent in Japanese.)

Regardless of what region they serve, all these societies — and the many others out there — promote the fun and skill of Dutch oven cooking, sponsor events and gatherings, and publish newsletters containing society news, recipes, and cooking tips for their members. On average, memberships fees range from $10 to $25 dollars annually.

Dutch Oven Main Dishes

Dutch ovens are great for main dishes. The deep sides and tight-fitting lids are great for roasting, braising, and slow cooking — cooking techniques that let the flavors of the foods you cook blend together in delicious combinations. The main recipes that follow in this section let you try out these and other cooking techniques that you can use easily adapt for other dishes. Keep the following few general recommendations in mind:

✔ When you roast meat in a Dutch oven, use a trivet. Dutch ovens don't have the raised bottoms that many traditional roasting pans have. To keep your meat or poultry out of its own juices and dripping, you need to use a trivet or a roasting rack.

✔ Brown your meat before you add the other ingredients, such as vegetables, sauces, and so on. If the recipe calls for you to cook your meat and vegetables at the same time, be sure to brown or sear the meat first. Doing so gives the meat a nice color and seals in the juices.

Pork Chops 'n Potato Sauce

Pork chops come from the loin portion of a hog, and where on the loin that they are determines both the quality of the meat and its price. So when you go shopping for pork chops, keep in mind these differences: *Loin chops* have meat on both sides of the bone and are the least fatty and the most expensive. A *center cut chop* has little to no meat on one side of the bone, but the meat on the other side of the bone is nice and lean. *End chops* are fattier and don't have the nice, lean meat portion that the other chops offer. These are the least expensive.

Briquettes: *28*

Preparation time: *10 minutes*

Cooking time: *45 to 60 minute*

Yield: *4 servings*

Vegetable oil	2 potatoes, sliced ¼-inch thick
4 pork chops, about ¼-inch thick	1 can (11 ounces) condensed cream of mushroom soup
1 medium yellow onion, chopped	

1 Add the oil to a 14-inch cast-iron camp oven, over 28 hot (gray) coals. Brown the pork chops on both sides. Remove the chops.

2 Sauté the onions. Pull out the onions, lay the chops back in, and spread the onions over the chops. Lay the potato slices evenly over the onions.

3 In a bowl, mix the condensed soup with a ½ can of water and pour the mixture over the ingredients.

4 Reduce the briquettes to about half and simmer until the chops and potatoes are fork tender.

Per serving: *Calories 340 (From Fat 149); Fat 17g (Saturated 4g); Cholesterol 64mg; Sodium 590mg; Carbohydrate 22g (Dietary Fiber 2g); Protein 25g.*

Enchilada Casserole

An enchilada is a tortilla wrapped around highly seasoned meat and often served with cheese and a sauce. In this recipe, instead of the traditional wrap, you layer the ingredients, which makes the final dish an easy one to serve and eat outdoors. Also note that you can make the sauce milder or hotter, simply by using the canned enchilada sauce with the degree of heat you prefer.

Briquettes: *24*

Preparation time: *5 minutes*

Cooking time: *50 to 60 minutes*

Yield: *8 servings*

2 pounds ground beef	*8 10-inch flour tortillas*
1 large onion, chopped	*3 cups grated cheddar cheese*
1 can (10 ounces) tomato soup	*1 cup sour cream*
2 cans (10 ounces each) enchilada sauce	

1 Cook the ground beef and onion in a 12-inch cast-iron camp oven over 24 hot coals until the beef is browned through and the onions are soft. Remove the cooked ground beef and onion from the oven and place it in a large bowl.

2 Stir the soup and enchilada sauce into the ground beef and onion. Spoon a ¼-inch layer of the meat, onion, and sauce mixture into the Dutch oven. Cover this mixture with a layer of tortillas, tearing to cover. Cover the tortillas with the grated cheese.

3 Repeat the layers of the sauce mixture, tortillas, and cheese until all the mixture is used up. Top with the cheese.

4 Place the lid on the oven. Pull 15 briquettes from the bottom and put them on the lid.

5 Bake for 35 to 40 minutes or until the mixture is bubbling and heated through. Serve with the sour cream.

Vary It! *To add even more spice to your dish, season your hamburger. Just use any taco or burrito seasoning packet to your hamburger and onion mixture (Step 1), following the directions on the packet. Then continue with the recipe as normal.*

Per serving: Calories 748 (From Fat 372); Fat 41g (Saturated 20g); Cholesterol 127mg; Sodium 1,051mg; Carbohydrate 53g (Dietary Fiber 4g); Protein 41g.

Campsite Beef Stroganoff

When you make traditional beef stroganoff, you prepare everything in stages, cooking the meat first, adding the sauce mixture next, and adding the sour cream last. The noodles you cook entirely separately, and then you combine everything during serving. In this recipe, after you brown the meat, you cook everything (including the noodles) together. The result is stroganoff that's as yummy and delicious as the original — without the work or attention.

Briquettes: *25*

Preparation time: *5 minutes*

Cooking time: *50 to 60 minutes*

Yield: *4 to 6 servings*

2 pounds extra lean ground beef	3 cans (8 ounces, each) tomato sauce
1 medium onion, chopped	1 teaspoon Worcestershire sauce
¼ teaspoon celery salt	½ cup sour cream
¼ teaspoon garlic salt	1 bag (12 ounces) egg noodles
Salt and pepper	

1 Brown together the meat, onion, celery salt, garlic salt, salt, and pepper in a 12-inch cast-iron camp oven over 25 hot coals.

2 While the meat is browning, mix together 1½ cups of water, the tomato sauce, Worcestershire sauce, and the sour cream in a medium bowl. (The sour cream won't be completely blended, and the mixture will have a few lumps.)

3 When the meat and onion are browned, spread the uncooked noodles evenly over the meat and onion. Pour the liquid mixture evenly over the noodles to moisten all the noodles well.

4 Cover with the lid and place the 15 briquettes on top, leaving 10 briquettes on the bottom.

5 Cook for approximately 30 to 45 minutes, or until the noodles are fully cooked.

Per serving: Calories 462 (From Fat 149); Fat 17g (Saturated 7g); Cholesterol 95mg; Sodium 1,032mg; Carbohydrate 46g (Dietary Fiber 4g); Protein 32g.

Mountain-Man Breakfast

Few pleasures are as delightful as a breakfast cooked outdoors, and this one gives you your meat, eggs, and hash browns without the hassle of cleaning separate pans.

Briquettes: *24*

Preparation time: *5 minutes*

Cooking time: *45 minutes*

Yield: *8 servings*

2 pounds breakfast sausage

2 pounds frozen hash brown potatoes

10 to 12 eggs, beaten with ¼ cup water

2 cups grated cheddar cheese

1 Fry and crumble the sausage in a 12-inch cast-iron camp oven over 24 hot coals. Remove the cooked sausage and drain on the paper towels.

2 Using the sausage drippings in the pan, brown the potatoes and spread them evenly in the bottom of the camp oven. Place the cooked sausage over the potatoes.

3 Pour the eggs over the sausage layer. Sprinkle the top with cheese.

4 Cook with 8 coals underneath the camp oven and 16 on top for 20 to 25 minutes, until the eggs are cooked.

Per serving: Calories 482 (From Fat 284); Fat 32g (Saturated 11g); Cholesterol 364mg; Sodium 887mg; Carbohydrate 21g (Dietary Fiber 2g); Protein 31g.

Sides: Always the Bridesmaid, Never the Bride

Side dishes are the unsung heroes of the dinner plate. That's because most people considered them filler: the thing that rounds out the meal or fills the empty space on the plate.

Sides, obviously, don't get the appreciation they deserve. But if you pair the wrong side dish with a meal (mashed potatoes with egg rolls, for example), you have a culinary disaster. But prepare the right side dish, and everything on the plate tastes better.

Don't limit your thinking on side dishes to vegetables. Sure, vegetables are the staples, but breads and fruits add a dimension all their own.

Dutch Oven Veggies

Many people cook their vegetables first and add any seasoning or butter afterward. The result is bland vegetables that get perked up as an afterthought. This recipe adds the seasoning and butter during the cooking process. Even without the cheese (which is a favorite of grown-ups and kids alike), the vegetables can stand on their own merits. Also keep in mind that, in a pinch, you can substitute pre-grated Parmesan cheese, but if you do, you'll sacrifice flavor. Freshly grated Parmesan beats pre-grated Parmesan hands down. Also, you can use virtually any vegetables you want with this recipe; simply make sure that you use 8 cups of veggies total and that you cut them into bite-size pieces.

Briquettes: *24*

Preparation time: *20 minutes*

Cooking time: *20 to 30 minutes*

Yield: *8 servings*

1 cup broccoli florets	*1 cup bite-size zucchini pieces*
1 cup cauliflower florets	*1 cup bite-size butternut squash pieces*
1 cup baby carrots	*Salt and pepper*
1 cup mushrooms	*¼ pound butter*
1 cup onions, cut into bite-size pieces	*2 cups shredded sharp cheddar cheese*
1 cup bite-size bell pepper pieces	*2 cups grated fresh Parmesan cheese*

1 Put ¼-inch water into the 12-inch cast-iron camp oven and add the veggies. Season generously with the salt and pepper — more than seems enough. Place the slices of butter on top of the veggies.

2 Put the camp oven over 24 hot coals until vegetable mixture is steaming, then pull out at least half of the coals. Steam the veggies until the carrots are tender.

3 Take the oven off the coals, remove the water with the baster, cover the veggies with the grated cheeses and put the lid on the oven. Serve when the cheese is melted.

Vary It! *To make a lighter version of this recipe, use cheese made with part skim rather then whole milk and use light butter. To make it lighter yet, take away the cheese entirely.*

Per serving: Calories 344 (From Fat 244); Fat 27g (Saturated 17g); Cholesterol 77mg; Sodium 639mg; Carbohydrate 9g (Dietary Fiber 3g); Protein 17g.

Creamed Corn Cornbread

Part cornbread, part vegetable side dish; Creamed Corn Cornbread is a way to sneak a few vegetables in on your little ones.

Briquettes: *20*

Preparation time: *5 minutes*

Cooking time: *20 minutes*

Yield: *6 servings*

1 cup yellow cornmeal	1 can (8 ounces) creamed corn
1 cup all-purpose flour	2 eggs
1 tablespoon baking powder	1 cup sour cream
2 tablespoons sugar	Honey (optional)
1 teaspoon salt	Butter (optional)
½ cup cooking oil	

1 In a large bowl, combine the cornmeal, flour, baking powder, sugar, salt, oil, creamed corn, eggs, and sour cream in a large bowl. Pour into a well-greased 10-inch cast-iron camp oven.

2 Bake with 6 hot coals under and 14 on top for about 20 minutes. Serve with honey and butter, if desired.

Per serving: Calories 475 (From Fat 263); Fat 29g (Saturated 7g); Cholesterol 88mg; Sodium 729mg; Carbohydrate 46g (Dietary Fiber 3g); Protein 8g.

Baked Pears

Unlike many fruits, pears should ripen off the tree. The only time that you want a tree-ripened pear is if the tree is in your front yard, and you're picking the pear yourself. A tree-ripened pear that's been boxed and shipped across the country will be unpleasantly mushy by the time it hits your grocer's produce section. When you're buying pears, select the ones that feel firm but give slightly at the stem. You can leave them at room temperature to ripen the rest of the way. You'll know they're ready when the skin lightens, and the aroma becomes noticeable.

Briquettes: *20 to 24*

Preparation time: *15 minutes*

Cooking time: *20 to 30 minutes*

Yield: *6 servings*

2 tablespoons butter	*½ cup pecan pieces*
6 tablespoons light brown sugar	*6 firm Bartlett pears*
1 tablespoon cinnamon	*Ground cloves*
6 crumbled butter cookies	*12 pecan halves*

1 Preheat a 12-inch cast-iron camp oven with the butter using 8 to 10 hot coals under the oven.

2 In a bowl, combine the brown sugar, cinnamon, crumbled cookies, and pecan pieces.

3 Cut the pears in half and gently scoop out the seeds, core, and stem. Sprinkle a pinch of ground cloves onto each pear half, being careful to not use much. Stuff each pear half with the brown sugar mixture.

4 Place pear halves cut side up in the camp oven. Dot with butter and place a pecan half on each pear.

5 Cover with the lid and add 12 to 14 briquettes to the top of the oven. Cook until hot, about 20 to 30 minutes. Serve while hot.

Per serving: Calories 291 (From Fat 126); Fat 14g (Saturated 4g); Cholesterol 16mg; Sodium 4mg; Carbohydrate 45g (Dietary Fiber 6g); Protein 2g.

Dutch Oven Desserts

Who doesn't like dessert? Dessert, after all, was the reason that the entree was invented. And cast iron is desserts' best friend. Just because you're camping — or roughing it out in the wide-open spaces of your RV — doesn't mean that you can't enjoy a few civilized niceties, such as Easy Pineapple Upside-Down Cake. If you can find a way to keep ice cream or whipped cream cold while hiking the trail, these delectable desserts become decadent delights when served à la mode.

Apple Crisp

This is a great recipe for fall, when apples are in season and at local produce stands. Of course, it's (almost) equally appetizing any time of year with store-bought apples. The key is the apple. Good cooking apples, which don't turn mushy or gritty, are Rome apples, Golden Delicious, and Winesap, varieties that are widely available.

Preparation time: *10 minutes*

Cooking time: *1 hour*

Yield: *8 to 10 servings*

10 cups peeled and sliced apples	*1½ cups brown sugar*
¼ cup lemon juice	*1¼ cups all-purpose flour*
3 tablespoon lemon zest	*1½ cups oats*
¾ cup sugar	*1 tablespoon cinnamon*
½ cup golden raisins	*1 teaspoon nutmeg*
¾ cup butter	*1 teaspoon cardamom*

1 Combine the apples, lemon juice, 1 tablespoon lemon zest, sugar, and raisins in a bowl. Spread the apple mixture in the bottom of a 12-inch cast-iron camp oven.

2 In a medium bowl, combine the butter and brown sugar. In another bowl, cut the butter mixture into the flour. Stir in the oats, cinnamon, nutmeg, cardamom, and the remaining 2 tablespoons lemon zest. Top the apple mixture with this topping mixture.

3 Place 8 coals under and 16 on top of the lid. Continue cooking until the apples are cooked and the topping is brown, about 1 hour. Serve warm.

Per serving: Calories 500 (From Fat 135); Fat 15g (Saturated 9g); Cholesterol 37mg; Sodium 18mg; Carbohydrate 91g (Dietary Fiber 5g); Protein 4g.

Lazy Cobbler

In a traditional cobbler, you prepare the fruit — peel, core, and slice — and the top crust (usually made of biscuit dough), a process that, in addition to several ingredients, takes a bit of time. This cobbler speeds things along. Instead of homemade biscuit dough, this cobbler uses a boxed cake mix, and instead of fresh fruit, it uses canned. You don't even need a spoon, because you don't even have to stir the ingredient together. Just dump them in your pan and let 'em cook.

Briquettes: *25*

Preparation time: *10 minutes*

Cooking time: *45 minutes*

Yield: *8 servings*

2 cans (30 ounces, each) peaches, sliced with syrup

1 package (18.25 ounces) white or yellow cake mix

1 to 1½ teaspoons ground cinnamon

⅓ stick butter or margarine

1 Place your 12-inch cast-iron camp oven over 15 hot coals.

2 Pour the contents of the peach cans into the oven. Spread the dry cake mix evenly over the peaches. Sprinkle the cinnamon over all. Cut the butter or margarine into equal slices and arrange on top.

3 Put the lid on top of the oven and place 10 hot charcoal briquettes in a checkerboard pattern on the top.

4 Bake for about 45 minutes or until done. Spoon into bowls.

Per serving: Calories 544 (From Fat 132); Fat 15g (Saturated 6g); Cholesterol 20mg; Sodium 453mg; Carbohydrate 105g (Dietary Fiber 3g); Protein 4g.

Baked Stuffed Apples

The flavor of baked apples comes from the apple (pick a good cooking variety, such as Golden Delicious or Rome), the filling you put in the hollowed out center, and the liquid. Many recipes call for plain water to be used. This recipe uses a mixture of water, honey, and orange juice, infusing the apple with subtle flavor as it cooks.

Briquettes: *35*

Preparation time: *15 minutes*

Cooking time: *50 minutes*

Yield: *6 servings*

6 apples

½ cup raisins

½ cup slivered almonds

½ teaspoon cinnamon

½ teaspoon nutmeg

6 ounces orange juice concentrate, thawed

3 tablespoons honey

1 Wash and dry the apples. Remove the core but don't cut all the way through the bottom of the apple.

2 In a small bowl, combine the raisins, almonds, cinnamon, and nutmeg. Using your fingers to stuff the filling into the apples, divide the filling among the apples.

3 In a small bowl, combine 2¼ cup of water, the orange juice concentrate, and honey. Mix until well blended.

4 Place the apples in a 12-inch cast-iron camp oven. Carefully pour the liquid mixture over the apples.

5 Bake with 9 hot coals on the bottom and 26 on the top for about 50 minutes, until the apples are tender. Spoon the excess sauce over the apples before serving.

Per serving: Calories 253 (From Fat 47); Fat 5g (Saturated 1g); Cholesterol Xmg; Sodium 3mg; Carbohydrate 54g (Dietary Fiber 6g); Protein 3g.

Almost Pumpkin Pie

Less a pie and more a crisp, this recipe eliminates the traditional pastry crust (and the work it takes to make one) for a crumbed mixture of cake mix, pecans, and butter. But, just as cutting shortening into the flour is the key to a flaky pastry crust, cutting the butter into the cake mix is key here. If you don't have a pastry cutter, can use a fork, two knives, or even your fingers. Whatever you use, don't stop until the cake mix-butter-pecan mixture is well blended and crumbly.

Briquettes: *24*

Preparation time: *10 minutes*

Cooking time: *1 hour*

Yield: *12 servings*

1 can (29 ounces) pumpkin	*1 teaspoon vanilla*
1 tablespoon pumpkin pie spice	*1 cup evaporated milk*
3 eggs	*1 cup butter*
1 cup sugar	*1 package (18.25 ounces) yellow cake mix*
½ teaspoon salt	*1 cup chopped pecans*

1 In a large bowl, mix together the pumpkin, pumpkin pie spice, eggs, sugar, salt, vanilla, and the evaporated milk. Pour this mixture into your greased 12-inch cast-iron camp oven.

2 Cut the butter into the cake mix with a pastry blender, then mix in the pecans. Sprinkle over the top of the pumpkin mixture.

3 Bake for 1 hour with 8 hot coals on the bottom and 16 on top.

Per serving: Calories 528 (From Fat 273); Fat 30g (Saturated 12g); Cholesterol 102mg; Sodium 425mg; Carbohydrate 60g (Dietary Fiber 4g); Protein 7g.

Easy Pineapple Upside-Down Cake

As delicious as the cake itself is, the best part of a pineapple upside-down cake is the topping: brown sugar, butter, and pineapple. To get a topping that's slightly caramel-y and not mushy, let the topping cook just a bit until slightly before you add the batter. For another Pineapple Upside-Down recipe, go to Chapter 13, and for more on why this cake is ideal for cast iron, go to Chapter 18.

Briquettes: *24*

Preparation time: *10 minutes*

Cooking time: *25 to 35 minutes*

Yield: *8 servings*

½ cup butter	1 package (18.25 ounces) yellow cake mix
1 cup brown sugar	3 eggs
1 can (20 ounces) pineapple slices	Juice from pineapple slices plus enough water to make 1¼ cups
8 maraschino cherries	

1 In a 12-inch cast-iron camp oven, melt the butter over 24 hot coals. Sprinkle the melted butter with the brown sugar. Place the pineapple slices over the brown sugar and reserve the juice. (There should be room for 7 to 8 slices.) Place a cherry in the center of each pineapple slice.

2 In a medium bowl, combine the cake mix, eggs, and reserved juice and water. Stir for 2 minutes. Spoon over pineapple slices.

3 Cook over 6 coals, transferring 18 coals to the lid, for 25 to 30 minutes.

4 When done (a toothpick inserted in the cake's center comes out clean), place the serving plate over the camp oven and carefully invert. Replace any pineapple slices that may have stuck. Serve warm.

Vary It! To enhance the flavor, add pecan halves randomly or in a decorative pattern to the brown sugar-pineapple mixture in Step 1.

Vary It! Prefer pears to pineapples? Use them instead. Simply peel, quarter, and core the pears and then cut each quarter lengthwise in half. Arrange the pears as you would the pineapple. Leave off the maraschino cherries.

Per serving: Calories 577 (From Fat 188); Fat 21g (Saturated 9g); Cholesterol 112mg; Sodium 470mg; Carbohydrate 94g (Dietary Fiber 1g); Protein 6g.

Chapter 15

Anyone Game?

Game is the meat of wild animals. You name it — deer, squirrel, pheasant, duck, wild turkey, and land turtles — if what you're eating is wild, it's game. And if you consider that until a few thousand years ago all meat-producing animals were wild (before they were domesticated by people who were tired of chasing them around), you realize that game's been an important part of the human diet for a long time.

And folks have been cooking game in cast iron since the Middle Ages in Europe. Of course, they probably caught their game themselves. You're just as likely to buy game, from a store, as you are to hunt it yourself.

This chapter includes information on what to look for when you go shopping for game, where you can find it (if you're not a hunter), and what you need to know to keep it from drying out as you cook it. And, of course, you can find several game recipes here, too.

Establishing the Game Rules

Most people don't eat game, or they don't eat it regularly, preferring the convenience and abundance of meat from domesticated animals. As a result, game isn't a main food source in American diets — or diets in any industrialized country for that matter.

Although game is generally tougher than meat from domesticated animals, fans say that it's also tastier. And because game generally has less fat, some folks argue that it's healthier, too.

Bluebloods and brown-baggers

Way back when people had to hunt for whatever meat they ate, hunting or eating game wasn't a matter of status, it was a matter of necessity. If you wanted meat, you went out and killed it, cleaned it, and hauled it home — usually in that order. Even after folks started domesticating animals as a food source (about 10,000 years ago), game still featured prominently in their diets.

Slowly, as these societies began to stratify into classes — those with, those with less, and those with practically nothing — hunting game evolved into a symbol of status. Those with — think of the ruling classes, whose main food consisted of the bounty from their own land and the labor from the people who worked it — hunted not for food as much as for pleasure. Hunting became a pastime and an indication of power. The thinking: "Real rulers" don't need to rely on domesticated animals; they're big and bad enough to go out and kill their own.

The middle classes, those who worked the land and who had other food sources (crops they could grow for their own use, as well as a few domesticated rabbits and chickens, for example), didn't need to hunt regularly and didn't have the leisure time to pursue it. For the lower classes, those who couldn't afford to keep domesticated animals, game remained an important part of their diet out of sheer necessity.

So, depending on where you fell in this system, eating game indicated that you were one of the powerful or one of the impoverished. The antagonism between these two groups spawned laws — poaching laws meant to protect the ruler's hunting grounds and other laws indicating who could kill what game. Rulers got the big game, such as deer, boar, and so on; peasants got the little stuff, such as squirrel and opossum. Think Robin Hood.

This pattern is still visible today. The types of restaurants that are most likely to serve game? High-class, pricey joints in metropolitan areas and mom-and-pop restaurants in rural areas.

To qualify as game, an animal has to be a mammal, a bird, or a reptile that lives on land. Fish are out. So are water reptiles. No matter how wild that bass was that you wrestled into your boat, it isn't game. At least not technically. Of course, you can argue this point with the many game-fishing associations around the world and the fishermen who wrangle marine creatures out of oceans and lakes everywhere.

Getting game

Obviously, if you're a hunter, you won't have trouble rounding up your own game, providing that your prey of choice is in season, the animals are willing, and you're not too bad a shot. But game isn't just for hunters. If you're not a hunter, the following sections outline several options you have for stocking up on the types of meat that I cover in this chapter.

Most game is *seasonal,* which means that it's available fresh only during the season when individuals are permitted by law to hunt each particular animal. If you don't happen to live in an area where game is present, you're going to have a more difficult time tracking it down.

Local stores

Check out your local grocery stores, markets, and specialty food stores. Your success rate for finding game in these locations will vary depending on the season, the area you live in, and the type of game you're looking for. You may have greater luck at specialty food stores. Any game that you buy from a market is federally inspected to be safe to eat.

Hunters

Some folks hunt game that they sell later. Check your local newspaper classified ads or try calling outdoor supply shops or hunting clubs. If you buy game directly from a hunter, make sure you trust the hunter and his abilities to *dress* game — that is, prepare the meat so that it's suitable for human consumption. That trust is the only indication you have that the meat is safe. (Check out the "More than you probably want to know" sidebar in this chapter if you *really* want to know more about dressing game.)

Game farms

Essentially a game farm is a controlled environment in which people have access to certain types of game animals. Some game farms support game birds, for example, like pheasant, wild turkey, and partridge. Other game farms may support game animals, like deer, bear, boar, and so on. On some of these farms, you participate in an actual hunt, in which you bring down your own game. On others, the folks who run the farm slaughter and dress the animals for you. Here are a couple of things to know about game farms:

- States have their own game commissions that oversee game farms within their jurisdiction. The oversight and rules governing game farms and the animals differ by state. To find out about the regulations in your area, contact your state's game commission (or similarly named department).

- Before you head out to a game farm thinking that you're going to bring home dinner, make sure the farm is one for that purpose. Some game farms are more like wildlife refuges where the only shooting comes from a camera.

To find game farms in your area, contact your local game commission or search the Internet. In your search engine, type in **game farms *your area*** or **game farms *type of animal*.** To find game farms in Utah, for example, enter **game farms Utah;** for game farms that offer pheasants, enter **game farms pheasant Utah.**

Internet suppliers

Internet suppliers may be your best bet. To find suppliers of particular types of game, in your search engine, type in *type of game* **supplier.** For example, typing **venison supplier** will generate a list of retailers who sell venison. Following are a few general Web sites that provide supplier information or links to sites with the information you're looking for:

- ✔ Specialty Food Suppliers at www.culinarysoftware.com/fooda.htm. This page provides an alphabetized list of specialty food suppliers, with contact information and brief descriptions of the foods available. In addition to game, you can find suppliers of various other foods.

- ✔ Chef Links at www.kieto.com/links/cheflinks.html. Here you can find links to game recipes and suppliers.

- ✔ Meat, Fish, Poultry, Seafood site at http://food.oregonstate.edu/f.html. Click the type of game you want information about to generate a list of resources and Internet sites containing both general information and supplier information.

- ✔ The Poultry Connection at www.poultryconnection.com/hatchery.html. This site offers a list of hatcheries and suppliers, with contact information and the type of poultry available. You can search for the type of game bird that you want.

Scoring general cooking points

As a rule, game is leaner than meat from domesticated animals. I guess looking for food and running away from hunters provides a bit more exercise than standing around down on the farm chewing your cud or laying in mud. Venison is leaner than beef, boar is leaner than pork, and wild turkey is leaner than the domesticated turkeys. Having less fat makes the meat less tender and prone to drying out when you cook it. In addition, the age of the animal affects how tender it is. Meat from young animals is more tender than meat from older animals.

When you cook game, particularly meat from older animals, slow cooking in moist heat (braising for example) is best. In addition, adding fat during cooking can make the meat more tender and flavorful. With game, you incorporate fat by basting, barding, or larding the meat.

- ✔ **Basting:** When you baste, you brush or spoon fat (usually melted butter, meat drippings, or stock) over the meat as it cooks. You can also use a bulb baster to drizzle the fat over the cooking meat.

- ✔ **Barding:** When you bard, you tie pieces of bacon or *fatback* (the strip of fat off the back of a hog) around the game animal and then remove it a few minutes before the meat is done so that the skin can brown.

✔ **Larding:** When you lard, you use a larding needle to insert *lardon* — long, thin strips of fat or bacon — into the meat itself.

For a variety of reasons (with the primary one being the animal's diet), meat from a wild animal tastes different from meat from its domesticated brother. So don't use the domesticated animal's flavor as the standard by which you judge the game meat.

Watching the Birdie

Game birds come in all shapes, sizes, and species. Large game birds include wild turkey and goose; medium game birds include wild duck and pheasant. Small game birds include dove, quail, and pigeon.

If you're not the hunting type, you can find some game birds on game farms. Many people around Thanksgiving time, for example, go to farms to select the bird for their holiday table. A few grocery stores, butchers, and markets also may sell game birds. Depending on the market and the season, you may be able to find freshly butchered birds, frozen birds, or canned birds (usually the smaller game birds).

When you select fresh game birds, pay attention to the following:

✔ **Age:** The meat of young birds is superior to older birds. It's more tender and has a milder flavor. Typically, young birds have pliable legs, feet, and breastbones and sharp claws.

✔ **Appearance and smell:** Quality birds don't give off an offensive odor, and the skin shouldn't be dry or dull.

When you go to cook your game bird, keep these points in mind:

✔ **Wild birds have much less fat than domestic birds of the same variety.** The lack of fat is even more pronounced in younger birds. For this reason, you need to work a little harder to keep the meat from drying out. (See the "Scoring general cooking points" section, earlier in this chapter, for details, including common techniques, such as basting, barding, and larding.)

✔ **The age of the bird impacts the cooking method.** Young birds, which are on the tender side, can be roasted, broiled, or fried. Cook older birds with moist heat — braising for example — or use them in soups and stews.

Dutch Cornish Hens

Rock Cornish hens, also called *Cornish game hens,* are miniature chickens that weigh between 1½ to 2½ pounds. Because of the relatively small amount of meat to bone, one bird feeds one or two people, depending on the size of their appetites. Rock Cornish hens are often broiled or roasted; sometimes, they're stuffed.

Wild rice is an excellent accompaniment to this recipe.

Preparation time: *5 minutes*

Cooking time: *1 hour*

Yield: *8 servings*

4 Rock Cornish hens, halved	*¼ teaspoon dried thyme*
4 teaspoons salt	*¼ teaspoon marjoram*
1 teaspoon pepper	*½ teaspoon chili powder*
6 tablespoons all-purpose flour	*¾ teaspoon paprika*
3 tablespoons butter	*¼ cup sherry*
3 tablespoons vegetable oil	*½ cup chopped fresh parsley*
¼ teaspoon sage	

1 Preheat oven to 375 degrees. Season the hens with the salt and pepper and coat with the flour.

2 Melt the butter and heat the oil in a 5-quart cast-iron Dutch oven over medium-high heat. Add the sage, thyme, marjoram, chili powder, and paprika.

3 Brown each half hen on all sides, a few at a time, without crowding. As each half browns, about 12 minutes, remove it from the Dutch oven and keep warm.

4 When all halves are browned, return them to the Dutch oven, and bake uncovered for about 20 minutes, or until fork tender. Remove hens to a serving platter.

5 Place the Dutch oven on the stovetop over medium heat. Add the sherry to the pan juices, scraping the bottom to deglaze the pan. Stir and cook for 2 minutes.

6 Stir in the parsley and pour the sherry mixture over the hens.

Per serving: Calories 498 (From Fat 329); Fat 37g (Saturated 13g); Cholesterol 223mg; Sodium 1,266mg; Carbohydrate 5g (Dietary Fiber 1g); Protein 35g.

Duck for dinner

When you shop for duck, pay attention to the U.S. Department of Agriculture (USDA) classifications. You can find the duck's classification on the package or on a tag attached to the duck's wing. Ducks are classified as A, B, or C. Ducks who earn an A, the best grade, are meatier than B-grade ducks. Generally, C-grade ducks aren't sold in markets.

You'll also see other classifications for ducks at the market that indicate the quacker's age and, consequently, the cooking method you should use:

- ✔ **Broilers and fryers:** Younger ducks, usually less than 8 weeks old. Their meat is suitable for broiling, frying, and other cooking methods that don't require slow cooking to tenderize the flesh.

- ✔ **Roasters:** Between 9 and 16 weeks old, these ducks benefit from slow roasting to tenderize them.

You may also see some broiler-fryers labeled as *ducklings*. This label doesn't mean much in terms of tenderness, because most ducks are butchered while they're still young and tender. Remembering that broiler-fryers are younger ducks (*ducklings*) and roasters are older ducks is key.

Fresh duck is usually available from late spring to early winter. Frozen duck is available year round. When you buy fresh duck, look for plump, broad breasts and skin that doesn't sag. When you buy frozen, make sure that the packaging is tight and unbroken.

To store fresh duck, remove the giblets. Then store the giblets and the duck separately in the coldest section of your refrigerator. You can leave them there for no more than three days. If wrapped tightly and kept frozen continuously at 0 degrees, you can keep your duck in the freezer indefinitely. The key is the 0 degrees. If you don't keep your freezer that cold (and most people don't), you can safely store your duck in the freezer for up to 3 months.

To thaw frozen duck, place it in the refrigerator a day or two before you need it. (The larger the duck, the longer it takes to thaw.) Don't refreeze the meat after it has thawed.

The mamas and the papa from China

Nearly half of all domestic ducks in the United States are Long Island ducks, which can trace their ancestry back to three ducks and a *drake* (male duck) that were brought to the United States from China in 1873. These descendents of the Peking duck, a variety of mallard and not just a delicious Chinese dish, are known for their succulent, dark meat.

Fried Duck Tenders

These marinated, fried strips of duck are great appetizers — just be sure to make more than this recipe produces! Or, if you're thinking dinner, serve them over rice. Toss in a few stir-fried vegetables (Chapter 10 has some recipes) and voila! You have a complete meal.

Preparation time: *10 minutes, plus overnight refrigeration for marinade*

Cooking time: *30 minutes*

Yield: *4 to 6 servings*

1 can (12 ounces) evaporated milk	4 to 6 boneless, skinless duck breasts
1 egg, beaten	Canola oil to fill skillet ½-inch deep
¼ cup soy sauce	Salt and pepper
1 tablespoon seasoning salt	1 cup all-purpose flour
1 tablespoon Worcestershire sauce	½ cup green onions, cut into ½-inch pieces
2 drops Tabasco sauce	

1 In a large, resealable freezer bag, combine the milk, egg, soy sauce, seasoning salt, Worcestershire sauce, and Tabasco sauce. Cut the duck breasts into finger-size strips and place them in the bowl with the marinade. Cover and refrigerate overnight.

2 When you're ready to fry, fill a 10-inch cast-iron skillet to ½-inch deep with oil over medium heat.

3 While the oil is heating, place the duck strips on wax paper and discard marinade. Salt and pepper the duck and then dredge in the flour.

4 Fry the strips in batches on medium heat, until the duck is golden brown, tender, and cooked through, about 3 to 5 minutes. Continue until all strips are fried. Fry the green onions for about 1 minute. Sprinkle green onions over strips and serve.

Per serving: Calories 700 (From Fat 391); Fat 44g (Saturated 14g); Cholesterol 276mg; Sodium 431mg; Carbohydrate 2g (Dietary Fiber 0g); Protein 71g.

Pheasant: A pleasant repast

You can sometimes find frozen pheasant in specialty meat markets, but you usually have to special order them or log onto the Internet. (See the "Getting game" section, earlier in this chapter, for some sites to start with.) Although *cocks* (male pheasants) weigh more than *hens* (females), they're less plump, less juicy, and less tender. A male can range from 2½ to 5 pounds compared to hen's average of 3 pounds. As with other game birds, the younger the bird (male or female), the moister and more tender the meat.

Pheasant Faisan

After an initial browning in butter, this recipe uses moist heat to cook the pheasant to doneness. This technique tenderizes the meat. To save some time, have the butcher cut up cut up your pheasant.

Preparation time: *5 minutes*

Cooking time: *30 minutes*

Yield: *4 servings*

2 pounds of pheasant, cleaned and cut into serving-size pieces	*1 bay leaf*
	½ teaspoon dried thyme
Salt and pepper	*¾ cup dry white wine*
6 tablespoons cold butter	*2 tablespoons fresh parsley, finely chopped for garnish (optional)*
1 clove garlic, peeled and crushed	

1 Season the pheasant with salt and pepper.

2 Heat 3 tablespoons of the butter in a 10-inch cast-iron skillet over medium-high heat.

3 Add the pheasant pieces skin-side down and cook until golden brown, about 5 minutes. Turn the pieces and cook another 3 minutes. If necessary, brown the pheasant in batches.

4 Reduce the heat to medium and add the garlic, bay leaf, thyme, and wine. Cover and cook 20 minutes or until the pheasant is fork tender. Remove the pheasant to the serving platter.

5 Swirl the remaining cold butter into the pan sauce, scraping the bottom of the skillet to deglaze.

6 Remove the bay leaf and pour the sauce over the pheasant and garnish with the parsley, if desired.

Per serving: Calories 508 (From Fat 317); Fat 35g (Saturated 16g); Cholesterol 185mg; Sodium 226mg; Carbohydrate 1g (Dietary Fiber 0g); Protein 45g.

Cooing for dove cooked in cast iron

Doves (and pigeons, their close cousins) have been a part of the human diet for thousands of years. You use these small game birds much the same way that you use chicken: You can cook it the same way and store it the same way. Head to Chapter 7 for details on storing chicken.

Love That Dove

If you don't have dove, substitute *squab,* a young domesticated pigeon that's never flown and, as a result, is *particularly* tender. You can find frozen squab year-round. This dish is excellent with rice.

Preparation time: *5 minutes*

Cooking time: *About 1½ hours*

Yield: *6 servings*

12 doves, cleaned	1 pint sour cream
Salt	1 cup sliced mushrooms
All-purpose flour	¼ cup white wine
½ cup butter	Paprika for garnish (optional)
1 onion, chopped	

1 Preheat your oven to 350 degrees. Season the doves with the salt and coat with the flour.

2 Heat ¼ cup of the butter in a 5-quart cast-iron Dutch oven over medium-high heat. Sauté the onion in the butter until golden. Remove the onions to a platter and keep warm.

3 In the remaining ¼ cup butter, brown the doves a few at a time, adding more butter if necessary. As the doves brown, about 7 minutes, remove to the platter with onions to keep warm until all the doves are brown.

4 Layer the browned doves and onion back into the Dutch oven. Bake, covered for 15 minutes at 350 degrees.

5 Meanwhile, in a bowl, combine the sour cream, mushrooms, and wine. Add to the doves and return it to the 350-degree oven, baking an additional 20 minutes, uncovered, or until done. Doves are done when meat thermometer inserted into thickest part of thigh registers 155 degrees. Be careful not to hit the bone: It throws off your reading.

6 Sprinkle with the paprika, if desired.

Per serving: Calories 1,082 (From Fat 842); Fat 94g (Saturated 42g); Cholesterol 324mg; Sodium 282mg; Carbohydrate 6g (Dietary Fiber 1g); Protein 52g.

Taking a bird's eye view

A few brief descriptions of other popular game birds that aren't included in the recipes in this chapter follow:

✔ **Grouse:** Medium- to large-size birds with plump bodies, grouse come in many varieties, including several varieties valued as game: the black grouse and hazel hen of Europe and Asia; and the prairie chicken, ruffed grouse, and others in America.

✔ **Partridge:** People in the United States use the term *partridge* to mean any number of game birds that aren't actually partridges at all. Although, technically speaking, partridges come in two main varieties — the gray and the red-legged — neither is native to North America. Americans consider grouse, quail, and bobwhites to be partridges. All these birds are plump and have white, tender flesh. You may be able to find frozen partridge at specialty grocery stores.

✔ **Plover:** Close cousins to the sandpiper, plovers are small, shore-inhabiting game birds. Ring plover, black-bellied plover, golden plover, dotterel, and lapwing, for example, are among the varieties of plover. Some claim that golden plover yields the best, most-delicate-tasting meat. Plover isn't too easy to come by, however. Hunting plover is illegal in the United States, so any plover not farm-raised must be imported from Europe. You may be able to find plover in specialty produce markets on a limited basis.

✔ **Quail:** Another case of mistaken identity: Colonists arriving in the New World saw birds that resembled the European quails of home and so christened them. In fact, American quail are not quail at all. Unlike the migratory birds they were named after, American quail don't migrate and hardly fly. To further confuse matters, people in different parts of the country call this already misidentified bird by different names: They're called *partridges* in the South, *bobwhites* in the East, and *quail* in the North. And folks in the Southwest know them as blue quail. Other names float around as well. Nevertheless, whatever these birds are called, they're white and have delicately flavored meat. Most quail for sale today have been raised on game farms. You can order quail through specialty butchers.

Other game birds: *coots* are similar to ducks; larks and thrushes are known for their singing; and woodcocks are cousins to the woodpeckers.

Game Animals

Game animals are divided into two categories: *Large* and *small*. Pretty scientific, huh? Common large game animals include venison and buffalo. (Boar and bear also qualify as large game animals, as do wild sheep and goats, kangaroo, and more.) The most popular small game animals are rabbit and squirrel.

The two types of game that you're most likely to find at your local market are rabbit and venison. However you obtain your game, keep the following in mind:

✔ **Wild game is generally leaner and therefore less tender than domesticated meat.** As a rule, meat from a younger animal is more tender than meat from an older animal, so be sure to card the deer before you kill it.

You can get a general idea about the tenderness of a cut by comparing it to a similar cut on beef or pork. For example, the sirloin portion on a deer would be more tender than the flank portion on that same deer, just as the sirloin portion on a cow is more tender than the cow's flank portion.

✔ **The fat on game animals usually has a rank taste.** Trim as much fat from the meat as you can before you cook it. To keep the meat from becoming too dry, you may have to baste, lard, or bard it. See the section "Scoring general cooking points" earlier in this chapter for info on those techniques of moistening up a dry piece of meat.

✔ **When the animal is killed affects the quality of the meat.** The meat is better when the animal has been killed in the fall, after it's had a chance to feed all spring and summer.

✔ **How the animal was dressed in the field affects the quality of the meat.** If the animal isn't bled and dressed out properly after being killed, the meat's flavor may be affected (it will taste "gamey" or wild) or it may be ruined and unfit for human consumption.

Game you buy from a market is federally inspected to be safe to eat. If you buy game from private individuals, you have to trust his or her ability in dressing and storing game.

✔ **To maximize the tenderness of your dish, cook the game slowly.** Braising is good. For particularly lean meats, or if you're cooking with dry heat (roasting for example), baste or lard the meat.

Venison: It's more than deer, dear

When you think of venison, the first — and only — animal that probably comes to mind is deer. But the *venison* category includes elk, moose, reindeer, caribou, and antelope.

More than you probably want to know

As soon as wild game is killed, the animal must be bled and dressed out. The carcass is usually elevated and two slits are made: One so that the blood can drain and another so that the internal organs can spill out and away from the animal. Skill and timing are important. If all the blood doesn't drain completely, the flesh takes on a strong gamey flavor. It won't ruin the meat, but it does make it less pleasant. More importantly, if the animal's bladder or intestines are ruptured during the dressing out process or even during the kill, the bacteria can spill into the cavity and contaminate the meat, ruining it for human consumption.

Hunter's Venison Bourguignon

This recipe has a fancy name, but the technique is actually simple. *Bourguignon* (boor-gee-*nyon*) is the French term for *prepared in Burgundy.* Although Burgundy *is* a region in France, the term speaks more to the technique of braising meat in red wine, which comes from Burgundy. Serve this dish over egg noodles or alongside simply prepared potatoes.

Preparation time: *10 minutes*

Cooking time: *About 2 hours*

Yield: *4 to 6 servings*

3 pounds venison, cut into 2-inch cubes	*½ teaspoon marjoram*
Salt and pepper	*2 sprigs thyme, crushed*
2 tablespoons butter	*2 tablespoons all-purpose flour*
1 onion, chopped	*1 quart beef stock or bouillon*
¼ pound ham, chopped or finely diced	*1 cup dry red wine*
2 cloves garlic, minced	*1 pound fresh mushrooms, sliced*
2 bay leaves	

1 Salt and pepper the venison. In a 5-quart cast-iron Dutch oven, heat the butter over medium heat. Add the venison and cook slowly for about 10 minutes, at which point the venison should have a little color. Add the onion and cook until tender.

2 Add the ham, garlic, bay leaves, marjoram, and thyme. Stir and simmer for about 3 minutes.

3 Add the flour and cook and stir another 3 minutes.

4 Add 1 cup of warm water and bring to a simmer by reducing the heat to medium-low.

5 Add the beef stock and wine. Simmer for about 1 hour.

6 Add the mushrooms and adjust seasoning, if necessary. Simmer another 45 minutes. Remove the bay leaves before serving.

Per serving: Calories 461 (From Fat 188); Fat 21g (Saturated 7g); Cholesterol 203mg; Sodium 1,108mg; Carbohydrate 8g (Dietary Fiber 2g); Protein 58g.

Wascally wabbits

You can find fresh and frozen whole rabbit or rabbit that's been cut into pieces in many grocery stores. Rabbit meat is almost all white. And like other game, meat from younger rabbits is more tender and has a milder flavor than meat from older rabbits. Young rabbits weigh between 2 and 2½ pounds; mature rabbits weigh between 3 and 5 pounds.

Rabbits taste much like chickens. You can substitute rabbit for chicken in just about any fried chicken or chicken stew recipe. Just allow a little more cooking time. However, rabbit meat has even less fat than poultry; the fact that it's so lean is probably why rabbit meat has become more popular of late.

Baked Rabbit

Slow cooking the rabbit in this recipe guarantees tender, succulent meat. Serve the dish in a bowl with rice, and you have an easy, delicious way to soak up the extra liquid. If you purchase a whole rabbit, have the butcher cut it into pieces for you.

Preparation time: *15 minutes*

Cooking time: *1½ to 2 hours*

Yield: *4 servings*

4 slices bacon	*1 cup chicken stock or bouillon*
2 pounds rabbit pieces	*½ cup dry red wine*
Salt and pepper	*1 teaspoon salt*
All-purpose flour for dredging rabbit	*1 teaspoon sugar*
3 to 4 tablespoons Canola oil	*¼ teaspoon dried thyme*
1 pound mushrooms, sliced	*¼ teaspoon dried rosemary*
8 ounces baby carrots	

1 Preheat your oven to 350 degrees. In a 10-inch cast-iron deep skillet (chicken fryer), fry the bacon over medium heat until brown. Remove the bacon and reserve for garnish.

2 Season the rabbit with the salt and pepper and dredge in the flour until coated. In the skillet, brown the rabbit pieces in the rendered bacon fat a few at a time over medium-high heat, adding additional oil if needed. Remove to platter to keep warm.

3 Add additional oil if necessary to cook mushrooms and carrots in the skillet over medium heat. Stir in the chicken stock, ¾ cup water, wine, salt, sugar, thyme, and rosemary; heat to boiling.

4 Return the rabbit to the skillet. Cover and bake in a 350-degree oven for about 1½ hours until fork tender. Garnish with the crumbled bacon.

Per serving: *Calories 622 (From Fat 307); Fat 34g (Saturated 8g); Cholesterol 173mg; Sodium 1,241mg; Carbohydrate 12g (Dietary Fiber 3g); Protein 64g.*

Good luck or good business?

It used to be that when you bought whole rabbit from a butcher, you'd get the whole rabbit, dressed as you would expect, *plus* a rabbit's foot. The reason that butchers left one rabbit foot on the carcass was to prove that the animal was, indeed, a rabbit. Well, what would it be if it weren't a rabbit? A cat.

Some unscrupulous butchers sold cats as rabbits to unsuspecting customers. Nowadays, the practice of leaving one foot intact is dying out, having given way to meat inspectors and USDA grading systems and all the other checks that ensure the safety and integrity of the food supply. If you do end up with a rabbit's foot the next time that you buy rabbit at the grocery store, just consider yourself lucky.

Chapter 16

Going Global with Recipes from Around the World

So many recipes do so well in cast iron that it would be a shame not to include recipes from around the world. This chapter offers all-American favorites that originated in far-off lands. Some are American versions of authentic dishes made famous elsewhere (the Chicken Parmigiana, for example, or the Arroz con Pollo); others are American dishes that have been inspired by cuisines from other countries (such as the fajita recipe).

This chapter includes recipes from Italy, Spain, Mexico, the Caribbean, and other far-off locations. But I think you'll agree that they round out your cast-iron repertoire quite nicely.

Pizza: An All-American Italian Favorite

Pizza is such a popular dish that you can be forgiven for not knowing that it hit U.S. shores only after World War II when American soldiers brought the idea back with them from Italy. Of course, American pizza is quite different from pizza as Italians know it. But still, cast iron's heating properties are great for crisp, golden American pizza crusts. (You can read more about cast iron's heating characteristics in Chapter 5.) **Note:** To make the pizza recipe included here, you need a cast-iron pizza pan.

Homemade Cheese Pizza

This recipe sticks to the traditional favorite: nice crisp crust, tomato sauce, and delicious melted cheese. To make your pizza, assemble the ingredients — pizza dough and tomato sauce (their recipes follow). Then bake as instructed.

Preparation time: *50 minutes, including time to make Quick Pizza Dough and Pizza Sauce*

Cooking time: *8 to 10 minutes*

Yield: *One 13-inch pizza, 8 slices*

Quick Pizza Dough (recipe follows)   2 cups shredded mozzarella cheese
½ to ¾ cup Pizza Sauce (recipe follows)

1 Preheat your oven to 450 degrees.

2 Spread, stretch, and shape your Quick Pizza Dough by hand onto a cast-iron pizza pan. Avoid tearing.

3 Spread ½ of the prepared Pizza Sauce onto the dough and sprinkle the cheese over the sauce.

4 Bake for 8 to 10 minutes or until the crust is golden brown. Cool 2 to 3 minutes before cutting or serving.

Vary It! *Add vegetable and meat toppings of your choice. Pile on pepperoni, sausage, onions, green peppers, mushrooms, and so on.*

Per serving: *Calories 313 (From Fat 97); Fat 11g (Saturated 5g); Cholesterol 25mg; Sodium 451mg; Carbohydrate 40g (Dietary Fiber 2g); Protein 13g.*

Quick Pizza Dough

If you're running short on time, skip making your own dough: Just buy ready-made dough from your grocer's freezer or refrigerator section.

Preparation time: *30 minutes*

Yield: *Dough for one 13-inch pizza crust*

3 cups bread flour, divided   1½ teaspoons honey
1 package dry rapid-rise yeast   1 tablespoon olive oil
1 teaspoon salt

1 In a large bowl, mix ½ cup of the flour with the yeast and salt. Dissolve the honey in 1¼ cup of lukewarm water and add to the dry mixture.

2 Add the olive oil and mix for 3 minutes with a wooden spoon. Mix in the remaining flour. (The dough should be only slightly sticky.) Turn the dough onto a floured surface and knead for about 5 minutes, until smooth.

3 Place the dough in a lightly oiled bowl and cover with the plastic wrap. Let it relax for 10 minutes in a warm place.

4 Punch down the dough. Allow to relax for another 10 minutes. Punch down.

Per serving: Calories 207 (From Fat 23); Fat 3g (Saturated 0g); Cholesterol 0mg; Sodium 292mg; Carbohydrate 39g (Dietary Fiber 1g); Protein 7g.

Pizza Sauce

Some people prefer a chunkier pizza sauce. If you're one of them, finely dice the tomatoes; don't blend them. Then continue with the recipe as written. If you're only making a pizza or two, you'll have some sauce leftover. Just freeze it for later use.

Preparation time: *10 minutes*

Cooking time: *30 minutes*

Yield: *About 8 ½-cup servings*

6 tablespoons olive oil	½ teaspoon salt
1 Spanish onion, minced	1 bay leaf
2 cloves garlic, chopped	2 tablespoons fresh basil, chopped
9 teaspoons tomato paste	2 to 4 teaspoons fresh oregano, chopped
1 can (28 ounces) plum tomatoes, blended smooth	½ teaspoon granulated sugar

1 In a 2-quart saucepan, heat the oil on the stovetop on medium heat. Stir in the onion and cook until translucent. Stir in the garlic and cook until wilted, about 1 minute. Add the tomato paste and cook, stirring constantly, for 30 seconds.

2 Add the blended tomatoes into the saucepan. Stir in the salt, bay leaf, basil, and oregano. Simmer, stirring occasionally, until the sauce is thickened, about 20 to 30 minutes.

3 Remove the bay leaf and adjust the seasoning with the sugar. Set aside until ready to use.

Per serving: Calories 126 (From Fat 92); Fat 10g (Saturated 1g); Cholesterol 0mg; Sodium 330mg; Carbohydrate 7g (Dietary Fiber 1g); Protein 2g.

Chicken Parmigiana

The term *parmigiana* describes food that's dredged in a mixture of bread-crumbs, grated Parmesan cheese, and various seasonings, and then sautéed. For chicken parmigiana, for example, pieces of chicken (usually boneless breasts) are pounded thin, dipped in egg, and then dredged in the cornmeal-parmesan mixture. You can prepare veal parmigiana, another common dish, in the same way. With cast iron, the breading is nice and crisp.

Classic Chicken Parmigiana

Classic parmigiana recipes are served over *vermicelli* (thin spaghetti) and covered in a tomato sauce. So grab a box of pasta and your favorite tomato sauce for this one. For added authenticity, top it off with melted mozzarella cheese.

Preparation time: *12 minutes*

Cooking time: *10 minutes*

Yield: *4 servings*

4 skinless, boneless chicken breast halves	*¾ cup breadcrumbs, plain or seasoned*
Salt and pepper	*¼ cup freshly grated Parmesan cheese*
½ cup all-purpose flour for dredging	*4 tablespoons butter*
1 egg	*1 tablespoon vegetable oil*

1 Wash the chicken breasts and pat dry. Pound the chicken breasts between two pieces of wax paper to ¼-inch thick. Season both sides of the chicken with salt and pepper.

2 Place the flour on a plate. Beat the egg in a large, shallow bowl. Combine the bread-crumbs and Parmesan cheese in another shallow bowl large enough for dredging.

3 Heat the butter and the oil over medium to medium-high heat in a 10-inch cast-iron skillet.

4 Dip the chicken in the flour to coat both sides, then dip it in the eggs, and then in the breadcrumb mixture.

5 Cook the chicken 5 to 7 minutes, turning once, until golden brown and cooked through. To serve, place the chicken on a bed of cooked pasta and pour over your favorite tomato sauce.

Per serving: *Calories 452 (From Fat 197); Fat 22g (Saturated 10g); Cholesterol 161mg; Sodium 494mg; Carbohydrate 27g (Dietary Fiber 1g); Protein 35g.*

A Vegetable Soufflé

Soufflés aren't just for dessert. The Calabasa Skillet Soufflé in this section is a savory rather than sweet soufflé that you can serve as a main dish.

Calabasa Skillet Soufflé

This squash soufflé is an Old Mexico recipe brought from a home kitchen in Chihuahua, Mexico. For information on types of squash and the difference between summer and winter squash, head to Chapter 10. If you have trouble finding the chayote squash, check out natural food stores.

Preparation time: *15 minutes*

Cooking time: *35 to 40 minutes*

Yield: *6 servings*

½ cup vegetable oil	*½ cup diced whole kernel corn*
½ cup diced chayote squash	*7 egg yolks*
½ cup diced summer squash	*2½ cups heavy whipping cream*
½ cup diced zucchini	*1 teaspoon salt*
½ cup diced onion	*1 teaspoon white pepper*

1 Preheat your oven to 350 degrees.

2 In a 12-inch cast-iron skillet, heat the oil over medium-high heat. Add the chayote squash, summer squash, zucchini, onions, and corn. Sauté until the vegetables are wilted, about 10 minutes.

3 In a mixing bowl, combine the egg yolks and cream. When the vegetables are wilted, remove the skillet from the heat and pour the egg mixture into the vegetables, blending thoroughly. Season to taste using the salt and pepper.

4 Cover the skillet and bake in the oven until the soufflé is set, about 35 to 40 minutes.

5 Remove from the heat and let rest for 10 minutes before serving.

Per serving: Calories 600 (From Fat 554); Fat 62g (Saturated 26g); Cholesterol 384mg; Sodium 437mg; Carbohydrate 8g (Dietary Fiber 1g); Protein 6g.

Famous Rice Dishes: Arroz con Pollo and Paella

Arroz con pollo (rice with chicken) and paella are two delicious and well-known rice recipes.

Arroz con pollo, a Spanish-Mexican dish, is commonly made with rice, chicken, green peppers, and seasonings. *Paella,* named after the pan that it's traditionally cooked and served in, is another rice dish. It often includes various meats and shellfish. The paella recipe in this chapter, Paella del Caribe, puts a Caribbean spin on a Spanish favorite. The rustic, dark look of cast iron really sets off the vibrant colors of the ingredients in these dishes.

Arroz con Pollo

The rich flavor of this recipe comes from its many ingredients. Assembling these many ingredients is probably the biggest challenge of the whole meal. Assemble all your ingredients beforehand. If you gather as you go, you'll invariably discover that you've misread or left a couple out.

Preparation time: 20 minutes

Cooking time: 2 hours

Yield: 8 servings

4 pounds of your favorite chicken pieces

Salt and pepper

2 strips bacon

½ pound sausage

½ cup peanut oil

2 cloves garlic, minced

2 medium onions, finely sliced

1 green bell pepper, seeded and finely sliced

½ pound mushrooms, sliced

2 cups long grain rice

2 cups peeled, seeded, and chopped fresh tomatoes

1 (2 ounce) jar diced pimentos, drained

1 (4 ounce) can chopped green chiles, drained

⅓ cup sliced green pitted olives

2 teaspoons wine or balsamic vinegar

2 teaspoons salt

1 teaspoon pepper

2 bay leaves

⅛ teaspoon saffron (optional)

2 cups chicken broth

1 cup vermouth or dry white wine

1 cup frozen peas (optional)

1 Preheat the oven to 325 degrees. Wash the chicken and pat dry. Lay on the wax paper and salt and pepper both sides of the chicken.

2 In a 12-inch cast-iron skillet, fry the bacon over medium-high heat and then drain on paper towels and crumble into your 7-quart cast-iron Dutch oven.

3 Fry the sausage in the bacon grease until it's brown. Remove the sausage to a Dutch oven with a slotted spoon to leave the drippings in a skillet. Add the peanut oil to the bacon and sausage drippings in the skillet.

4 Add a few pieces of the chicken at a time to the skillet and brown on both sides. With tongs, remove the chicken pieces to the Dutch oven as they're browned.

5 In the same skillet and drippings, sauté the garlic, onions, bell pepper, and mushrooms until slightly tender. Remove to the Dutch oven with a slotted spoon to leave the drippings in the skillet.

6 In the skillet drippings, brown the rice and add to the Dutch oven.

7 Into the Dutch oven, add the tomatoes, pimentos, green chiles, olives, vinegar, salt, pepper, bay leaves, saffron (if desired), chicken broth, and vermouth.

8 Place the cover on the Dutch oven and bake for about 2 hours, checking every 30 minutes to add more chicken broth if necessary. The mixture should not be soupy, but neither should it be dry.

9 Add the peas (if desired) during the last 15 minutes. Remove the bay leaves before serving.

Per serving: *Calories 683 (From Fat 324); Fat 36g (Saturated 8g); Cholesterol 133mg; Sodium 1,332mg; Carbohydrate 49g (Dietary Fiber 3g); Protein 39g.*

Paella del Caribe

This dish gets its distinctive flavor and golden color from saffron, the world's most expensive spice. Fortunately, because of the expense, a little bit of saffron goes a long way. Saffron comes powdered or in threads. You can use either for the recipe. If you have threads, crush them right before you add them to the dish.

Preparation time: *20 minutes*

Cooking time: *45 minutes*

Yield: *6 servings*

¼ cup olive oil	2 sprigs of thyme
1 cup chicken breast, diced	2 (7-ounce) fish fillets, cubed
1 teaspoon saffron	¼ cup sliced green onions
1 cup onions, diced	¼ cup chopped parsley
1 cup tomato, diced	1 tablespoon lime juice
1 cup carrots, diced	Salt and pepper
12 young okra, whole	2 cups long grain rice
1 quart chicken stock	1 cup bay scallops
1 bay leaf	1 cup small shrimp, peeled and deveined
2 whole cloves	

1 In a 15-inch cast-iron skillet, heat the olive oil over medium-high heat.

2 Add the chicken and sauté until lightly browned, about 7 minutes. Remove the chicken from the pan and keep warm.

3 Add the saffron, onions, tomato, and carrots. Sauté for 10 minutes or until the vegetables are wilted. Add the okra, chicken stock, bay leaf, cloves, and thyme. Bring the mixture to a rolling boil, stirring occasionally, and reduce the heat to simmer.

4 Add the fish, chicken, green onions, parsley, and lime juice. Season to taste using salt and pepper. Stir in the rice into the seafood mixture. Cover and simmer for 10 minutes.

5 Stir in the shrimp and scallops, cover and cook for and additional 10 to 15 minutes until the rice is tender and the shrimp and scallops are cooked through. Remove the bay leaf before serving.

Per serving: *Calories 526 (From Fat 130); Fat 14g (Saturated 3g); Cholesterol 99mg; Sodium 952mg; Carbohydrate 62g (Dietary Fiber 3g); Protein 34g.*

Fabulous Fajitas

Fajitas have gained popularity in recent years. A combination of marinated strips of meat, caramelized vegetables, steaming hot tortillas, and a variety of sauces and dips, fajitas offer something to please just about anyone. Of course, serving fajitas that live up to their promise can be a challenge.

The biggest hurdle is keeping all the ingredients at their proper temperature until everything is ready to be served. Fajitas include several dissimilar ingredients, each with different cooking requirements and preparation methods. Your best method of attack is to prepare the items that hold up well *before* you need them. Tortillas, for example, don't hold up well. They get dry and hard. The sauces, however, hold up very well and, in some cases, are better chilled. So have them already prepared before you even begin cooking your fajita meal.

Then, as you cook, you need to put the ingredients in a spot that will keep them warm. For the vegetables and meat, that spot is a preheated oven. For the tortillas, the area *isn't* the oven, which will dry them out. After you cook the tortillas, stack the hot tortillas in aluminum foil and then wrap a towel around them to keep them warm.

Assembling the parts

To prepare the various parts of your meal, use the following timetables as a guide:

- **Marinades:** Prepare at least two hours before. Prepare even earlier if you want really pungent meat with a fuller flavor; you can prepare it a day in advance if you like. Marinate your meat in the refrigerator.

- **Guacamole:** Prepare as early as the day before, and store it in an airtight container in the refrigerator until ready to use. ***Note:*** Guacamole doesn't save well (it discolors easily and goes bad fairly quickly) so be sure to use up all that you've made within two or three days.

- **Pico de gallo:** Prepare this condiment up to a day before and store it in the refrigerator in an airtight container until ready to use. Although pico de gallo can be stored in the refrigerator for a few days, it tastes and looks fresher if used shortly after being prepared.

Marinades

Marinating (soaking meat in seasoned liquid) serves two purposes: First it imbues the meat with flavor. Second, it acts as a tenderizer. The marinade in this section is homemade. If you're short on time, you can buy marinade sauce and skip preparing the marinade, itself, or you can buy already marinated meat and skip the marinating process entirely.

Because most marinades include acidic ingredients (such as vinegar), always marinate in glass, ceramic, or stainless steel containers. Even plastic storage bags are a good, mess-free alternative. Never use aluminum, which reacts with the acid.

One of the keys to flavorful fajitas is how long the meat marinates. The longer the meat marinates, the more intense the flavor of the meat. When you make the fajita recipe in this chapter, be sure to work the marinating time into your plans.

Marvelous Fajita Marinade

Use a zester or hand grater to get the orange and lemon peel that you need. Be careful not to get into the pith (the white part of the peel), which is bitter. This marinade is great for beef, pork, or chicken.

Preparation time: *5 minutes*

Chilling time: *Up to 2 hours*

Yield: *Enough for 4 fajitas*

1 large orange	1 clove garlic, minced
1 lemon	1 teaspoon pepper
¼ cup pineapple juice	1 dried chile, left whole
¼ cup white wine	3 tablespoons butter, melted
1 to 2 tablespoons soy sauce	

1 Grate 1 tablespoon of the peel from the orange and 2 teaspoons of the peel from the lemon, set it aside. Squeeze the orange and lemon to get ¼ cup of juice each.

2 Combine the zest, orange juice, lemon juice, pineapple juice, wine, soy sauce, garlic, pepper, chile, and butter in a large resealable plastic bag.

3 Place approximately 2 to 2½ pounds flank steak, pork tenderloin, or chicken breast (pounded to ½-inch thickness) in the marinade, and seal the bag.

4 Place the bag in the refrigerator to marinate for at least 30 minutes and up to 2 hours, turning occasionally.

Per serving: Calories 113 (From Fat 77); Fat 9g (Saturated 5g); Cholesterol 23mg; Sodium 233mg; Carbohydrate 7g (Dietary Fiber 1g); Protein 1g.

Sauces and condiments

A Mexican specialty, *guacamole* is made from mashed avocado mixed with lemon or lime juice and various seasonings. Look for fresh avocados that aren't too soft (these are too ripe) or too firm (not ripe enough). When you press gently, you should be able to feel the fruit give slightly.

If you buy an avocado that needs ripening, leave it at room temperature for a couple of days. If you're in a real hurry, put the avocado in a brown paper bag with a ripe tomato. It'll be ripe in less than a day.

Fortunately, the Spanish dish *pico de gallo,* which means *beak of the rooster,* is 100 percent beak-free. But originally, folks partook of this tangy tomato condiment by using their thumb and index finger, in a motion resembling a pecking rooster — an impression that was heightened, no doubt, by freely flowing Madeira.

In addition to serving guacamole and pico de gallo with your fajitas, include sour cream alongside the other sauces and condiments.

Pico de Gallo

Traditional pico de gallo is finely chopped. You can make yours as chunky as you want. Just try to keep the size of the chopped onion, pepper, and tomatoes proportionally the same so that the flavors are evenly distributed.

Preparation time: *5 minutes*

Cooking time: *3 to 5 minutes*

Chilling time: *Until cold or overnight*

Yield: *4 ¼-cup servings*

1 cup peeled, seeded, and diced tomatoes	*1 poblano pepper, seeded and finely chopped*
2 tablespoons olive oil	*¼ to ½ small onion, grated*
2 clove garlic, minced	*2 tablespoons lime juice*

1 Place the tomatoes in a medium bowl.

2 Combine the olive oil, garlic, and the pepper in a small saucepan over medium heat for 3 to 4 minutes, stirring constantly. Pour over the tomatoes.

3 Add the onion and lime juice. Chill overnight or until cold.

Per serving: Calories 89 (From Fat 67); Fat 7g (Saturated 1g); Cholesterol 0mg; Sodium 7mg; Carbohydrate 6g (Dietary Fiber 2g); Protein 1g.

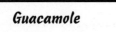

Guacamole

The most important ingredient in guacamole is the avocado. Fresh avocado is best, but if avocados aren't in season, aren't available in your area, or aren't ripe, your best bet is buying canned avocado. Trying to pit and mash an unripe avocado yields about as much edible fruit as a withered vine. So go for the canned variety.

Preparation time: *5 minutes*

Yield: *4 ¼-cup servings*

3 medium, ripe avocados, peeled, pitted and mashed	*1 tablespoon lime juice*
	½ teaspoon salt
¼ small onion, grated	*2 tablespoons chopped fresh cilantro*
1 small ripe tomato, peeled, seeded and chopped	*Juice from 1 lemon*
4 slices jalapeno pepper, seeded and chopped	

1 Combine the avocado, onion, tomato, jalapeno, lime juice, salt, and the cilantro in a medium bowl.

2 Add the lemon juice. Taste the combined ingredients and adjust the seasoning as necessary.

3 Place plastic wrap directly on the surface of the mixture and let it stand for a few minutes.

4 Refrigerate in an airtight container until it's time to serve.

Per serving: *Calories 220 (From Fat 170); Fat 19g (Saturated 4g); Cholesterol 0mg; Sodium 294mg; Carbohydrate 15g (Dietary Fiber 12g); Protein 4g.*

Making the fajitas

You need at least three pans for this recipe: One to cook the stovetop ingredients, another to broil the meat, and a third preheated pan (or several small pans for individual servings) for serving the fajitas. You can find specific details in the following fajita recipe.

When preparing fajitas, prepare sauces and condiments so that they're ready to go. After you start cooking the meat, fajitas come together quickly.

Fabulous Fajitas

Most fajita recipes include marinated strips of beef or chicken. Although this recipe calls for marinated beef, you can substitute marinated chicken or pork for the beef.

Preparation time: *20 minutes*

Cooking time: *30 minutes*

Yield: *4 servings*

8 10-inch flour tortillas

2 to 2½ pounds marinated flank steaks, pounded to ¼-inch thickness (see the Marvelous Fajita Marinade recipe earlier in this chapter)

4 tablespoons butter

2 large onions, sliced and separated into rings

2 green bell peppers, sliced and separated into rings

1 package (8 to 10 ounces) sliced mushrooms (optional)

4 tablespoons butter

2 limes, halved

Pico de Gallo (recipe earlier in this chapter)

Guacamole (recipe earlier in this chapter)

1 Place the top rack of the oven 4 inches below broiler. Place the bottom oven rack in the lowest position. Place a cast-iron griddle on the bottom rack. Set your oven to 425 degrees. Heat your cast iron for 30 minutes.

2 Heat another cast-iron griddle or skillet on the stovetop on high heat for a few minutes; then reduce the heat to medium.

3 Place one tortilla on the griddle; cook until the bottom blisters (about 30 seconds). Turn with tongs and repeat until the second side is blistered. Stack the tortillas on the foil and wrap to keep warm.

4 Set your oven to broil — the griddle is still on the bottom rack. Place the meat in a pan on the top rack and broil for approximately 5 to 6 minutes on each side.

5 While the meat is cooking, melt the butter in a cast-iron skillet. Add the vegetables and sauté until the onions are translucent. Season with the salt and pepper. Remove from the heat but leave in the pan to keep warm.

6 Remove the meat from the broiler and cut against the grain into finger length strips.

7 Using potholders, remove the griddle from the oven and place on wooden underliners or a hot pad. Place the meat and vegetables on the griddle to serve. Serve with tortillas, lime halves, Pico de Gallo, and Guacamole.

Vary It! *Cook the meat on a gas or charcoal grill for even more flavor.*

Per serving: *Calories 1,573 (From Fat 798); Fat 87g (Saturated 36g); Cholesterol 220mg; Sodium 1,398mg; Carbohydrate 122g (Dietary Fiber 22g); Protein 77g.*

Pitting and mashing an avocado

To prepare the avocado for guacamole, you have to first pit it and then mash it. Follow these steps (you need a cutting board and a paring knife):

1. Cut the avocado lengthwise down to the pit and slide your knife all the way around; then twist to separate the halves.

2. Keeping your fingers well out of the way, swing the blade of a knife (preferably a heavy one) down into the pit, then twist the knife to remove the pit

3. Slide a large spoon between the skin and the flesh, and scoop out the flesh.

4. Using a fork or potato masher, mash the avocado.

Putting it all together

Okay, so you've pulled off the preparation of your fajitas. All the ingredients are steaming hot or nice and chilled as they should be. Now it's time to dig in. You can put the fajita together any way that you like; most people assemble them as they would a burrito:

1. Put the heated flour tortilla on plate.

2. Place the meat and marinated vegetables down center of tortilla.

3. Add the sour cream, Pico de Gallo, and Guacamole on top of that.

4. Fold the tortilla over the contents.

5. Enjoy!

Feeding That Sweet Tooth

Only a few treats are better than sweets. And only a few sweets are better than pastries. And few pastries are more enjoyable than those that don't require a plate, a fork, and a linen napkin, such as Beignets, fried yeast pastries from New Orleans (via France), and Aebleskivers — Danish pancake balls that don't need syrup.

Okay, so I know that New Orleans is part of the United States. But, really, it's so unlike any other U.S. city, so culturally varied and interesting (having been settled by the French, taken over by the Spanish, and not considered part of the United States until the Louisiana Purchase of 1803), and so down-right fun to visit that it really should qualify as a foreign port of call.

Beignets

Beignets are deep-fried pastries. Although they can be savory (including ingredients like crab meat and herbs), most beignets are sweet. This recipe calls for a generous dusting of confectioners' sugar.

Preparation time: *1 hour, 40 minutes*

Cooking time: *2½ minutes*

Yield: *4 dozen beignets*

1 package dry yeast	3 eggs beaten
3½ cups all-purpose flour	¼ cup melted butter
1 teaspoon salt	Oil for deep-frying
¼ cup sugar	1 cup confectioners' sugar
1¼ cups milk	

1 Dissolve the yeast in 4 tablespoons of warm water or according to package directions. Set aside.

2 In a mixing bowl, combine the flour, salt, and sugar and mix well to ensure proper blending. Fold in the dissolved yeast, milk, eggs, and butter. Continue to blend until the beignet dough is formed.

3 Place the dough in a metal, glass, or ceramic bowl, cover with a towel, and allow to rise for 1 hour. Remove to a well-floured surface and roll out to ¼-inch thickness. Cut into rectangular shapes, cover with a towel, and allow dough to rise for 30 minutes.

4 In a deep-sided (3 to 4 inches) cast-iron skillet or pot, preheat the oil to 375 degrees.

5 Deep-fry, turning once, until the beignet is golden brown, about 2½ minutes. Drain and dust generously with confectioners' sugar.

Per serving: *Calories 106 (From Fat 56); Fat 6g (Saturated 1g); Cholesterol 17mg; Sodium 56mg; Carbohydrate 11g (Dietary Fiber 0g); Protein 2g.*

Aebleskiver (Pancake Balls)

To make this recipe, you really need a specialty pan called a *Danish cake pan,* an *aebleskiver pan,* or a *munk pan.* With several rounded wells, this pan is designed for stovetop use — a necessity because you have to turn the pancake balls as they cook.

Preparation time: *10 minutes*

Cooking time: *2 to 3 minutes*

Yield: *4-dozen balls*

2 cups all-purpose flour	⅔ cup milk
2 tablespoons sugar	3 egg yolks, beaten
1 teaspoon baking soda	2 tablespoons melted butter
1 teaspoon cardamom	3 egg whites, beaten
¾ teaspoon salt	2 tablespoons melted butter or vegetable oil for greasing wells
1 cup sour cream	

1 Set the aebleskiver pan on the stove burner on medium-low heat.

2 In a large bowl, sift the flour, sugar, baking soda, cardamom, and the salt together and set aside. In a smaller bowl, combine the sour cream, milk, egg yolks, and 2 tablespoons melted butter.

3 Make a well in the center of the dry ingredients and add the liquid mixture, stirring until well blended.

4 Gently fold the beaten egg whites into the batter.

5 Test the pan by dropping a few drops of water on it. If drops dance in small beads, then the temperature is correct.

6 Add about ½ teaspoon of melted butter or vegetable oil into the wells and heat. Pour the batter into the wells, filling slightly over ½ full. (Re-oil the wells with each batch.)

7 With knitting needles or fork, turn the aebleskiver frequently to brown evenly. Do not pierce.

8 Aebleskivers are done when a wooden pick inserted in the center comes out clean.

9 Remove from the pan and sprinkle immediately with the confectioners' sugar. Serve with the jam.

Vary It! *Pare and dice 2 medium apples. Sprinkle about 1 teaspoon diced apple over batter in each well while cooking.*

Per serving: *Calories 63 (From Fat 39); Fat 4g (Saturated 3g); Cholesterol 24mg; Sodium 47mg; Carbohydrate 5g (Dietary Fiber 0g); Protein 1g.*

Part V
The Part of Tens

The 5ᵗʰ Wave   By Rich Tennant

"I like cooking with cast iron. It's durable, heats evenly, and for adding iron to your diet, it's a lot easier than stirring my stews with a crowbar."

In this part . . .

You have arrived at the often imitated but never dupli-
cated *For Dummies* Part of Tens. This part offers
quick lists of info that you may find both interesting —
dishes that taste better cooked in cast iron, for example —
and helpful, such as tips to ensure that your recipes turn
out the way that you want them to.

Chapter 17

Ten Ways to Make Your Cast Iron Last a Lifetime (or Longer)

• •

In This Chapter

▶ Seasoning dos and don'ts

▶ Lasting through generations

• •

*U*nlike just about any other pan out there and certainly unlike any other pan in the same price range, cast iron can literally last for generations. But you do need to take care of it, because it isn't indestructible. Follow certain rules and your heirs will be fighting over who gets your glorious pans. This chapter puts all those rules in one place.

Reseasoning After Each Use

You know that you need to season cast iron before you use it the first time. (If this is news to you, head to Chapter 3 to find out why preseasoning is important and for instruction on how to do it.) Reseasoning your pans *after* each use is also important. The reason is that each time that you clean your cast iron, you remove a little seasoning. If you clean your cast iron enough times without reseasoning, the pans will lose the patina that makes them nonstick, and the metal will become vulnerable to rust.

Fortunately, reseasoning isn't nuclear physics. After you clean and dry your pan, simply wipe a thin coat of vegetable oil over the pan's surface.

Never Put Cold Water in a Hot Pan

All metals are susceptible to *thermal shock,* a large and rapid change in temperature. If you put a cold pan on a hot burner, a hot pan under cold running water, or subject your cookware to any other combination of extreme and sudden temperature differences, you run the risk of warping or even breaking it.

Whether a pan is hot or cold depends on how quickly the molecules in the metal are moving. Cold molecules move slowly; hot molecules move quickly. The hotter the pan, the quicker the molecules move and all the more haphazardly; the colder the pan, the more sluggish they are. Force an instant temperature change and the molecules don't have time to transition from one state to another. The result? The metal equivalent of a human hissy fit.

The key is *gradual* temperature change. Pouring batter into a hot pan is safe. Putting a room temperature pan into a warm oven? Safe. Taking a pan from your refrigerator and putting it in a cold oven and preheating both together? Safe. Remember. Easy does it.

Don't Use Soap

For a society that has practically made *antibacterial* the new religion of clean, the idea of not using any soap at all sounds practically heretical. But you don't need soap to clean cast iron, and using it can break down the seasoning.

The only time that you need soap is when your pan is brand-spanking new and you have to wash it before you season it. (See Chapter 3 for details on that.) Beyond that, you don't need much cleaning paraphernalia — just hot water and a stiff-bristled brush. Some people don't even use water. If they have a cast-iron pan that they reserve solely for breads, for example, they simply wipe it out with a paper towel to clean it. (Not using soap doesn't present a health hazard. When you cook with cast iron, the pan gets hot enough to kill any germs on its surface.)

If you absolutely, positively can't stop yourself from sticking your cast iron in a sink full of soapy water, go ahead, but use mild soap and remember that

- ✔ You'll need to season your pan more frequently — maybe even after every use.

- ✔ Bringing out your cast iron's patina — a cook's dream — is going to take you longer. To find out about patina and why your success as a cast-iron cook is important, head to Chapter 1.

Don't Even Think about Using the Dishwasher

If soap is bad for cast iron (see the preceding "Don't Use Soap" section), running it through the dishwasher is practically the kiss of death. First, dishwashing detergents are more abrasive than dish soap and cause more damage to the seasoning. Second, in a dishwasher, water bombards your cast iron from every angle. Third, dishes essentially air dry in a dishwasher, which means that the water that bombarded your pan stays on it until it finally evaporates. (Check out the "Keeping Water Away" section, later in the chapter.)

If convenience is your excuse for putting your cast iron in the dishwasher, think about how inconvenient sanding off rust spots and then reseasoning your pan is. Two minutes of hand cleaning is nothing compared to the toil required to resurrect a prized piece of cast iron.

Keeping Water Away

Water is one of cast iron's enemies. One of your prime objectives as a cast-iron cook is to expose it to the least amount of water as possible in the least time. To minimize exposure to water, follow these suggestions:

- ✔ Wipe your cast iron dry immediately after you clean it. To make sure that all the moisture is gone, put your cast iron in a warm oven or on a warm burner for a couple of minutes.

- ✔ Other pans are better for water-intensive cooking, so don't use your cast iron as a boiler or steamer — at least not until it's well seasoned. Then, too, be sure to put a nice coat of vegetable oil on the inside of your cast iron.

- ✔ If you live in a humid environment, put a crumpled up paper towel into the pan before you store it and leave the cover off or ajar.

You can find more tips for caring for your cast iron in Chapter 4.

Using It Often

Unlike other cookware, cast iron actually gets better the more that you use it. Every time you cook with it, you're enhancing the pan's cooking properties. You can see this improvement as its color darkens. New cast iron is a gunmetal gray color and porous; old cast iron is black and satiny smooth. (In days gone by, cast-iron, new or old, was referred to as *black iron* because of the black color that cast iron took on as it aged.)

The black, satiny patina is the result of seasoning — layer upon layer of seasoning — that comes from using, reusing, and caring for your cast iron. The *only* way to get this black, satiny patina is to use the pan often. Preseasoned cast iron, which comes from the factory already seasoned and ready to use, gives you a head start on this process, but even these pans don't compare to old, well-used cast-iron pans.

When you're breaking in a new pan, be sure to cook fatty foods the first few times. Sausage, bacon, hamburgers, macaroni, and cheese — any dish with a high-fat content deepens the initial seasoning. After the pan is nicely cured, however, you can cook anything you want in it. So do!

Don't Let Teens Threaten Each Other with It

True story. When I was 14 and my angry older sister chased me around my mother's kitchen table, I grabbed my father's 15-inch cast iron skillet off the wall, held it over my head in both fists, and told her to back off. To her credit, she did. But to make my point — I had a weapon and was willing to use it — I slammed the indestructible pan down on the linoleum and watched as it broke into two halves. The fight ended at the shocking realization that cast iron was *not* indestructible and that my sister and I had some explaining to do.

If your kids need a mace or club to protect themselves in the sibling wars, buy them one. Don't let them use your cast iron.

Storing Appropriately

Cast iron doesn't require much care in the storage department. You can keep it in a cupboard, or you can hang it on a wall or from an overhead pan rack if you're so inclined. Just make sure that it's anchored well to the wall.

The most important storage directive is to make sure that, wherever you store your cast iron, the area is cool and dry. You don't want to hang cast iron, even purely decorative cast iron, on the wall above your stove, for example, because of the steam that rises from the stovetop. If you're stacking your cast iron, make sure that you leave the covers off or ajar so that air can circulate to keep moisture from forming.

For additional information about caring for your cast iron, head to Chapter 4.

Avoiding Acidic and Alkaline Foods at First

Certain foods — acidic foods, such as tomatoes and citrus products and alkaline foods, such as beans — can react to the iron in your pan. When your pan is new and before it's had a chance to develop the protective patina, such a reaction isn't particularly good for the pan (these foods can pit the surface), and it's disaster for your meal, which will end up tasting less like the food and more like the pan. (If you can't see why this is bad, lick your cast iron for a quick taste.)

This doesn't mean that you can *never* cook these foods in cast iron. Chili is a cast-iron favorite, as are old-fashioned green beans. It just means that the pan should be well seasoned before you do so. The seasoning protects the metal and the flavor of your food.

Appreciating Its True Value

In some families, the cast iron is passed down through generations as a valued family heirloom — even though most cast iron isn't worth a significant amount of money and, heaven knows, isn't particularly pretty. Cast iron is a treasure because it brings to mind good times, good food, and family. So when you cook with your cast iron, have fun.

If you enjoy cooking in it and you enjoy what you cook, these old, black-iron pans can appreciate in value far beyond their market value, their cooking properties, and all the other practical reasons people use them. Then you'll have a pan that not only *can* last generations but *will* last generations.

Chapter 18

Ten Dishes Best Suited to Cast Iron

In This Chapter

▶ Frying up the best chicken and potatoes

▶ Pineapple upside-down cake and more

*I*f you're into cast iron — you like cooking with it, you like the taste of the tempting edibles that you prepare in it, and you've had success with cast-iron cooking — you probably have some dishes that you swear are just *better* when they're cooked in cast iron. And I'd have to agree. You may attribute this preference to taste, texture, or any of the other traits that make particular dishes stand out as your cast-iron favorites.

Most folks don't have the scientific data to support their claims — "I don't know what it is, but *[insert the name of your dish here]* is better, rises higher, has a nicer crust, and seems tastier when I cook it in cast iron." All cast-iron cooks have dishes that they prefer to prepare in cast iron. This chapter lists ten. And if you're relatively new to cast iron, you may want to think about giving these a try — early and often.

Biscuits

Most biscuit recipes have the same four ingredients as their base: flour, shortening, leavener, and milk. From these ingredients, you can produce light, fluffy biscuits with flaky crusts or hockey-puck biscuits (you know; those biscuits that have the shape and density of a hockey puck). The difference between these two results hinges on the amount and measuring of the ingredients and the technique that you use to mix them. (You can find out all that you need to know about biscuit ingredients and technique in Chapter 11.)

Beyond the recipe and the technique, however, the type of pan has an impact, too. Many people — even those who bake in cast iron for other dishes — use regular aluminum baking sheets when they make biscuits. But cooks who use cast iron claim that the same recipes come out better.

Being a firm member of the cast-iron camp, I recently decided to hold a little bake-and-taste test. I made two batches of the same biscuit recipe, cooking one batch on aluminum baking sheets and the other in my cast-iron skillet. Both batches turned out well, but the cast-iron batch had a flakier crust, a moister interior, and a slightly better rise. Scientific evidence that cast iron makes better biscuits? No. But my family preferred the cast-iron biscuits, and that's enough for me.

Cornbread

The best cornbread is crusty on the outside and moist on the inside. For this reason, cast iron is cornbread's best friend. When you cook cornbread in an aluminum pan, the top crust has a nice golden appearance and the texture you want, but the sides and bottom have a texture more consistent with cake: golden but not crusty. That's fine if that's the way you like your cornbread. For many cornbread aficionados, however, the crust is the best part, and cast iron's heating characteristics — even heat distribution and no hotspots — produces the crusty exterior on the sides and bottom as well.

Whenever you make cornbread in cast iron, be sure to preheat and grease the pan. This produces a delightfully golden and scrumptiously crisp crust.

For a whole slew of cornbread recipes — traditional and otherwise — head to Chapter 11. If you want to know how to make complete meals out of cornbread, go to Chapter 9.

Fried Chicken

Fried chicken is fried chicken. Take chicken, season it, dredge it in flour, corn-meal, or some other substance, fry it until it's done, and there you go. Fried chicken.

Southern fried chicken, on the other hand, is more than fried chicken; it's the epitome, the culinary archetype — the *Platonic ideal.* Tell people you're fixing Southern fried chicken for dinner, and immediately, they imagine crisp golden skin and moist flavorful chicken. Their captive imagination should also con-jure up a cast-iron pan, because *you can't make Southern fried chicken without cast iron!* It's just not the same.

Cast iron's ability to safely retain heat and distribute it evenly is key. The consistent high temperature keeps the oil hot enough that the moisture in the chicken stays above the boiling point (which is key to nongreasy fried chicken because the pressure of the steam wanting to escape is enough to stop the chicken from absorbing the oil). And the even distribution of heat helps the chicken cook evenly. Head to Chapter 7 for a Southern Fried Chicken recipe and tips on how to make any fried chicken better.

Fried Eggs

Eggs fry best in nonstick, heavy bottomed skillets that hold a constant temperature. You can't get much heavier bottomed than cast iron. A well-seasoned cast iron pan is nonstick, and few pans retain heat as well. So cast iron is a perfect match for fried eggs.

Fried Potatoes

Okay, nobody ever said fried potatoes are good for your health. But, boy, are they a treat. Although fried potatoes may not be a regular part of your diet, you can splurge periodically, and when you do, be sure to fry in cast iron. Frying potatoes in a well-seasoned cast-iron skillet is easy — the skillet is nonstick and the hot pan fries the potato slices to a golden, buttery crisp. Sure, you can do the same with other nonstick skillets, but potatoes fried in cast iron just taste better — maybe it's the pan's seasonings.

So get out the potatoes, onions, butter, shortening, and a cast-iron skillet, and head to Chapter 10, where you'll find a couple fried potato recipes.

Game — Any Kind

Game, meat from wild animals, is less lean and less tender as a rule than meat from domesticated animals. Slow cooking is often vital when you cook game, because the long cooking time tenderizes the meat. Cast iron, being the first slow cooker, is a great option for cooking game.

It has another benefit, too: You can use any cast-iron skillet or pan for outdoor cooking. Cooking game over an open fire imparts a flavor all its own.

Chapter 15 is devoted to game recipes. To find out about outdoor cooking, go to Chapter 14.

Old-Fashioned Green Beans

Unless you live in parts of the country where old-fashioned green beans are still made regularly, you may think that the way to prepare green beans is to toss them into a pot of hot water and boil or steam them until they're tender — a process that takes all of 5 to 10 minutes. Serve with a dab of butter and a sprinkle of salt and pepper and — voila! — a quick, albeit uninspired, vegetable dish.

Old-fashioned green beans, however, take time to cook. Slow simmered with bacon, salt pork, or ham hock until the flavors blend, they beat the quick boiled/steamed version hands down. Cook them in cast iron, and they're even more flavorful. Go to Chapter 10 for a Southern Green Bean recipe that will put steamed green beans to shame.

Pineapple Upside-Down Cake

The most crucial parts of a pineapple upside-down cake are the brown sugar, butter, and pineapple topping. Not only does it provide flavor, but it also provides necessary texture — a rich contrast to what's essentially a plain, old white cake.

If you make this cake in a regular cake pan, the topping lacks the slightly caramel-y texture that really yummy pineapple upside-down cake has. Recipes calling for cake pans usually instruct you to melt the butter in the oven, add the brown sugar, place the pineapple on top of the sugar-butter mixture, and then immediately pour the batter on top of that. Often, you end up with a tasty but mushy cake.

In a cast-iron pan, you heat the concoction on the stovetop. This step allows the brown sugar and butter mixture to cook briefly over direct heat, melting the butter as an oven can but also slightly melting the brown sugar. When you add the pineapple, the juice from the fruit flavors the mixture, and the fruit begins to caramelize. Pour the batter into the now-heated pan over this mixture. The result is a rich and gooey but not mushy topping and a golden, flavor-infused cake.

By varying how long you let the brown sugar and butter mixture cook, you can control how caramel-y your toppings texture is. Cook it less, and the mixture is less caramel-y; cook it more, and it's more so.

You can find two pineapple upside-down cake recipes: One in Chapter 13, for when you're cooking indoors, and another in Chapter 14, for the outdoor cook.

Steak

Steak doesn't require much preparation and cooking, and it doesn't need extraordinary efforts to make it taste good. For that reason, your challenge isn't mastering a series of complicated cooking techniques or memorizing a long list of dos and don'ts. Your challenge is simple: Don't mess it up. Don't turn a perfect piece of meat into a mediocre one.

To cook steak, you generally sear the steak to seal in the juices and then finish it in the oven. Cast iron is great for steaks, because you can use it for both tasks. Preheat your cast iron over medium-high heat (don't worry, it won't warp) to prepare for searing and then stick it in the oven to finish.

 The location on the cow is what determines steak quality as well as the proper cooking technique. Steaks that are on the tender side, which come from the rib and sirloin areas, have different cooking requirements than less tender meat, coming from other areas of the cow. (Refer to Chapter 6 for details about types of meat and cooking requirements and several steak recipes.)

Stew — Any Kind

When you make soup, you begin with stock and then add various ingredients to provide flavor and texture. When you make stew, you begin with the meat, the key component of the broth's flavor, and vegetables. Then you add stock, as necessary, to make the broth the consistency that you want. Although you're using stock, the heart of a stew broth is the meat itself and the juices that come from it as it stews.

Cast iron is ideal for making stews, because you can use the same pan for browning your meat, which is often your first step, as you use for cooking the stew in. This is important, because you don't lose any of the juices or bits and pieces of meat or any of the flour for that matter. Many stew recipes instruct you to dredge the meat in flour, the key to thick broth, before browning.

In addition, whether you're cooking on the stovetop, in the oven, or outdoors over an open fire, you need to slow cook the stew for a long time. Most stew meat is naturally tough and needs the extra cooking time to become tender. Because cast iron retains heat so well and distributes it evenly, you avoid hot spots that can burn or scorch your food during the long cooking time.

Finally, a great dinner is a great dinner, but a dinner with ambience is a culinary experience. Sure, the ingredients may just add up to stew, but when you put them all together in a black iron pot and then ladle big helpings of the thick, rich concoction into crockery bowls or tin plates, the dish not only looks better but tastes better, too.

For a pretty good stew recipe, if I do say so myself, head to Chapter 9.

Chapter 19

Ten Tips for Surefire Success

. . . .

. . . .

Much of cast-iron cooking is about *feel*. Many cast-iron cooks don't even measure. They judge quantities by a dollop of this, a dab of that, a pinch here or a sprinkle there, or — my favorite — "just until," as in "just until the smell burns the back of your nose" or "just until the spoon leaves a trail when you stir the batter." Precise? No, but descriptive enough to get the results you want.

Of course, the recipes in this book are more precise, offering actual measurements and instructions where necessary for cooking in cast iron. But you can cook any recipe in cast iron. Although this chapter can't help you ferret out how much exactly a dollop is, it does offer guidelines to ensure that your recipes come out right whenever you cook in cast iron.

Seasoning and Reseasoning

I can't say this strongly enough: Any cast iron you cook in has to be seasoned. An unseasoned cast-iron pan is a disaster in the kitchen. Food sticks to it like you wouldn't believe. And what doesn't stick is inedible — unless, that is, you happen to like the taste of metal. Seasoning eliminates these problems: It makes the surface nonstick and ensures that your food doesn't taste like metal. It also protects the pan from rust.

As the seasoning deepens, as it will over time, the pan's cooking characteristics become that much greater and more desirable. So season your new pan and then reseason your pan again after every use by wiping a thin coat of vegetable oil on the inside of it. If your pan shows signs that the seasoning is breaking down, you'll want to reseason it in the oven. Chapter 3 tells you everything that you need to know about seasoning your cast iron.

You can buy preseasoned cast iron now. This preseasoning takes care of the initial seasoning for you, but you still need to reseason your pans after using them.

Preheating Your Pan

Cast iron is an efficient heat conductor. After it reaches the given temperature, the whole pan — bottom, side, and even the handle — is at that temperature. This is one of the great characteristics of cast iron, because it means that the heat distribution is even and that hot spots, the bane of every cook, don't exist.

It also means that, for most recipes, you need to allow the pan to preheat completely before you add your food. This is especially important for baked dishes, such as cakes and cornbreads, dishes that rely on consistent oil temperatures, such as fried chicken, and recipes that require a quick application of high heat, such as seared steaks. The preheated pan gives your baked goods a nicer crust, it keeps your fried foods from absorbing too much oil and getting greasy, and it seals in the juices of seared meats without overcooking them.

Using the Right Size Pan

You can make any recipe in just about any cast-iron pan. This versatility means that you don't need many cast-iron pans — one or two is usually sufficient — but it also means that you have to be willing to adjust the recipe as necessary to accommodate cooking times and cooking methods. If you don't have the pans you need and don't have a suitable substitute, adjust the cooking times or the preparation method. Cornbread that you put in a skillet takes longer to cook than cornbread made in a cornstick pan, for example, so be sure to take that into account when you make your cornbread. Similarly, if you have only shallow pans, don't try to deep-fry your dish, even if that's what the recipe calls for. Pan-fry instead.

Controlling Your Temperature

Cast iron conducts heat well, so you'll want to control the cooking temperature. You need to keep cast iron's heating characteristics in mind as you set and adjust temperatures:

✓ With cast iron, you often don't need to use temperatures as high as those specified in recipes that aren't designed with cast iron in mind. So start out at the temperature the recipe states but always be willing to adjust the heat downward.

✓ If you're using an electric range, remember that turning off the burner isn't enough to stop the cooking process. You also need to remove the cast-iron pan from the burner; otherwise, even though the burner's off, your dish will continue to cook.

You can read about the heating characteristics of cast iron and how to adjust temperatures accordingly in Chapter 5.

Modifying Cooking Times

When you cook in cast iron, the actual cooking times may be slightly less than that specified in your recipes. As you cook, don't rely solely on your kitchen timer; look for other signs of doneness.

When you roast meat, for example, use a meat thermometer. If you're baking a cake or quick bread, test for doneness with a cake tester or toothpick. Yeast breads sound hollow when you thump them. Meat should be at appropriate internal temperatures: Poultry should register 170 to 185 degrees, pork should come in at 170 degrees, and beef should tip the scales at 140 to 170 degrees. Head to Chapter 5 for more tips on testing for doneness.

Coating with Oil or Cooking Spray

Until your cast iron has a dark, satiny patina, some foods may stick. (See Chapter 1 for a description and illustration of what the patina looks like.) For that reason, always use a little bit of oil or cooking spray to ensure a nonstick surface. This advice can even benefit those folks whose pans are well seasoned, because, in addition to making food release easily, the oil or cooking spray also adds flavor.

Cooking with Quality Cast Iron

The quality of your cast iron matters. Quality affects not only how long the pan lasts — poorer quality cast iron is brittle and prone to warping or breaking — but also how well they take seasoning and what their cooking characteristics are. Some of the characteristics of top grade cast iron are as follows:

- ✔ **It has a finer grain and is easier to season.** This is important for producing a nonstick surface and eliminating the possibility of rust.
- ✔ **The metal has a uniform thickness.** This is important because it makes for even heating and reduces the likelihood of hot spots that can burn or scorch your food. Uniform thickness also reduces the likelihood of the pan warping because of temperature changes.

You can find more information about how to judge the quality of cast iron in Chapter 2, and the implications quality has to cooking and safety.

Using Quality Ingredients

What you cook with is as important as what you cook *in*. When you're planning your menu, choose ingredients that will enhance rather than detract from your dish. A great roast, for example, starts out as a bright red, well-marbled piece of meat. Similarly, unless a recipe calls specifically for canned or frozen vegetables, opt for fresh for optimal flavor.

Sometimes, the best ingredient for the task at hand isn't the freshest, prettiest, most expensive, and so on. The ripest fruit — even overripe fruit that you'd be tempted to throw away if you were just going to eat it on its own — is often the best choice for fruit desserts and fruit breads. (For a great banana bread recipe, go to Chapter 12. Chapter 13 has several wonderful desserts using fruit.)

Sticking Around

Obviously, if you're deep-frying, pan-frying, simmering, sautéing, searing, grilling, and so on, you need to be nearby. But even recipes slow-cooked in cast iron need some attention. You may not need to be in the room standing watch over the stove, but you need to be nearby. You may have to check the simmering liquid to make sure it doesn't steam away, or maybe the recipe requires that you periodically rearrange the ingredients to ensure that everything cooks evenly. Roasting is probably the most hands-off cast-iron cooking technique, and even that path requires you to be around if you want to baste.

Having Fun

You bought this cookbook (or, at least, you're reading it now), so I'm guessing you enjoy spending time in the kitchen. Don't forget that. I know from experience that preparing dinner (or lunch, or breakfast) can too often morph from a pleasurable experience into a hectic race against the clock. When you pull out your cast-iron pan, let it serve as a reminder that, "Hey, this is supposed to be fun." Let your creativity flow by creating a five-star dish that would be at home on a table in the trendiest bistro; or whip up a simple recipe that has a couple hundred years of history behind it. But regardless of the direction your cast-iron cooking takes you, enjoy yourself.

Metric Conversion Guide

• •

*N**ote:* The recipes in this cookbook weren't developed or tested using metric measures. Quality may vary in some cases when converting to metric units.

Common Abbreviations

Abbreviation(s)	What It Stands For
C, c	cup
g	gram
kg	kilogram
L, l	liter
lb	pound
mL, ml	milliliter
oz	ounce
pt	pint
t, tsp	teaspoon
T, TB, Tbl, Tbsp	tablespoon

Volume

U.S Units	Canadian Metric	Australian Metric
¼ teaspoon	1 mL	1 ml
½ teaspoon	2 mL	2 ml

(continued)

Volume *(continued)*

U.S Units	Canadian Metric	Australian Metric
1 teaspoon	5 mL	5 ml
1 tablespoon	15 mL	20 ml
¼ cup	50 mL	60 ml
⅓ cup	75 mL	80 ml
½ cup	125 mL	125 ml
⅔ cup	150 mL	170 ml
¾ cup	175 mL	190 ml
1 cup	250 mL	250 ml
1 quart	1 liter	1 liter
1½ quarts	1.5 liters	1.5 liters
2 quarts	2 liters	2 liters
2½ quarts	2.5 liters	2.5 liters
3 quarts	3 liters	3 liters
4 quarts	4 liters	4 liters

Weight

U.S. Units	Canadian Metric	Australian Metric
1 ounce	30 grams	30 grams
2 ounces	55 grams	60 grams
3 ounces	85 grams	90 grams
4 ounces (¼ pound)	115 grams	125 grams
8 ounces (½ pound)	225 grams	225 grams
16 ounces (1 pound)	455 grams	500 grams
1 pound	455 grams	½ kilogram

Measurements

Inches	Centimeters
½	1.5
1	2.5
2	5.0
3	7.5
4	10.0
5	12.5
6	15.0
7	17.5
8	20.5
9	23.0
10	25.5
11	28.0
12	30.5
13	33.0

Temperature (Degrees)

Fahrenheit	Celsius
32	0
212	100
250	120
275	140
300	150
325	160
350	180

(continued)

Temperature (Degrees) *(continued)*	
Fahrenheit	*Celsius*
375	190
400	200
425	220
450	230
475	240
500	260

Index

Notes

Notes

FOR DUMMIES®

The easy way to get more done and have more fun

PERSONAL FINANCE

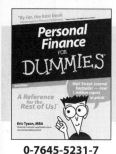

0-7645-5231-7

0-7645-2431-3

0-7645-5331-3

Also available:

Estate Planning For Dummies
(0-7645-5501-4)

401(k)s For Dummies
(0-7645-5468-9)

Frugal Living For Dummies
(0-7645-5403-4)

Microsoft Money "X" For
Dummies
(0-7645-1689-2)

Mutual Funds For Dummies
(0-7645-5329-1)

Personal Bankruptcy For
Dummies
(0-7645-5498-0)

Quicken "X" For Dummies
(0-7645-1666-3)

Stock Investing For Dummies
(0-7645-5411-5)

Taxes For Dummies 2003
(0-7645-5475-1)

BUSINESS & CAREERS

0-7645-5314-3

0-7645-5307-0

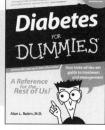

0-7645-5471-9

Also available:

Business Plans Kit For
Dummies
(0-7645-5365-8)

Consulting For Dummies
(0-7645-5034-9)

Cool Careers For Dummies
(0-7645-5345-3)

Human Resources Kit For
Dummies
(0-7645-5131-0)

Managing For Dummies
(1-5688-4858-7)

QuickBooks All-in-One Desk
Reference For Dummies
(0-7645-1963-8)

Selling For Dummies
(0-7645-5363-1)

Small Business Kit For
Dummies
(0-7645-5093-4)

Starting an eBay Business For
Dummies
(0-7645-1547-0)

HEALTH, SPORTS & FITNESS

0-7645-5167-1

0-7645-5146-9

0-7645-5154-X

Also available:

Controlling Cholesterol For
Dummies
(0-7645-5440-9)

Dieting For Dummies
(0-7645-5126-4)

High Blood Pressure For
Dummies
(0-7645-5424-7)

Martial Arts For Dummies
(0-7645-5358-5)

Menopause For Dummies
(0-7645-5458-1)

Nutrition For Dummies
(0-7645-5180-9)

Power Yoga For Dummies
(0-7645-5342-9)

Thyroid For Dummies
(0-7645-5385-2)

Weight Training For Dummies
(0-7645-5168-X)

Yoga For Dummies
(0-7645-5117-5)

Available wherever books are sold.
Go to www.dummies.com or call 1-877-762-2974 to order direct.

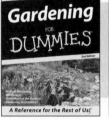

FOR DUMMIES®

A world of resources to help you grow

HOME, GARDEN & HOBBIES

Feng Shui
FOR DUMMIES
A Reference for the Rest of Us!
0-7645-5295-3

Gardening
FOR DUMMIES
A Reference for the Rest of Us!
0-7645-5130-2

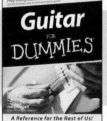

Guitar
FOR DUMMIES
A Reference for the Rest of Us!
0-7645-5106-X

Also available:

Auto Repair For Dummies
(0-7645-5089-6)

Chess For Dummies
(0-7645-5003-9)

Home Maintenance For
Dummies
(0-7645-5215-5)

Organizing For Dummies
(0-7645-5300-3)

Piano For Dummies
(0-7645-5105-1)

Poker For Dummies
(0-7645-5232-5)

Quilting For Dummies
(0-7645-5118-3)

Rock Guitar For Dummies
(0-7645-5356-9)

Roses For Dummies
(0-7645-5202-3)

Sewing For Dummies
(0-7645-5137-X)

FOOD & WINE

Cooking
FOR DUMMIES
A Reference for the Rest of Us!
0-7645-5250-3

Cookies
FOR DUMMIES
A Reference for the Rest of Us!
0-7645-5390-9

Wine
FOR DUMMIES
A Reference for the Rest of Us!
0-7645-5114-0

Also available:

Bartending For Dummies
(0-7645-5051-9)

Chinese Cooking For
Dummies
(0-7645-5247-3)

Christmas Cooking For
Dummies
(0-7645-5407-7)

Diabetes Cookbook For
Dummies
(0-7645-5230-9)

Grilling For Dummies
(0-7645-5076-4)

Low-Fat Cooking For
Dummies
(0-7645-5035-7)

Slow Cookers For Dummies
(0-7645-5240-6)

TRAVEL

Italy
FOR DUMMIES
A Travel Guide for the Rest of Us!
0-7645-5453-0

Hawaii
FOR DUMMIES
A Travel Guide for the Rest of Us!
0-7645-5438-7

Las Vegas
FOR DUMMIES
A Travel Guide for the Rest of Us!
0-7645-5448-4

Also available:

America's National Parks For
Dummies
(0-7645-6204-5)

Caribbean For Dummies
(0-7645-5445-X)

Cruise Vacations For
Dummies 2003
(0-7645-5459-X)

Europe For Dummies
(0-7645-5456-5)

Ireland For Dummies
(0-7645-6199-5)

France For Dummies
(0-7645-6292-4)

London For Dummies
(0-7645-5416-6)

Mexico's Beach Resorts For
Dummies
(0-7645-6262-2)

Paris For Dummies
(0-7645-5494-8)

RV Vacations For Dummies
(0-7645-5443-3)

Walt Disney World & Orlando
For Dummies
(0-7645-5444-1)

FOR DUMMIES®

Helping you expand your horizons and realize your potential

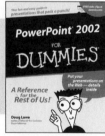
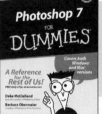

FOR DUMMIES

The advice and explanations you need to succeed

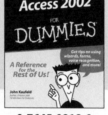